A Comprehensive Guide to Readers Theatre

Enhancing Fluency
and Comprehension
in Middle School
and Beyond

Alison Black

Anna M. Stave

INTERNATIONAL
Reading Association
800 BARKSDALE ROAD, PO BOX 8139
NEWARK, DE 19714-8139, USA
www.reading.org

The International Reading Association attempts, through its publications, to provide a forum for a wide spectrum of opinions on reading. This policy permits divergent viewpoints without implying the endorsement of the Association.

Executive Editor, Books Corinne M. Mooney
Developmental Editor Charlene M. Nichols
Developmental Editor Tori Mello Bachman
Developmental Editor Stacey Lynn Sharp
Editorial Production Manager Shannon T. Fortner
Production Manager Iona Muscella
Supervisor, Electronic Publishing Anette Schuetz

Project Editors Stacey Lynn Sharp and Christina Lambert

Art Cover Design, Linda Steere;
Cover and Interior Student Photography, Alison Black and Anna M. Stave

Library of Congress Cataloging-in-Publication Data

Black, Alison, 1950-

A comprehensive guide to readers theatre : enhancing fluency and comprehension in middle school and beyond / Alison Black & Anna M. Stave.

p. cm.

Includes index.

ISBN 978-0-87207-590-0

1. Reader's theater--Study and teaching (Middle school) 2. Drama in education. 3. Language arts. I. Stave, Anna M., 1943- II. Title.

PN2081.R4B58 2007

371.39'9--dc22

2006101622

To Hal Herber and Don Leu, who have greatly contributed
to our own literacy development and to our understanding
of how to develop our students' literacies

Alison Black is Assistant Professor in the Division of Education at the State University of New York at Oneonta where she teaches literacy courses at the graduate and undergraduate level. She has published articles ranging from teaching via online asynchronous discussion to the NCATE review process to preservice teacher concerns.

Alison was a K–12 teacher, media specialist, and storyteller before moving into higher education. Her interest in children's literature and storytelling and her work with children of all ages led naturally to Readers Theatre and continues to guide her use of this instructional method in the college classroom. She has presented numerous workshops nationally and within New York State modeling the use of children's literature and Readers Theatre in the K–12 classroom.

Anna M. Stave is Associate Professor of Adolescence Education and English at the State University of New York at Oneonta. Before moving into university and college education programs, she was a middle and high school English and drama teacher. She directed youth theater programs at Karamu Youth Theatre, Karamu House, Cleveland, Ohio; Salt City Playhouse, Syracuse, New York; and Playhouse on the Hill, Clinton, New York. She was also Associate Professor of Drama at

Onondaga Community College, Syracuse, New York. Anna has offered international, national, and state publications and presentations related to Readers Theatre, interdisciplinary programs, writers' perceptions of writing, preservice teachers' perceptions of teaching, and drama in the classroom. She was also a New York State English Council Educator of Excellence.

As a middle and high school teacher, Anna developed Readers Theatre performance using poetry. As Director of Youth Theatre Programs and as a college drama professor, she taught courses in Readers Theatre, directed Readers Theatre productions, and used Readers Theatre as a part of school arts programs and in workshops for elementary, middle, and high school teachers. She continues to model and use Readers Theatre performance in her courses and workshops for teachers.

Over the past 30 years, we have had the opportunity to observe and facilitate the use of Readers Theatre in classrooms spanning all grade levels from preschool to college. We have seen it bring language and literature to life, provide a voice for the quietest students, and allow all students the opportunity to be successful readers. We have also seen how the process of Readers Theatre supports state and national English language arts standards.

Recently, it has been our good fortune to observe and participate in the Readers Theatre performances of several middle school classrooms. The work of the teachers and their students in these classrooms has informed and illuminated our description and development of the processes and products of Readers Theatre found in this book. All of the elements that we describe herein may not necessarily have been implemented in those classrooms, but we believe we inspired the teachers' use of Readers Theatre through our work with them in the college classroom—and fittingly, their use of Readers Theatre in their middle school classrooms has served as an inspiration for this book.

Our experiences have prompted us to write this book as a way to encourage the use of Readers Theatre in the classroom and to provide a structure for teachers to follow that will facilitate meeting U.S. state and national standards. Because accountability is an ever-increasing mandate in our schools today, the knowledge and use of state and national standards in our teaching is of greater importance. This book goes beyond the scope of other books on Readers Theatre; in addition to providing both a general and a specific discussion of the process, it also offers a detailed emphasis on standards, assessment, activities, and adaptations—all issues of growing concern in today's schools.

How to Use This Book

This book is more than a basic "how-to" text on Readers Theatre. Its style provides easy access to specific information and yet is also of use to the reader looking for general information regarding Readers Theatre. This comprehensive guide offers a detailed and comprehensive presentation of the products, processes, benefits, and research foundations for Readers Theatre and a detailed approach to both *why* and *how* to use this strategy. It focuses attention on the connection of Readers Theatre to literacy development and national standards as described by the International Reading Association (IRA) and the National Council of Teachers of English (NCTE) and to state standards such as those of California and New York. It also presents a variety of assessment tools applicable to the literacy skills enhanced by Readers Theatre as well as supplementary activities that extend the use of Readers Theatre in the classroom. The book's focus on research as well as the benefits of using Readers Theatre for literacy, personal development, and communication skills—specifically in promoting active reading fluency, comprehension, and critical thinking—makes it the definitive handbook for Readers Theatre.

Intended Audience

This book is based on current research, theory, and practice within the field of literacy with an emphasis on middle school and with adaptations for younger and older students, English-language learners (ELLs), struggling readers, and gifted students. Because the emphasis of this book is on reading, speaking, listening, meaning making, and viewing as opposed to writing, *Readers Theatre* is geared toward practicing teachers in the field, specifically middle school teachers and teacher educators whose major interests are in reading, English language arts, and literacy.

Though the descriptions of creation and performance in the classroom are directed at the middle school teacher, we have included adaptations and suggestions for other grades and skill levels so that, by using the middle school level as a starting point, we can extend the practice of Readers Theatre to the elementary and the high school classroom. The theoretical perspectives that ground Readers Theatre as well as the practical guidelines for implementation will encourage the teacher who wishes to facilitate students' reading fluency and comprehension, motivate students to read, and develop their vocabulary. Observations, quotes, and reflections from the middle school classrooms in which the authors have worked provide an immediacy to this work.

Text Organization

Chapters 1 through 3 and 7 through 10 provide a wide-angle lens into the use of Readers Theatre. They are of relevance to anyone using or thinking of using this strategy, regardless of content or grade level. Chapters 4 through 6, however, offer a microscopic view of three specific genres: fiction, nonfiction, and poetry.

The first section, "Getting Started," introduces the reader to the concept of Readers Theatre and offers a theoretical base for its use. Chapter 1 provides an introduction and rationale for using Readers Theatre in the middle school classroom, revealing its research base and theoretical foundations. Chapter 2, "Launching Readers Theatre in the Middle School Classroom," provides the reader with the "nuts and bolts" of the initial process. This chapter serves as the general how-to section, paying attention to the elements required for successful Readers Theatre, including group dynamics, selection of materials, and preparation time. An overview of what is required of the teacher is presented in the form of a continuum that moves the process from teacher-directed to student-directed. Chapter 3, "Developing the Performance," finishes the process, focusing on audience, performance time and space, rehearsal, staging, and dress rehearsal. These two major chapters give the novice user of Readers Theatre guidelines and suggestions and offer the experienced user a wealth of ideas as well as confirmation of what they already may be doing. The broad look at the strategy of Readers Theatre provided in Part I is of use to all readers. In addition, this section features teacher and student quotes that illustrate classroom responses to Readers Theatre and add a student and teacher presence to the text. Photographs depicting students using Readers Theatre in the classroom also provide a student presence to the book and are included in this section and also Parts II and III.

"Exploring Genres Through Readers Theatre" is Part II, giving an in-depth look at the explicit use of three genres. In an attempt to provide models for a variety of texts, this section focuses on three different text formats—fiction, nonfiction, and poetry. Each of the chapters in this section offers concrete examples of scripts and staging with reference to the elements discussed in chapters 2 and 3 and how they relate to that text format. This detailed approach is necessary in a guide that serves to model explicitly how Readers Theatre may be used with fiction, nonfiction, and poetry.

Part III is "Extending Readers Theatre Applications." It includes chapter 7, with suggested activities that enhance a teacher's use of Readers Theatre, and chapter 8, which looks at Readers Theatre beyond the middle school classroom, addressing adaptations to other classrooms and to ELLs, struggling readers, and gifted students.

State standards (California and New York) and national standards (IRA and NCTE) are discussed in Part IV, "Accountability," beginning with chapter 9. This chapter provides a matrix illustrating how Readers Theatre performances address all three of these sets of standards. A second matrix breaks down the steps involved in two-day, five-day, and ten-day schedules set for Readers Theatre and how each of these steps applies to the various standards. A third matrix details how each of the extension activities in chapter 7 addresses the various standards. One way in which accountability is made visible by teachers is the acknowledgment of state and national standards in their instruction. Often, best practice embodies the standards, and yet the connection between the two is not understood or acknowledged. By making clear connections in these matrixes between the many aspects of Readers Theatre and the standards, it is our hope that teachers will realize not only the ways in which Readers Theatre can help them address standards but also the ways in which they are already addressing standards. Chapter 10 in this section includes assessment tools for both individuals as well as groups involved in performances.

Several appendixes are included. Appendix A offers the reader sources and resources for scripts. Appendix B provides a discussion of cross-curricular connections, and Appendix C provides reproducible forms. Finally, to provide more convenient access to the standards discussed in detail in chapter 10, Appendix D compiles those standards in list form.

A Note on Copyright Issues

We believe it is imperative to briefly discuss the copyright issues regarding fair use within the classroom. While it is necessary to know the law about copyright issues, Readers Theatre as described in this book looks at the purpose of reading aloud as educational—to increase students' fluency and comprehension of a text while allowing them to actively demonstrate that fluency and comprehension. This text comprehension is gained through the repeated and purposeful reading of a text and demonstrated through fluent and expressive reading. The listeners or audience may be the teacher, classmates, students in other grades, school personnel, students' families, and community members. Such fair use for educational purposes usually is allowed as long as no admission fee is charged for the performance.

The purpose of Readers Theatre performance as described in this book is a variation of existing educational practices and is not intended as performance for a paying public or in any way as a commercial enterprise. However, teachers regularly use materials in their classroom that are authored and may be under copyright, and copyright laws are not always clear. It is recommended that, if a teacher is in doubt as to material used, he or she should contact the publisher's permissions department for clarification. The following is an excerpt from the U.S. government copyright website (U.S. Copyright Office, n.d.) at www.copy right.gov/title17/92chap1.html#107 that specifically addresses fair use.

> § 107. Limitations on exclusive rights: Fair use
>
> Notwithstanding the provisions of sections 106 and 106A, the fair use of a copyrighted work, including such use by reproduction in copies or phonorecords or by any other means specified by that section, for purposes such as criticism, comment, news reporting, teaching (including multiple copies for classroom use), scholarship, or research, is not an infringement of copyright. In determining whether the use made of a work in any particular case is a fair use the factors to be considered shall include—
>
> (1) the purpose and character of the use, including whether such use is of a commercial nature or is for nonprofit educational purposes;
>
> (2) the nature of the copyrighted work;
>
> (3) the amount and substantiality of the portion used in relation to the copyrighted work as a whole; and
>
> (4) the effect of the use upon the potential market for or value of the copyrighted work.

The fact that a work is unpublished shall not itself bar a finding of fair use if such finding is made upon consideration of all the above factors. (n.p.)

In addition to being aware of fair use guidelines, teachers should also be familiar with the benefits of using materials in the public domain. Any work published in the United States before 1923 or any work where copyright has expired becomes part of the public domain (Stanford University, 2003). Literature that is in the public domain is not protected by intellectual property laws (such as copyright, trademark, or patent law). Therefore, these works may be used without obtaining permission. For more information on public domain, we recommend viewing Stanford University's website discussing copyright and fair use at http://fairuse.stanford.edu/Copyright_and_Fair_Use_Overview/chapter8/index.html.

This information is provided to readers as a courtesy of the authors in an attempt to help them navigate the waters of copyright issues. However, we are not experts on this topic and encourage readers to seek their own legal advice regarding copyright if necessary.

Acknowledgments

We wish to thank our families, friends, and colleagues for their continuing encouragement and support during all phases of this project.

We could not have completed this book without the extraordinary cooperation and enthusiasm of Ann Olmstead and her students at Cooperstown Middle School and Stephanie Hulbert and her students at Sidney Middle School. Their willingness to share their experiences and performances with Readers Theatre has enabled us to describe how Readers Theatre can operate effectively in classroom settings.

Wayne Wright, New York State Historical Association, Special Collections, deserves a special thank you for introducing us to Dora Walker's diaries, and J.O. Green for her collection and careful transcription of these diaries.

We would like to express our appreciation for Alfresco's Italian Bistro for providing excellent Italian food and a comfortable and cheerful place to develop our ideas.

We also thank Stacey Sharp, our Developmental Editor, and Teresa Curto, Assistant Director of Publications at the International Reading Association, for their support, guidance, and patience throughout the publishing process.

Permissions Granted

These publishers have generously given permission to use extended quotations from the following copyrighted works.

"The Tortoise and the Hare," from *Fables From Aesop* retold and illustrated by Tom Lynch, copyright 2000 by Tom Lynch. Used by permission of Viking Children's Books, A Division of Penguin Young Readers Group, A Member of Penguin Group (USA) Inc., 345 Hudson Street, New York, NY 10014. All rights reserved.

From *Wisdom Tales From Around the World* by Heather Forest, copyright 1996 by Heather Forest. Reprinted by permission of Marian Reiner on behalf of August House Publishers, Inc.

From *The True Confessions of Charlotte Doyle* by Avi, copyright 1990 by Avi. Reprinted by permission of Orchard Books, an imprint of Scholastic, Inc.

From *The Papers of Dora Walker* courtesy of the New York State Historical Association, Special Collections, Cooperstown, New York.

From *...If Your Name Was Changed at Ellis Island* by Ellen Levine, copyright 1993 by Ellen Levine. Reprinted by permission of Scholastic, Inc.

From *Ellis Island Interviews: In Their Own Words* by Peter Morton Coan, copyright 1997 by Peter Morton Coan. Reprinted with permission of the Carol Mann Agency.

From *Ellis Island*. Originally published in French as *Recits d'Ellis Island: histoires d'errance et d'espoir* by P.O.L. editeur, Paris, France, copyright 1994 P.O.L. editeur. English translations by Harry Mathews and Hessica Blatt, copyright 1995 by The New Press. Reprinted with the permission of The New Press.

From *I Was Dreaming to Come to America* by Veronica Lawlor, copyright 1995 by Veronica Lawlor. Used by permission of Viking Penguin, A Division of Penguin Young Readers Group (USA) Inc., 345 Hudson Street, New York 10014. All rights reserved.

Universal Declaration of Human Rights: An Adaptation for Children by R. Rocha and O. Roth, copyright 1995. Used by permission of United Nations Publications, 2 UN Plaza, DC2 Room 856, New York, NY 10017, USA.

"In Beauty May I Walk," p. 59 (trans. J.K. Rothenberg) in P. Abbs and J. Richardson, *The Forms of Poetry*, copyright 1990. Reprinted with the permission of Cambridge University Press.

REFERENCES

Stanford University. (2003). The public domain. In *Copyright & Fair Use Overview* (chap. 8). Retrieved from http://fairuse.stanford.edu/Copyright_and_Fair_Use_Overview/chapter8/index.html

U.S. Copyright Office. (n.d.). Copyright law of the United States of America and related laws contained in Title 17 of the *United States Code*. In *Copyright Law* (chap. 1, #107). Retrieved from http://www.copyright.gov/title17/92chap1.html

PART 1

Getting Started

This section provides you with the background necessary in order to begin using Readers Theatre in your middle school classroom. Chapter 1 of this section, "An Introduction to Readers Theatre," familiarizes you with the concept of Readers Theatre and its theoretical base, placing it within the specific context of a middle school classroom. Chapter 2, "Launching Readers Theatre in the Middle School Classroom," and chapter 3, "Developing the Performance," offer a general overview of the key elements of Readers Theatre and provide guidelines and suggestions for their implementation. This broad look at Readers Theatre serves as a preview to the next section, which provides a microscopic look at the processes involved in Readers Theatre as it is enacted through the genres of fiction, nonfiction, and poetry.

CHAPTER 1

An Introduction to Readers Theatre

In 1999, the International Reading Association (IRA) Commission on Adolescent Literacy declared there was an "ever-deepening crisis in adolescent literacy" (Moore, Bean, Birdyshaw, & Rycik, 1999, p. 3). The 1998 Reading Report Card by the National Assessment of Educational Progress (NAEP) reported that only 60% of adolescents in the United States could comprehend factual statements and that less than 5% could elaborate on the meaning of material they had read (Donahue, Voelkl, Campbell, & Mazzeo, 1999). The NAEP's study of the long-term trend in reading indicates that since 1971 there has been improvement in 9-year-olds, but little improvement seen in 13-year-olds and no improvement seen in 17-year-olds (Donahue et al.).

A bill introduced in the U.S. Congress in 2003 to reduce high school dropout rates cited illiteracy as the major cause for high dropout rates, noting that most students who drop out read below the ninth-grade level and that one quarter of those who graduate are barely able to read training manuals (Davis, 2003). Further, as students move through school, they are expected to read more and to comprehend more challenging text. The stagnant NAEP scores and the growing concern among educators regarding adolescent literacy make a strong case for a focus on effective literacy strategies for adolescents. Readers Theatre has proven to be one such strategy.

What Is Readers Theatre?

Readers Theatre is a strategy that showcases the power of language. It is an interpretive reading activity in which readers bring characters, story, and even content area or textbook material to life through their voices, actions, and words. Allowing for interpretation through multiple modes, Readers Theatre is often described as "a stylized form of dramatization" (Trousdale & Harris, 1993, p. 201). Regardless of formatting and purpose, it is based on script reading and the suggestive power of language (Shepard, 1994). Readers Theatre has been called "radio drama" and a "play for voices," and its ability to adapt to specific texts, ages, performance styles, and language is one of its strengths. The form of Readers Theatre most familiar to educators today was originally developed by Chamber Readers, a nonprofit Readers Theatre company in California that has promoted reading and literature since 1975.

Readers Theatre provides an oral interpretation of literature, becoming an integrated language event in the classroom. Students may adapt and present self-selected material. A story, poem, scene from a play, song, or even material from a textbook, newspaper, historical document, or biography can provide ingredients for a script. Readers Theatre makes a unique contribution to the language arts through its integration of thinking, reading, writing, speaking, listening, and viewing experiences.

Readers Theatre emphasizes the oral performance of a text. Its conventions require that the performers read from a text. The physical presence of the text or script visually reinforces that the performance is centered in the text, and the performance is a reading of the text. Through their expressive reading, posture, limited actions, and carefully selected production elements, the performers are suggesting and enhancing meaning and creating pictures. The audience is also a partner in making and visualizing meaning from the same text as the performers. It takes the text, the performer, and the audience to make complete meaning from the performance text, and it is this combination that brings the text alive.

This form of reading aloud goes beyond the traditional forum of round robin. It is an interpretive presentation of a text by a group of readers in a nonthreatening, controlled, and prepared setting. Readers Theatre creates an opportunity for students to explore a text and to become involved with the process of rehearsal and repeated readings (Herrell & Jordan, 2002).

Roles of the Teacher and Students

In Readers Theatre, the students are always the readers and performers of the scripts and, once acquainted with Readers Theatre, can become the directors and producers. The teacher is first and foremost the director of the performance and initially serves as the producer and writer of the scripts. The goal is to scaffold student independence with Readers Theatre scripts and performances. The roles of both teacher and students are somewhat fluid and should be tailored toward the needs and abilities of individual classrooms. (For further discussion on the roles of teachers and students, see chapter 2, page 19.)

Setting

Though many Readers Theatre performances take place in the classroom, the performance aspect can also move student readers and performers beyond the classroom. Readers Theatre performances may be developed for a wide variety of settings (see Figure 1). These can include other classes within the school or district, local libraries, historical societies, museums, art galleries, theaters; nursing homes; and community centers in connection with specific community events. Travel beyond classroom walls is also possible through the use of technology (audio/radio broadcast format, videotapes, public access broadcast

networks, website development, and the publication of scripts) and publication of Readers Theatre scripts in school newspapers or journals for students and educators.

The Audience

In addition to the teacher and the performers, the audience plays a vital role in Readers Theatre. Within the classroom, the students themselves may comprise the audience. This flexibility, which allows students to move between the roles of performer and audience, allows for the participation of all students.

The audience may shift from within the class to the classroom down the hall, generating interactions among a variety of ages, grades, and abilities. Readers Theatre may also include other school personnel as well as parents, either as active participants in Readers Theatre or as observers of the performance or both.

Readers Theatre enables reading aloud with intent and purpose, where individuals are reading to and for an audience. Individuals read aloud with understanding because the material is familiar to them through repeated readings of the script. This process may also reinforce familiar content material that has been written or adapted by the readers themselves.

The readers are interpreting character, action, motivation, mood, and tone by doing and experiencing them, and not simply talking about them (Trousdale & Harris, 1993). The reading becomes theater because of the many voices of both group and individual readers reading aloud, a way to make books come alive. The audience becomes part of the theater by listening to and imagining the details of scene and action communicated through those voices, sentences, and words. In fact, one of the performer's goals in Readers Theatre is to read a script aloud effectively, enabling the audience to visualize the action. This "shared happening between performers and audience" (Coger & White, 1982, p. 5) gives each individual a vital part to play. The readers perform through dramatic speech while the audience members create mental images of what they hear. For some, watching and listening to such performance enables them to understand literature or written text beyond the medium of print. This dramatic interpretation of text through Readers Theatre provides avenues for many ways of knowing.

Reading aloud may be enacted through Readers Theatre in a variety of ways. At one extreme, Readers Theatre is simply the reader and the script, without props, costumes, memorization of lines, or required movement. At the other extreme is the full-blown Readers Theatre performance with script and reader as well as mime, movement, props, costumes, and whatever else is needed or wanted. It is this versatility that makes Readers Theatre difficult to define, yet also ensures that reading aloud remains at its core where the script is constantly visible and used.

The setting itself may determine the method of presentation. "Students are free to sit or stand, in formal or informal arrangements, communicating primarily through the use of vocal inflection, gestures, and facial expressions" (Herrell & Jordan, 2002, p. 166). Scripts may be written for as many students as possible, involving them in the production solo, with a partner, or in a small group or groups. Those not participating as readers become the audience so that listening skills may be emphasized and reinforced to facilitate their future roles as readers.

Regardless of *how* it is implemented, Readers Theatre relies on a reader's prior knowledge and experience to read the script and focuses on repeated readings for fluency and comprehension. In addition, the audience role is that of a reader of "living text," and their prior knowledge combined with this living text will create personal meaning and understanding. Through performance, actors in Readers Theatre suggest a complete vision of the text with voice, body, posture and limited movement, music or sound effects, and limited props and stage settings.

Research Base and Theoretical Background

To fully grasp the potential of using Readers Theatre in the classroom, it is important to know how it affects students. The concept of Readers Theatre is grounded in a strong theoretical foundation. Combining research from both reading and creative dramatics, Readers Theatre helps defeat stereotyping, allows for variety in roles as well as learning modalities and levels of communication, and makes connections to learning standards (see chapter 9). Readers Theatre offers a forum for a process and a product, and places teachers in a range of roles, from model to facilitator. Readers Theatre not only supplies an unusual and creative approach to drama, but also provides an intense focus on fiction and nonfiction texts, making available the poems, narratives, and expository writings of the finest authors. The very performance of Readers Theatre allows these writings to come to life.

The following section explores studies and applications of Readers Theatre, lending a foundation of support to its many benefits. Discussion revolves around six major areas: oral communication skills, reading fluency and comprehension, reading motivation, vocabulary development, story schema, language structure, and collaboration.

Oral Communication Skills

Oral communication skills are enhanced through the use of Readers Theatre (Ediger, 2002). The need to speak clearly and enunciate so that listeners understand what is said and the emphasis on proper grammar and its usage are vital to Readers Theatre and serve as strong indicators of successful speaking skills. Although rereading is essential for fluency and comprehension, oral rereading has even greater potential: "A student having difficulties with a selection when he reads it silently may find it much easier to grasp when he reads it out loud or when it is read to him by a student who understands it" (Post, 1971, p. 170).

Oral reading "more than silent reading can make clear to readers such literary elements as the role of narrator and characters" (Post, 1971, p. 169). Readers focus on their voices to portray a character. Therefore, they pay attention to articulation, pronunciation, fluency, and projection.

> "You can use your voice to stand out."
> MIDDLE SCHOOL STUDENT

Both fiction- and nonfiction-based scripts make frequent use of dialogue, including narration and conversation. Narration creates setting or movement and imparts other essential contextual information. Conversations are based on what the characters say; therefore, the language they use is especially important for understanding motivation and perspective. For example, a character with high social stature may use complex, formal language while a character without this high social stature may use humble, informal, or even incorrect language. Just as in real life, language changes according to the status, role, or mood of the character, and the language used in conversation allows the listener to "get inside" the story as well as the characters. Martinez, Roser, and Strecker (1999) found that students initiated discussion regarding oral interpretation of how characters should sound. They recorded two second-grade students talking about the characters Hansel and Gretel from the folktale:

Vicky: Your voice is too sweet. I don't think Gretel would talk nice to her stepmother.

Jessica: That's what I'm doing. Gretel is being too sweet because she can't stand her. I want it to sound like phoney, not like I'm really trying to be nice. (p. 332)

The components of language in speaking and listening give life to stories and ideas. "The sound of the language adds a new dimension of meaning" (Harste, Short, & Burke, 1988, p. 138). Through Readers Theatre, students also develop listening skills: both the basic skills as performers required for listening for cues and the listening skills of an audience. As audience members, students develop both aesthetic and efferent listening skills. They listen for pleasure, and they listen to learn and understand. Knowing that they will also be performers, they listen critically to evaluate the reading and performance, the script and language used, and the story or content.

Reading Fluency and Comprehension

Regardless of content or format, the key component of Readers Theatre is reading, specifically repeated reading that has been shown to foster fluency and to deepen students' understanding of text. Because the focus of Readers Theatre is reading, the list of Readers Theatre vocabulary in Table 1 presents key reading

Table 1. Readers Theatre Vocabulary

Aesthetic Listening:	Listening for pleasure.
Automaticity:	A decoding of text automatically so that attention focuses on comprehension.
Decoding:	Identifying words by attaching appropriate sounds to specific letters or letter sequences. A child decoding the word *cat* would read the letters with the appropriate sounds for /c/, /a/, and /t/.
Efferent Listening:	Listening for information.
Fluency:	The ability to read accurately with expression, pacing, and phrasing.
Guided Reading:	Teacher, as facilitator, listens to students read and guides them with questions to enhance their comprehension of text.
Intertextuality:	Making connections between texts.
Semantic Clues:	Clues to the meaning of words that focus on vocabulary and context. A child using semantic clues would read "The cat ran up the tree" and not "The cow ran up the tree" because of the context and the child's understanding of *cow* and *cat*.
Shared Reading:	Students observing the teacher reading from a shared text; then, when familiar with the text, reading it themselves.
Syntactic Clues:	Clues to the meaning of words that focus on sentence structure, grammar, and word order. A child using syntactic clues would read "She likes her new hat" rather than "She her hat new likes" because the structure of the latter sentence does not sound correct.

terms and definitions of the reading skills often utilized throughout the implementation of Readers Theatre. Opportunities for oral performance and interventions focused on reading fluency have been previously limited to the elementary grades. However, Readers Theatre is a viable strategy to be used with all grades, but especially middle school and high school where specific oral reading skills have been neglected (Goodson & Goodson, 2005).

Decoding, comprehension, fluency, and automaticity combine to create a successful reader, and each component is enhanced through the use of repeated readings in Readers Theatre. When readers first attempt to read, they must decode or translate print into sound. This process includes the use of phonics, context clues, sight words, and structural analysis. Next, the combinations of sounds or printed letters become words and then word groups and then sentences. For most readers, these first steps of decoding are automatic, as is the next step: focusing on the meaning within and between words, sentences, and paragraphs. Reading also requires decoding and making meaning from graphic elements of the text as well as connecting these visuals with the printed letters and words. These actions are the basics of the comprehension process. For an individual to be a successful reader, however, these actions must be combined with fluency (Ambruster, Lehr, & Osborn, 2001).

Fluency—the ability to read accurately and with expression, pacing, and ease—allows students to read aloud effortlessly and animatedly. As a fluent reader, they read with automaticity: They decode text automatically so their attention may be focused on comprehending what they read (Samuels, 1979). However, students who struggle with reading are usually unable to quickly identify most of the words in a text often because of a lack of automaticity. These students read in stilted, word-by-word delivery that sounds unnatural, and they are unable to pay attention to text meaning. They are also often unable to comprehend what they have read. These students have not had the experience or the practice of processing words and meaning automatically and fluently and may not have heard or paid attention to fluent and expressive reading.

> "Thanks to Readers Theatre, their speaking aloud is clearer and their rate and pacing are good."
> MIDDLE SCHOOL TEACHER

The reading component of the No Child Left Behind Act (2002), Reading First, declares that building fluency is one of its five major dictates. *Put Reading First* (Armbruster et al., 2001) states that "readers theatre provides readers with a legitimate reason to reread text and to practice fluency" (p. 29). Other studies also have found Readers Theatre to be a viable means of fostering fluency (Bidwell, 1990; Hoyt, 1992; Martinez et al., 1999; Rasinski, 2001; Rinehart, 1999; Tyler & Charad, 2000). Because research has shown that "many adolescents would benefit from additional time with the same text" (Goodson & Goodson, 2005, p. 24), repeated readings or rereading, a strategy inherent in Readers Theatre, will facilitate reading fluency and text comprehension. When students are reading fluently, their attention is no longer focusing on decoding but on comprehension (Allington, 1983; Dowhower, 1987, 1994; Homan, 1993; Samuels, 1979).

Readers Theatre offers a way for teachers to incorporate repeated readings in a motivating and meaningful context within their classrooms. Readers remember and understand more as they reread a story; their word recognition and pronunciation skills increase. Reading practice within the context of Readers Theatre becomes rehearsal with "the lure of performance" (Busching, 1981, p. 334), providing an incentive for students to return again and again to a specific passage with the goal of reading it fluently. The repeated reading involved in Readers Theatre affords practice needed for reading to become automatic and concurrent while creating a motivating forum to do so.

Reading Motivation

Students are given a meaningful context to read, write, speak, listen, and view through Readers Theatre. It serves as a motivational tool for them, developing their schema of specific texts, concepts, and language. In addition, Readers Theatre requires collaboration among students, establishing a valid and purposeful reason for students to work together for its creation and implementation. Rehearsals foster a confidence in and comfort level for all students and lead to a performance that provides a space where anything may happen.

Through repeated readings as well as performance with others, students make close contact with the text. They experience the text firsthand, no longer observers or even merely readers. This experience of performing a text serves as a major motivating factor for students to read (Bidwell, 1990; Martinez et al., 1999; Millin & Rinehart, 1999; Rinehart, 1999). "Repeated readings become rehearsals, and those rehearsals before their peers, and an eventual performance provide the incentive to practice reading the same passage repeatedly" (Goodson & Goodson, 2005, p. 25).

"Readers Theatre is a very fun way of learning things by acting them out. I like how you have to use body movements and your imagination instead of props. That helps you get into the reading more."

MIDDLE SCHOOL STUDENT

To enter on cue during rehearsals and performance, readers must carefully read and listen to the text. This challenge, or "the lure of performance" (Busching, 1981, p. 334), serves as an incentive for revisiting the text constantly, as students strive to bring the written words to life. Not only does Readers Theatre provide a meaningful context in which students read, write, speak, listen, and view, it also includes the bodily-kinesthetic intelligence as a physical aspect of learning (Larkin, 2001), supporting teachers' observations that many students have a desire to perform and express themselves orally (Prescott, 2003).

Readers Theatre also allows students to have a voice in decision-making and collaboration. Students should be allowed to select the role in which they are most comfortable, and this means allowing students to be readers, performers, and organizers. Each of these roles requires reading, speaking, listening, and preparing. Decision making regarding roles, choice of text, choice of language, pacing and expression, experimentation, and performance empowers students and sparks enthusiasm because they are in control of the process and it becomes their own.

Bidwell (1990) found that struggling middle school students were especially motivated by Readers Theatre. Her work with eighth graders included turning a trade book with which they were struggling into a script, then rehearsing and videotaping it. She discovered that students came alive, concentrating "so much harder because they were going to be performing in front of their class or parents, or sometimes the whole school" (p. 40).

Readers Theatre motivates students to read, to read expressively, and to read for understanding. Research (Bidwell, 1990; Chomsky, 1976; Martinez et al., 1999; Ranger, 1995; Uthman, 2002) has found a significant increase in students' motivation to read when participating in Readers Theatre. Students once viewed as poor readers were seen in a positive light by peers after participating in Readers Theatre. Students remained on task for longer periods of time and found a purpose for the repeated readings required for performance. The motivating aspects of Readers Theatre are key to its success in the classroom. In addition, the performance aspect of Readers Theatre motivates students to develop their vocabulary.

Vocabulary Development

Over a century of research on vocabulary has helped educators to understand that vocabulary knowledge is one of the best indicators of verbal ability (Sternberg, 1987; Terman, 1916) and that lack of vocabulary may be a crucial factor underlying school failure (Becker, 1977). Therefore, vocabulary development is essential, and, because words are best learned in context, vocabulary development may be facilitated through reading (Nagy, Herman, & Anderson, 1985). By encouraging students to develop and use well-organized scripts—scripts then used to verbally enact the story or present information—Readers Theatre creates a meaningful context in which students may learn new vocabulary and word usage.

Through Readers Theatre, students are introduced to texts of good literary quality and exposed to varied, rich, and colorful vocabulary. The promotion of word play where words "feel good on the tongue, sound good to the ear, and incite a riot of laughter in the belly" (Graves & Watts-Taffe, 2002, pp. 147–148) gives students pleasure while it develops their vocabulary. Creating a forum within the classroom where students are "immersed in a situation in which rich, precise, interesting, and inventive use of words is valued" (Graves & Watts-Taffe, p. 150) encourages students to develop their vocabulary. Such a forum is Readers Theatre. It gives students the responsibility of reading, speaking, listening, and writing language in a performance medium. Because the goal of performance is to engage the audience, Readers Theatre serves as an excellent vehicle for word play and vocabulary development.

In their writing of a script, students may borrow vocabulary from their reading. For example, young children developing scripts for Readers Theatre were found to use vocabulary from fairy tales they had heard frequently read aloud. Older students are able to

> extend their vocabularies when they have sustained interactions with a well-written text. Just as big, shared books provide a model for the language children use in their own stories, so does Readers Theatre (with its repeated readings of a text) perform a similar function. (Hill, 1990, p. 3)

Performance demands attention and so does the need for students to find the right words to gain that attention.

Beyond motivation is the manner in which vocabulary is learned. As noted earlier, vocabulary is best learned in context, but even context is not enough unless there are repetitive encounters. Especially beyond the elementary grades, "the need for repetition or redundancy is an important idea to hold on to in developing vocabulary as well as comprehension" (Early & Sawyer, 1984, p. 337). Vocabulary development occurs, not through assigned word lists, but through repeated encounters with words in natural contexts. Therefore, one of the essential elements of Readers Theatre, the concept of repeated readings, has applicability for vocabulary development. Because Readers Theatre uses repetition, activity, and reinforcement, three facets of the basic procedure for developing vocabulary (Smith & Barrett, 1975), it may be beneficial in increasing students' sight vocabulary.

Many middle school struggling readers are word-by-word readers. They may read and understand an individual word, but they do not anticipate what is coming next or realize that the word they have read is part of a sentence that must be understood as a whole. Both semantic and syntactic clues enable the reader to read and comprehend each word as well as the complete sentence. Through script read-alouds and repeated readings, Readers Theatre gives students the opportunity to get beyond reading word by word. Becoming familiar with the script and understanding both its meaning and use of language provides readers with experience in the use of semantic and syntactic clues.

Vocabulary development, critical for students of all ages, but especially for middle and high school students, is facilitated through reading (Nagy et al., 1985), word play (Graves & Watts-Taffe, 2002), and instruction that includes the repetition of a word, an activity, and reinforcement (Smith & Barrett, 1975). The forum of Readers Theatre, through the use of repeated readings, word play, semantic and syntactic clues, and peer feedback, all within a performance venue, is able to provide strong support for the development of students' vocabulary. Readers Theatre also has the potential to increase students' sense of story schema and language structure.

Story Schema

Reading from a shared text or creating or adapting scripts within the forum of Readers Theatre has the potential to increase students' knowledge of story schema and intertextuality. The sustained interactions with a well-written text during Readers Theatre provide a model of good writing and help to extend students' vocabulary (Hill, 1990).

Moving into the text, students come to recognize both its details and major themes. If reading fiction, students' story schema (expectations of the organization of story, including setting, characterization, theme, and plot) is developed. If reading dialogue, students also come to learn about point of view (Ratliff, 2000), allowing them to consider another's thoughts or perceptions. The elements of drama, such as movement, sound, and energy, as enacted through Readers Theatre, help students see things from different perspectives. Taking on the role of a character challenges students to develop empathy for that character or to better understand what motivated the character to act in a specific way.

> "Readers Theatre is a very expressive way to show feelings. I like this because instead of expressing my own feelings, I have the chance to express a character's feelings."
>
> MIDDLE SCHOOL STUDENT

If reading nonfiction, students begin to recognize specific organizational patterns of the text. Students reading both fiction and nonfiction focus on the content and the process of reading the text. Their schemata of prior life experiences and prior reading experiences with similar texts interact with the reading context. This interaction helps students to predict text and aids in their processing of letters and sounds. Concurrently, the development of schemata is facilitated by the recognition of letters, sounds, and words. This constant circular processing continues smoothly for successful readers and is supported and enhanced by Readers Theatre. As students continue to read, they also begin to grasp intertextuality (making connections between texts) and recognize how a narrative or expository text can be written in the form of a Readers Theatre script.

Language Structure

Readers Theatre may help students become more aware of language and its structure, especially syntax or the knowledge of word order, phrasing, and grammar. Students involved in dramatic activities such as Readers Theatre constantly explore ways of talking and using language. Pellegrini (1980) observed dramatic play with young children and discovered a correlation between such play and the children's understanding of syntactic structure. Using text in Readers Theatre to actively engage children allows them to examine word order, phrasing, and grammar for both literal and emotional meanings (i.e., "I do not fear…" versus "Can't scare me").

If students create or adapt a text for a Readers Theatre script, they learn to discriminate between trite or contrived language and effective language (Hill, 1990; Ratliff, 2000). They begin to consider the rhythm of the words, the length of the sentence, and the use of rhyme and repetition. Whatever makes an effective narrative or nonfiction text becomes obvious when students read aloud in Readers Theatre. Working on a script for performance allows students to grasp the use of language to describe ideas, to organize text, to create a mood, and to make a point. Devices such as repetition of a theme, key word, or phrase are incorporated into the script, and students become aware of pacing, sequencing of ideas, and editing needed to give the audience enough information to understand the characters, story, or concepts.

This exploration and use of language often leads to a greater awareness of the variations in language and a more critical use of syntactic patterns. The creation or adaptation of scripts for Readers Theatre also reinforces syntactic knowledge (DeRita & Weaver, 1991). Constant editing, rereading, reading aloud, and group feedback provide opportunities for students to discuss and better understand language structure as well as to become accurate and fluent readers of text.

Students engaged in Readers Theatre use "literate language" (McMaster, 1998, p. 575) and play with words, selecting the language they believe best fits. Through the implementation of Readers Theatre in the classroom, the power of story and the power of language are demonstrated. Students begin to realize that the written and the spoken word have the power to entertain, to create, to think, to reflect, to change, and to communicate.

Collaboration

All students in the class may be a part of Readers Theatre, and all readers rely on one another to succeed. This means that students not only have to work cooperatively, but they also have to communicate what they understand as well as what they want and be able to articulate reasons to support what they want. This cooperative process has both social and intellectual benefits, helping students to better communicate and work together and to better understand, ask, request, suggest, and test ideas.

The collaboration required of students to successfully create, practice, and implement Readers Theatre not only helps to eliminate labels of reading ability (Wolf, 1993), but it also helps students work together toward shared goals (Goodman, 1978; National Institute for Literacy, 2001; Sloyer, 1982). As students work together, their confidence grows, they begin to see themselves as part of a successful project, and they gain a sense of pride and satisfaction. Because Readers Theatre is an experience that may last only a few days or a few weeks, students are able to complete a project and see their efforts rewarded.

"You get to work with different people."

MIDDLE SCHOOL STUDENT

A lack of gender or racial discrimination in roles is possible in Readers Theatre. It is appropriate for a girl to read a boy's part, a student to read an adult's words, and conversations to be read by students from a variety of cultures. In fact, the very turning of these roles upside down and sideways often provides insights and humor for the reader and the audience.

One of the more appealing possibilities of Readers Theatre, in juxtaposition to the collaboration it requires, is the elimination of labels of reading ability through its adaptation to a variety of learning styles. Dewey (1944) advocates the combined use of sensory, motor, and mental processes for effective learning. Hoyt (1992) asserts that there are "many ways of knowing" (p. 580), and that students develop greater reading comprehension when they are able to integrate reading with drama and oral language. Trousdale and Harris (1993) discuss many ways Readers Theatre includes different kinds of intelligences beyond verbal intelligence in the interpretation of literature. In her yearlong study using Readers Theatre, Wolf (1993) found that interpretative behaviors such as language use, body movement, and affective interpretations allowed for a more fluent reading and for stronger comprehension as the students enacted self-created literary texts.

> "I like Readers Theatre because you express yourself in many ways, like when we were reading *The True Confessions of Charlotte Doyle*. I made a paper wig so I could read Charlotte's part. It was awesome!"
>
> MIDDLE SCHOOL STUDENT (MALE READING A FEMALE CHARACTER'S LINES)

Drama provides a context for students to employ the language arts (Pappas & Brown, 1987). Struggling students especially are often able to be successful through Readers Theatre because there is a physical aspect of learning (bodily, kinesthetic intelligence) as well as the development of interpersonal, social, and collaborative skills. The use of these modalities allows students to weave together many possible text interpretations in addition to providing practice and purpose for the actual reading of text.

The integrated language event of Readers Theatre—with its focus on speaking and listening and opportunities for reading, writing, thinking, and viewing—promotes cooperative interaction with peers and enables students to read expressively and with confidence (Prescott, 2003). Further, the concept of repeated readings has been shown to lead to significant gains in fluency and increased student motivation to read. Readers Theatre provides a context for vocabulary development; it immerses students in story schema and the structure of language by providing examples of diverse quality literature that is both read and heard. Finally, the oral communication skills required in Readers Theatre prompt students to reread orally, engage in discussion and dialogue with attention to pronunciation and fluency, and comprehend what is read and heard more clearly. The impact that the process and performance of Readers Theatre have on students' language development and literacy skills as noted here is enormous. The benefits are many and varied, and, perhaps most importantly, the use of Readers Theatre is easily integrated into the classroom and its curriculum.

Adaptability and Practicality of Readers Theatre

In addition to being supported by a solid research base, Readers Theatre is practical and can be implemented by classroom teachers. Because of its adaptability to age, audience, and ability, Readers Theatre is more approachable for most classroom teachers. In addition, its emphasis on reading and the use of quality text allows for a smooth integration into content areas.

Because students may devise roles and select their own parts in Readers Theatre, there exists a noticeable lack of emphasis on reading ability. The wide spectrum of roles and the process of Readers Theatre itself allow students with special needs, struggling readers, and/or emergent readers to play a part. Teachers recognize students' varying abilities and are able to structure performance groups, select appropriate materials to be performed, and suggest or assign roles that will create successful reading and performance situations for all students. A performance may have one person reading each part or groups of students reading parts as a chorus. The latter format gives each student a role and allows the group to set a pace that helps struggling or emergent readers to successfully experience reading. With mixed-ability classrooms becoming more and more common, the adaptability of Readers Theatre for all levels of students is extremely beneficial for teachers.

Readers Theatre makes accessible a variety of texts. It also engages students with text through discussion, reading aloud, listening, visualization of text, and assessment of their work in relation to the text content, and provides the time for students to be engaged beyond simply discussion. It allows students to play with language, words, and concepts, and to share what they have learned. Through Readers Theatre, teachers are able to involve their students in "an interactive, interpretive process without the constraints of typical theatrical endeavors involving elaborate props, costumes, memorization of lines, lengthy rehearsals, and scenery" (Herrell & Jordan, 2002, p. 166). Given the time constraints of the school day, this very simplicity makes Readers Theatre more approachable and possible for the classroom teacher.

REFERENCES

Allington, R.L. (1983). Fluency: The neglected reading goal. *The Reading Teacher, 36*, 556–561.

Armbruster, B., Lehr, F., & Osborn, J. (2001). *Put reading first: The research building blocks for teaching children to read. Kindergarten through grade 3*. Jessup, MD: National Institute for Literacy.

Becker, W.C. (1977). Teaching reading and language to the disadvantaged—What we have learned from field research. *Harvard Educational Review, 47*, 518–543.

Bidwell, S.M. (1990). Using drama to increase motivation, comprehension, and fluency. *Journal of Reading, 34*, 38–41.

Busching, B. (1981). Readers Theatre: An education for language and life. *Language Arts, 58*, 330–338.

Chomsky, C. (1976). After decoding: What? *Language Arts, 53*, 288–296, 314.

Coger, L.I., & White, M.R. (1982). *Readers Theatre handbook: A dramatic approach to literature*. Glenview, IL: Scott Foresman.

Davis, S. (2003, September 17). Congresswoman Susan Davis introduces bill to reduce high school dropout rates [Press release]. Retrieved from http://www.house.gov/susandavis/press/pr091703hsdropoutrate.html

DeRita, C., & Weaver, S. (1991). Cross-age literacy program. *Reading Improvement, 28*, 244–248.

Dewey, J. (1944). *Democracy and education*. New York: Macmillan.

Donahue, P., Voelkl, K.E., Campbell, J.R., & Mazzeo, J. (1999). *The NAEP 1998 reading report card for the nation and the states*. Princeton, NJ: National Assessment of Educational Progress.

Dowhower, S.L. (1987). Effects of repeated reading on second-grade transitional readers' fluency and comprehension. *Reading Research Quarterly, 22*, 389–406.

Dowhower, S.L. (1994). Repeated reading revisited: Research into practice. *Reading & Writing Quarterly: Overcoming Learning Difficulties, 10*, 343–358.

Early, M., & Sawyer, D.J. (1984). *Reading to learn in grades 5–12*. New York: Harcourt Brace Jovanovich.

Ediger, M. (2002). *Oral communication in the reading curriculum* [Opinion paper]. (ERIC Document Reproduction Service No. ED470700)

Goodman, J.A. (1978). *Teaching the total language with Readers Theatre*. (ERIC Document Reproduction Service No. ED191321)

Goodson, F.T., & Goodson, L.A. (2005). You oughta use the periods and stuff to slow down: Reading fluency through oral interpretation of YA lit. *Voices From the Middle, 13*(2), 24–29.

Graves, M.F., & Watts-Taffe, S.M. (2002). The place of word consciousness in a research-based vocabulary program. In A.E. Farstrup & S.J. Samuels (Eds.), *What research has to say about reading instruction* (3rd ed., pp. 140–165). Newark, DE: International Reading Association.

Harste, J.C., Short, K.G., & Burke, C. (1988). *Creating classrooms for authors: The reading–writing connection*. Portsmouth, NH: Heinemann.

Herrell, A., & Jordan, M. (2002). *Fifty active learning strategies for improving reading comprehension*. Englewood Cliffs, NJ: Prentice Hall.

Hill, S. (1990). *Readers Theatre: Performing the text*. South Yara, VIC, Australia: Eleanor Curtain.

Homan, S.P. (1993). Effects of repeated readings and nonrepetitive strategies on students' fluency and comprehension. *Journal of Educational Research, 87*, 94–99.

Hoyt, L. (1992). Many ways of knowing: Using drama, oral interactions, and the visual arts to enhance reading comprehension. *The Reading Teacher, 45*, 580–584.

Larkin, B.R. (2001). "Can we act it out?" *The Reading Teacher, 54*, 478–481.

Martinez, M., Roser, N., & Strecker, S. (1999). I never thought I could be a star: A Readers Theatre ticket to fluency. *The Reading Teacher, 52*, 326–333.

McMaster, J.C. (1998). "Doing" literature: Using drama to build literacy classrooms: The segue for a few struggling readers. *The Reading Teacher, 51*, 574–584.

Millin, S.K., & Rinehart, S.D. (1999). Some of the benefits of readers theater participation for second grade Title I students. *Reading Research and Instruction, 39*, 71–88.

Moore, D.W., Bean, T.W., Birdyshaw, D., & Rycik, J.A. (1999). *Adolescent literacy: A position statement for the Commission on Adolescent Literacy of the International Reading Association*. Newark, DE: International Reading Association.

Nagy, W.E., Herman, P.A., & Anderson, R.C. (1985). Learning words from context. *Reading Research Quarterly, 20*, 233–253.

National Institute for Literacy. (2001). *Put reading first*. Washington, DC: Office of Educational Research and Improvement.

No Child Left Behind Act of 2001, Pub. L. No. 107-110, 115 Stat. 1425 (2002).

Pappas, C., & Brown, E. (1987). Learning to read by reading: Learning how to extend the functional potential of language. *Research in the Teaching of English, 21*, 160–177.

Pellegrini, A.D. (1980). The relationship between kindergartners' play and achievement in prereading, language, and writing. *Psychology in the Schools, 17*, 530–535.

Post, R. (1971). An oral interpreter's approach to the teaching of elementary school literature. *The Speech Teacher, 20*, 167–173.

Prescott, J.O. (2003). The power of Readers' Theater: An easy way to make dramatic changes in kids' fluency, writing, listening, and social skills. *Instructor, 112*(5), 22–26, 82–84.

Ranger, L. (1995). *Improving reading comprehension through multi-faceted approach utilizing drama*. Unpublished master's thesis, Keane College, Union, NJ.

Rasinski, T. (2001, April). *Revisiting reading rate as a diagnostic tool for reading difficulties*. Paper presented at the annual meeting of the American Educational Research Association, Seattle, WA. (ERIC Document Reproduction Service No. ED453246)

Ratliff, G.L. (2000, November). *Readers Theatre: An introduction to classroom performance*. Paper presented at the 86th annual meeting of the National Communication Association, Seattle, WA. (ERIC Document Reproduction Service No. ED455550)

Rinehart, S.D. (1999). "Don't think for a minute that I'm getting up there": Opportunities for readers' theater in a tutorial for children with reading problems. *Reading Psychology, 20*, 71–89.

Samuels, S.J. (1979). The method of repeated readings. *The Reading Teacher, 32*, 403–408.

Shepard, A. (1994). From script to stage: Tips for Readers Theatre. *The Reading Teacher, 48*, 184–186.

Sloyer, S. (1982). *Readers Theatre: Story dramatization in the classroom*. Urbana, IL: National Council of Teachers of English.

Smith, R.J., & Barrett, T.C. (1975). *Teaching reading in the middle grades*. Reading, MA: Addison-Wesley.

Sternberg, R.J. (1987). Most vocabulary is learned from context. In M.G. McKeown & M.E. Curtis (Eds.), *The nature of vocabulary acquisition* (pp. 89–105). Hillsdale, NJ: Erlbaum.

Terman, L.M. (1916). *The measurement of intelligence*. Boston: Houghton Mifflin.

Trousdale, A.M., & Harris, V.J. (1993). Missing links in literary response: Group interpretation of literature. *Children's Literature in Education, 24*, 195–207.

Tyler, B., & Charad, D.J. (2000). Using Readers Theatre to foster fluency in struggling readers: A twist on the repeated reading strategy. *Reading and Writing Quarterly: Overcoming Learning Difficulties, 16*, 163–168.

Uthman, L.E. (2002). Readers' theater: An approach to reading with more than a touch of drama. *Teaching PreK–8, 32*(6), 56–57.

Wolf, S.A. (1993). What's in a name? Labels and literacy in Readers Theatre. *The Reading Teacher, 46*, 540–545.

CHAPTER 2

Launching Readers Theatre in the Middle School Classroom

Now that you are ready to implement Readers Theatre in your classroom, this chapter will lay the groundwork of the entire process, providing you with a general understanding of all the basic steps involved in Readers Theatre, from script generation to performance. This chapter is divided into five sections. The first section, Establishing Group Dynamics, describes the changing roles and responsibilities of you and your students as you move through the process, and the subsequent sections guide you through the remaining steps: Selecting Material, Understanding the Material, Adapting the Material to a Script, and Casting. Chapter 3 expands on this foundation, focusing on developing and building the performance.

Establishing Group Dynamics

Changing Roles and Responsibilities of the Teacher

Because student independence is the eventual goal of any activity, the teacher's role in creating a Readers Theatre experience follows a continuum that moves from teacher-directed to student-directed with the goal of student independence. Figure 2 illustrates this continuum, depicting a possible road map to help teachers facilitate that independence. However, because students' needs and abilities differ, and because the process of Readers Theatre is dependent upon the students, the range of roles a teacher may play will vary. Some teachers may run through the entire continuum for each Readers Theatre performance, some may work through the continuum over the course of the school year, and some may stay at one of the stages because that is what works for them and for their students. What is important to remember is that teachers do have an indispensable role in Readers Theatre, one that will shift and change according to the students.

Figure 2. Changing Role of the Teacher in Readers Theatre

Teacher-Directed	Shared Reading	Guided Reading	Student-Directed

Teacher-Directed Performances: Teacher as Writer, Producer, and Director. In order for students to *be* successful, they must understand what it is they need to *do* to be successful. This basic tenet of teaching holds true for the use of Readers Theatre in the middle school classroom. Introducing the concept and creating a structure for its implementation is purely teacher-directed. An introduction may include a video of Readers Theatre, overheads of basic staging and scripts, or a teacher-led discussion of reading aloud and how that practice becomes Readers Theatre. Structure in Readers Theatre includes the creation or selection of a script, basic staging, and the roles of both readers and audience. An initial attempt at Readers Theatre would have the teacher create or select a script, choose the readers and assign roles to them, make time for rehearsal, position the readers on stage, and serve as director for the rehearsals and performance.

It is imperative to allot students time for rehearsal, especially for the reading of their script. Teacher-directed lessons where students spend the maximum amount of time engaged in reading text are necessary to develop fluency (Berliner, 1981). Teachers need to provide time for reading and repeated reading, time that may be spent reading the script for fluency and expression.

Part of this teacher-directed stage is the teacher's role of producer/director. Regardless of student independence, this specific role is almost always teacher-directed. It includes the selection of theme or curricular connections for Readers Theatre and the creation of an array of thematic materials from which students may choose. The teacher often identifies and works with the performers, monitoring the group process and helping to decide who does what (see Figure 3).

Figure 3. Teacher Meeting With Students in Groups

Adapting a script will often become the teacher's responsibility because of time constraints in the school day. (See chapter 3 for a list of different schedules so that you may choose the time frame most appropriate for implementing Readers Theatre in your classroom.)

As producer/director, the teacher identifies important structural elements and vocabulary essential to understanding the context, content, and emotions within the text. The teacher organizes and schedules space and time for rehearsals and the final performance and may seek additional resources (including extra materials and even other staff) to help with the performances. Finally, the teacher may invite an audience from outside the classroom. Overall, as producer/director, the teacher serves as coach, mentor, and facilitator throughout the process of Readers Theatre. These roles are specifically focused on modeling and eliciting fluent and expressive reading from the students.

Shared Reading: Teacher as Fluent-Reading Model. *Shared reading* is defined as students first observing the teacher reading fluently from a shared text and then reading along with the teacher (Tompkins, 2005). Readers Theatre is dependent upon students' reading with expression. Teachers need to be effective reading models so that students understand what expressive reading sounds like. The use of a model text allows students to see what is being read and hear how it is being read.

Moving beyond the teacher-directed mode in Readers Theatre, the teacher at the shared reading level reads the text or script aloud while the students follow by reading silently. Then, once the text is familiar, students participate by reading aloud. It is during shared reading that the teacher may focus attention on specific vocabulary, text organization, or word and letter combinations to enhance students' oral reading of the text. This stage on the continuum focuses on students' reading fluency. Beyond demonstrations of expressive reading, teachers also need to provide instructional support and feedback to students. This task is addressed in the third stage, guided reading.

Guided Reading: Teacher as Facilitator. In guided reading, the teacher moves to the role of facilitator, stepping in and out of the reading, demonstrating specific reading strategies, clarifying misconceptions, and taking advantage of teachable moments (Tompkins, 2005). The focus here continues to be on fluency but also moves to student comprehension of the text. By meeting with students individually or in small groups, the teacher creates a forum for students to talk about how good readers sound and how a certain script can be brought to life.

As students read, the teacher listens and asks questions that enable students to get inside the story. For example, when one seventh-grade teacher used Readers Theatre to instruct students on narrative poetry, she sat and listened to each group read. At certain points she checked students' comprehension by asking them questions such as, "What does that mean?" She focused on specific vocabulary, key phrases, and symbolism, and also addressed their expressiveness in reading. In one group, a student read the verse in a monotone. The teacher said, "All right, but can you hear him bragging? Listen!" and she read the same verse with great feeling. Then she asked, "Now why is he bragging?"

As a facilitator, teachers may ask students about bringing dialogue to life, how to use punctuation in their reading, and the difference between the narrator and character texts. The use of punctuation in this context focuses students' attention on how it may help to guide their expressive reading. For example, a comma means to take a pause for logical meaning or emphasis. An exclamation point indicates an important or exciting statement that could be said louder and faster. Specific questions may include the following:

- Do you pause for dramatic effect? Where? Why?
- What tone should you use when reading that line?
- What is that punctuation telling you?
- What is the narrator's role? How should he or she sound?

As a guide, the teacher poses thoughtful questions and comments that move students toward a better understanding of the text as well as a more expressive reading of it. Teachers serve both as a model and resource, allowing students to discuss their own ideas or questions regarding the text and the reading. Also, the collaborative nature of Readers Theatre requires the teacher to help facilitate successful group work through the selection of group members, assignment of roles within each group, and assistance or mediation in problem solving.

Student-Directed Performances: Students as Writers, Producers, and Directors. As students become more familiar with the process of Readers Theatre and more proficient at reading the script and enacting specific roles, the teacher may intercede only when needed. Often, when students have experience with Readers Theatre, the teacher's main role is to help with the creation or selection of the script and to serve as stage director, offering explicit advice.

Observations of middle school classrooms engaged in Readers Theatre found the teachers moving in and out of numerous roles. They admitted that knowing their students well enabled each teacher to group students so that they would work together effectively. When each group began to work on their rereading, the teachers observed and constantly helped specific individuals and groups problem solve.

Student independence is evident in students' ability to work more autonomously in groups and to raise and address questions that focus on their comprehension of the text. For example, a group of seventh-grade boys were rehearsing the poem "Casey at the Bat" for a Readers Theatre presentation. After hearing a strong reader read the last several stanzas, one boy asked, "So he struck out? How come the umpire didn't say 'strike three'?" There was silence as the group mulled this over. Finally, another boy responded, "Maybe the writer didn't want you to know what happened until the very end." Then another chimed in, "Yeah! Like *out* is the very last word in the poem!"

Selecting Student Performance Groups

Readers Theatre requires that students work well together in groups to make meaning from texts and to communicate that meaning. To be most effective, each group should have four or five members. In a class of 25 students, there would be five groups of five students. A primary consideration for teachers is the amount and type of group-work experiences students have had.

If the class has worked frequently and productively in groups, there is little preparation needed for the move to Readers Theatre performance groups. In this case, group members might be selected on the basis of interest in a particular text for performance (some good examples for starting out are already well-known stories, such as Little Red Riding Hood, Goldilocks and the Three Bears, and The Three Little Pigs). The story line of Little Red Riding Hood is used as an example in both this chapter and chapter 3. It is not adapted from any one text or a completed script for a performance; it is only used as a possible adaptation because it is a familiar story and can be used as a simple illustration of script development and staging for performance. Each student would list a first and second choice. Students might also identify at least three out of the five group members with whom they would like to work on the project. The teacher would then assemble groups based on students' interest in the text, choices for group members, and knowledge of how well the students read, comprehend, and work with others.

> "If you are with groups, listen to what they have to say and don't do everything that you want to do."
> MIDDLE SCHOOL STUDENT

If the class has had limited or no experience working in groups, it will be necessary to provide practice with the traditional roles used in groups: facilitator, recorder, presenter, illustrator, researcher, and so forth. In this case, the teacher would ask students to select their top three choices for a text from a teacher-developed list of texts. Then, the teacher would determine group members based on students' interests and knowledge of students' ability to work in groups. When students are comfortable working together, they can then move into performance groups. These groups are cooperative but also serve as a focus group for a specific script. Students in performance groups work through a variety of roles to bring a text to life. Because grouping is such an important aspect of successful participation, it is essential that struggling readers and ELLs are placed in a group whose members are supportive, helpful, and respectful. It is important to identify in what ways the struggling reader can make positive and unique contributions to the group roles (sound, visuals, etc.). Further, the group's director should be able to act as a coach for the struggling reader, or there might be several class coaches who can work on vocal performances with struggling readers.

Roles and Responsibilities of the Students

Regardless of the level of experiences with group work, each group needs an effective facilitator, a reliable recorder, and students who can get along with one another. More specifically, each group needs one reader who has good comprehension and one reader who reads fluently. These may or may not be the same reader. Depending upon both the text and the personality of the class, the number of males and females in a group may influence text selection as well as group relationships. Gender, however, is not a consideration when casting. For example, in casting for a performance of Little Red Riding Hood, a girl could read the part of the Wolf or the Hunter; a boy could read the part of Little Red Riding Hood or Grandmother. The performance is about verbally and visually suggesting the character's thoughts, emotions, and actions, and is not a literal interpretation of characters and not necessarily a gender match with the reader. It is helpful to assign or elect group roles or tasks and to give each member a folder for the script and other materials. The roles are director, stage manager, artist, sound creator, and researcher.

> "Make sure your whole group knows what's going on."
> MIDDLE SCHOOL STUDENT

Director. The director is the most able reader, one who can understand and communicate the meaning of the text. The director might also suggest who reads which part of the text. For example, Elizabeth reads all the direct quotes for Little Red Riding Hood ("Granny, what big teeth you have!"); Susan reads the first two paragraphs, which describe the setting; John reads the introduction and the Hunter.

Stage Manager. The stage manager is essentially a recorder. On a master script, the stage manager marks the reader and name of character for each section of the script, writes the reader's postures and actions, and the whole-picture floor plans (see the scripts in chapters 4, 5, and 6 for examples). The stage manager and the researcher make and keep a list of all production elements (costume pieces, props, music or sound) and the order of events (introduction of performers, background information for the text, transitions, conclusions). The stage manager records the group schedule and a list of tasks that need to be done.

Artist. The artist is responsible for finding and creating any background visuals (murals, slides, photos, posters) or objects (costume pieces and props) used in performance. The artist also works with one or more group members to develop these production elements.

Sound Creator. The sound creator has three tasks: (1) selection, recording, and playing of any music that may introduce or conclude the performance; (2) selection and rehearsal of parts of text that are read by two or more readers as a chorus; and (3) listening in rehearsals for appropriate volume, rate, pronunciation, and feeling in each group member's reading. Each group member should also listen carefully and add comments to those made by the sound creator.

Researcher. The researcher finds information about the text and its author. The researcher also reports the group's questions and concerns to the teacher for suggestions or explanations.

Because class size and dynamics vary, these roles are flexible. Additional roles may be created as teacher or students see fit, and the same roles may be handled by two or more students. Students may discuss the roles and determine which student would be most interested in or best for each role. The teacher should make the final decisions on the assignment of group roles based upon students' choices and students' abilities. The key to the function and assignment roles in the performance group is to keep the focus on the final Readers Theatre performance.

Although it is important to form groups whose members have the potential to work well together and who have clearly defined roles and tasks, it is important for the teacher to regularly observe and work with each group. Working with a group may include helping to solve group and performance difficulties, observing and commenting constructively on understanding and interpretation of text, or making performance suggestions for each member of the group and for the whole group. It is also a good idea to help the group create a plan if a group member is absent on the day of performance.

Selecting Material

Material for Readers Theatre performances can come from many sources. These include fiction (sections of novels, short stories, fables, folk tales, myths, and legends), nonfiction (diaries, letters, memoirs, oral histories, sections of a biography or autobiography, newspapers, and historical documents), and poetry. Teachers can use texts in their own classrooms and school libraries for sources of material. There are also many community resources (librarians, poets, storytellers, historians, community sources of oral histories, state historical associations, newspapers, and museums) who can provide rich materials for presentations.

Whatever the form or content, students need to have read, explored, discussed, analyzed, and elaborated with a text genre similar to one they will be performing. For example, students' first introduction to narrative poetry should not be for a Readers Theatre performance. That genre should be introduced prior to Readers Theatre implementation so that when students select or are assigned a narrative poem they are familiar and comfortable with it.

Materials should also reflect the interests of the students (adventure, sports, nature, relationships, fantasy, etc.) and their prior experiences with the genres and general content. Part of the text-selection process is clearly determined by the students' familiarity with similar genres, their interests, and their reading levels. The material should be complex enough to engage students for an extended period of time and to require group participation to make meaning clear; however, material should not be so complicated in terms of context, vocabulary, or concepts that the teacher must explain the entire text.

"Pick something you want to do so Readers Theatre is something fun to do."

MIDDLE SCHOOL STUDENT

Material for Readers Theatre can also extend and further engage students in an area already studied. If the class is reading young adult novels in literature circles or as a whole class, each group (literature or performance) could select one chapter for Readers Theatre performance. If the class is studying poetry, students could develop performances of additional poems on similar themes or topics. If students are studying other cultures, an extension of this study might include performances of myths, folk tales, or legends of that culture. If discussing a social studies unit on immigration or the Civil War, students might develop performances based upon oral histories, letters, diaries, newspaper articles, or other documents of that time period.

Once the general content, genre, text complexity, and students' interests are determined, the teacher selects 5 to 10 possible texts for performance. The school librarian and other content area teachers can be a great resource in finding materials both in print and on the Internet. The texts used as the basis for scripts in chapters 4 through 6 are great sources, and Appendix A lists other recommended sources for scripts. Depending on time schedule and students' experiences with group work, students can be given an opportunity to read all of these teacher-selected texts and select one, two, or three they would like to work on for performance.

To give students easy access to these materials, they may be placed in a classroom library, in the school library on reserve, or online through the school's website. The teacher may want to preview the texts with the whole class before students read them. This preview is much like a book talk, which offers some connection to the students' experiences and highlights key points of interest, action, and information. It may also be necessary to provide some information on the context, concepts, or vocabulary used in a particular selection.

In addition to considering the texts for the students as readers and performers, the texts should also be considered for the audience members. The student groups may perform for only their classmates or for an invited audience (younger students, peers, or community groups). The selected audience should be able to understand and enjoy the performance for its variety of topics, perspectives, and potential performance styles. Based on student choices of material, potential performance groups, and time of performance, the teacher develops a program of text performances that is engaging for audiences *and* performers. The development of successful groups and the selection of appropriate texts are the foundation for a successful Readers Theatre performance.

Understanding the Material

After the performance groups and their texts have been selected, students must develop an understanding of the selected materials before developing a script for performance. There are two types of understanding of text necessary for Readers Theatre: content and emotional. Content understanding includes identifying and describing ideas, information, events, and actions that occur in the text or script. Emotional understanding is an identification and description of the speakers' feelings when saying or conveying the content understanding. It is important for students to possess both types of understanding of the texts selected for performance as each contributes to the fluent and expressive reading of the performance materials.

Developing a Content Understanding of Text

Content understanding refers to comprehension of the basic plot or storyline of the text, identification of the main ideas and key supporting details, and an understanding of the features of a genre (e.g., fables conclude with a statement of moral; short stories and poetry compress actions and experiences). Understanding the text also involves some understanding of the context of the work to be performed and the author's background in relation to the text. Finally, understanding meaning of important vocabulary words that relate to main ideas and key details is also necessary.

Often, key vocabulary words and text-specific word groupings or phrases need to be pulled out and examined in the context of the work and in relation to a dictionary meaning. This vocabulary work may be developed by the teacher, the teacher and the group, or the group depending on the students' abilities with learning new vocabulary words. Regardless of how the words are learned, it is important that the teacher work with the students to develop proper pronunciation of the new words for the performance. This can be done through word repetition (say it correctly three times in a row, and it is yours). Teacher and students could also use phonetics or create their own phonetic way of writing the word so it can be remembered and, if needed, written directly over the word in the scripts. Vocabulary cards with the word, its definition, a pronunciation key, and the sentence in which it appears can be created by the group. The stage manager records and keeps a master list of all the vocabulary and phrases, and the individual performers also have a list of the words and phrases that they read.

The following questions may aid in understanding content and may be used either for individual students or for group discussion:

- What is the main idea?

- What are some words or phrases from the text that describe that idea?

- What are some words that are new or whose meanings are not clear? What do you need to do to find the meanings and pronunciations of those words?

- Why do you think the writer created the text? Who was the intended audience?

- What ideas, phrases, or words will need particular emphasis or explanation for your audience?

- How can you connect the main idea to your experiences? Your audience members' experiences?

Developing an Emotional Understanding of Text

In addition to content understanding, the performers should also have an emotional understanding of the text. *Emotional understanding* means that students need to be able to identify the feelings and motivations of the speaker and what words or phrases suggest those feelings. One way to develop an emotional understanding would be for each student to list the emotions that he or she finds in the text and its context (the word, phrase, sentences). When the lists are completed, the students compare their lists with others in the group and make an agreed-upon master list for each speaker's emotions found in the performance script.

The following questions are useful for both individual student use and for the group discussion:

- Who is the person speaking?

- What kind of person is the speaker?

- Who is the speaker talking to?

- What is the feeling of the speaker?

- What words, phrases, or sentences in the text suggest that feeling?

- What could make the speaker feel this way?

- Have you experienced similar situations or feelings?

- What feeling do you want to express to your audience?

When the group has determined both the content and emotional meanings of the text, the stage manager and researcher should record the conclusions on the script. These conclusions might be responses to the questions mentioned previously on content understanding and emotional understanding. For example, in a script for Little Red Riding Hood, the phrase "Grandmother, what big eyes you have!" could have written beside it the feelings "fear" and "surprise," or each speaker could list emotions like these next to their parts. The information about the speakers will eventually become part of each performer's folder for use in developing both ideas and feelings in performance.

Adapting the Material to a Script

In Readers Theatre performances, most, if not all, of the script is already written. Whether the story is fiction, nonfiction, or poetry, most of the work already exists as a novel chapter, poem, diary, or other document. The script for performance can be copied or retyped from the original materials. It may be necessary to cut and paste sections together to reduce the number of script pages. If retyping the script, it may also be necessary to enlarge the print so that the script materials are large enough to be seen and read easily during the performance.

Each section is marked with brackets to indicate a section and labeled with the name of the speaker. For example, in Little Red Riding Hood, the words of Little Red Riding Hood would appear in the text as: LRH [Grandmother, what big teeth you have!]. LRH is an abbreviation for the character name and is placed in the left margin and is connected with an arrow to the brackets. The stage manager keeps a list of the speaker name abbreviations and marks a master script with the brackets and margin notes of speakers' words (see the side for Mr. Keetch on page 33 of this chapter and chapters 4, 5, and 6 for scripts of various genres and how margin notes and brackets are used to assign roles and provide stage directions).

Dividing the Material for Script Adaptation

The major work involved in script adaptation is dividing the text into units of meaning for performance. It is not necessary or appropriate to do major rewriting to adapt or develop a script because the focus of Readers Theatre is on reading more than writing. The job of the performers is to communicate that existing work and to provide needed introductions, transitions, and conclusions, which will enhance the performers' and audience's understanding of and engagement with the work. Summarizing or editing of a text may be necessary for audience understanding or to fit materials into a performance time. For example, a short story or novel chapter may need to have elaborate descriptions shortened, summarized, or deleted if they are not central to the performance.

The teacher and students also need to divide the scripts into clear meaningful sections for reading aloud.

Decisions on how the text should be divided for script adaptation should be based on the material to be performed, the time needed for script development, and the abilities of the students. Division can be based upon single paragraphs or stanzas; description or narration based upon point of view or content; direct dialogue with or without related narration or description, repeated words or phrases, which may be read by two or more performers; or whole-group responses or refrains (see chapters 4, 5, and 6 for examples). Whether the text is complex or simple, the students should spend most of the preparation time making and communicating meaning, not developing or adapting a script. If the material to be performed is relatively complete and needs little introduction and minimal internal restructuring (e.g., Little Red Riding Hood), the students in the group can divide the script with limited teacher input. Once completed, students discuss their choices with the teacher and together they make final script divisions.

If material is complex, not highly structured (such as oral histories), or not easily divided into logical or emotional sections, it is better to have the teacher make the script divisions. Therefore, with complex materials, the teacher's task is to adapt the script; the students' task is to understand and to communicate the script. The teacher can meet with each performance group and explain the reasons for the script divisions. The teacher summarizes, paraphrases, or edits sections of the selected text for performance (see the script in chapter 4 adapted from *The True Confessions of Charlotte Doyle*, for example). The teacher would explain to the performance group the reasons for the divisions, the editing, and the sources for the introduction and conclusion.

> "I am not very good at public reading. Readers Theatre is good practice though."
>
> MIDDLE SCHOOL STUDENT

Necessary Script Additions

In addition to script divisions for readers, the performance will need to have some combination of introduction, transitions, and conclusion that are not part of the existing text. For example, in a performance of Little Red Riding Hood, an introduction might explain the time period, talking animals, and the nature of the fable form. Depending upon the materials, the students' background knowledge, and easy-to-use resources, the students may develop an introduction and conclusion. The teacher could provide the background materials, which group members could summarize, paraphrase, or quote directly. Teacher and students could provide transitions within the text. Regarding internal changes within the original text, it might be necessary to condense or summarize narration or change a few words that are key elements for understanding and that the audience might not recognize. Because there is a clear ending to the story, it would not be necessary to develop an ending statement as a conclusion.

In a second example, a performance based upon oral histories needs an introduction that establishes a context for the speakers and a description about who gathered the histories and under what conditions. Each history also briefly identifies and describes the speaker and connects his experiences to a larger context. For example, the speaker is a 10-year-old boy from Italy arriving with his mother and younger sister at Ellis Island around 1920 (see the Immigrant Voices Unit in chapter 5). This script would have some additional oral histories based on a timeline or similar themes. The Ellis Island oral histories could be arranged by date of arrival, age or country of the immigrant, or topic (first view of the island, medical exams, the dining room). The conclusion might be a particular history that in some way summarizes or emphasizes the content of the performance, or it might be a teacher- or student-created conclusion. These elements may be simple or complex depending upon the works to be performed, the abilities of the students, and the needs of the audience. Unless there is a long rehearsal and development period for the Readers Theatre performances, the teacher develops the introductions, transitions, and conclusions, and inserts them at appropriate points in the script or text to be performed (see examples in chapters 4, 5, and 6).

Casting

Once the script has been completed, the student director, as facilitator of the group, will work with the group to decide who will read which parts. Stronger readers may wish to read more, weaker readers to read less. It is important for the teacher and the group director to remind students that they will have time to practice and become comfortable with reading from the text rather than just reading it out loud only once. In discussing casting, the students may volunteer to read certain parts and suggest that others read particular sections. The content and emotional understandings of the text, including character motivations and emotions, have already been identified by the group. In the casting process, the students can read one or more sections to see what it is like to read the script out loud. The casting discussion incorporates a combination of student choices and teacher suggestions with opportunities for students to try out reading a section. Although this is an ideal way of casting, there may need to be some adaptations based on the students in the group or new understanding of the material based on casting discussions or rehearsing.

When the casting is completed, the stage manager lists the names of the readers next to the speaker names from the divided text (e.g., Jim—N1, Mike—Intro, Michelle—LRH). All group members should receive a complete copy of this script. It is often helpful to give copies of the script to struggling readers and ELLs before it is presented to the whole class or group and to provide a summary and paraphrase of the material and vocabulary words. In addition, the classroom teacher, reading teacher, or special education teacher can preview the materials with the struggling readers and help them to identify key ideas and emotions. The print should be large and easy to read with few visual distractions. One or two pages should be marked for specific readers and the marking system explained to the students. Finally, struggling readers and ELLs should work on correctly pronouncing new words. They should have plenty of time to practice their readings so that they can deliver smooth and expressive interpretations of the script.

Once a cast is determined, each performer should receive a copy of the script in which the teacher or the students highlight the parts they speak. The performers should also underline three or four sentences that precede or cue their parts. These markings make it easy for the reader to find their parts on the page without reading the whole page.

If the script is more than three or four pages, it is often easier for a performer to handle fewer pages of script. For example, if a performer reads only pages 2, 3, and the conclusion of a six-page script, it is easier to read from a side. A *side* is a partial script that contains only the sections each character reads (for example, all of Little Red Riding Hood's dialogue) and the four or five lines before and three or four lines after the particular section of dialogue in the script. On the following page is a side for Mr. Keetch, excerpted from *The True Confessions of Charlotte Doyle* (Avi, 1990; the complete script begins on page 67 in chapter 4).

Once these beginning steps of the preparation process have been completed, the teacher and students shift focus and energy into the development of their Readers Theatre performance.

REFERENCES FOR SCRIPTS

Avi. (1990). *The true confessions of Charlotte Doyle* (pp. 52–59). New York: Scholastic.

REFERENCES

Berliner, D.C. (1981). Academic learning time and reading achievement. In J.T. Guthrie (Ed.), *Comprehension and teaching: Research reviews* (pp. 203–226). Newark, DE: International Reading Association.

Tompkins, G. (2005). *Language arts: Patterns of practice*. Upper Saddle River, NJ: Pearson.

Side for Mr. Keetch
Speakers' Roles
CD—Charlotte Doyle
CAPT—Captain Jaggery
N—Narrator
K—Mr. Keetch

CD → [From the forecastle deck we crossed to the quarterdeck and then to the helm.] ~~Foley, a lean, bearded man, was at the wheel. Mr. Keetch, as unsmiling as ever, stood by his side. The wheel itself was massive,~~ with ~~hand spikes for easier gripp~~ing.

~~When the captain and I approached, the two men stole fleeting glances in our direction but said nothing.~~

~~Captain Jaggery released my arm and gazed up at the sails. At length he said,~~ ["Mr. Keetch."] ← CAPT

~~The second mate turned to him.~~ ["Yes, sir."] ← K

CAPT → ["I believe," ~~the captain said,~~ "we shall soon have a blow."]

~~Mr. Keetch seemed surprised.~~ ["Do you think so, sir?"] ← K

CAPT → "I hardly would have said so otherwise, now would I, Mr. Keetch?"

K → [The man darted a glance] [at me as if I held the answer.] ~~All he said however was,~~ ["I suppose not, sir."] ← K   CD

CAPT → ["Thank you, Mr. Keetch. Now, I want to take advantage of it. Tighten all braces, and be ready with the jigger gaff."]

K → ["Aye, aye, sir."]

CAPT → ["And bring the studding sails to hand. We may want them to make up for lost time."]

K → ["Aye, aye, sir."] [After another glance] [at me,] [Mr. Keetch marched quickly across the quarterdeck ~~and at the rail bellowed,~~ "All hands! All hands!"] ← K

[Within moments the entire crew assembled on deck.] N

K → ["Topgallant and royal yardmen in the tops!"] ~~he cried.~~

N → [The next moment the crew scrambled into the shrouds and standing rigging, high amidst the masts and spars.] ~~Even as they ascended Mr. Keetch began to sing out a...~~

CHAPTER 3

Developing the Performance

In chapter 2, the emphasis was on the roles and responsibilities of the teacher; the roles and responsibilities of the students; and selecting, understanding, and adapting the materials to be performed. In this chapter, the emphasis is on developing the performance. In developing a performance for Readers Theatre, it is important to organize, visualize, and develop the entire process from the beginning through the final performance. This chapter has five sections: Preparing for Performance, Practicing Vocal Performance Through Repeated Reading, Staging the Script Reading, Dress Rehearsal, and Performance Celebration.

Preparing for Performance

Because Readers Theatre is not a full-scale theatrical production, the preparation time needed is shorter than that for a play, and the performance space can be more limited in size (a classroom or an open meeting space) and technical supports. Performers do not memorize their lines, and their actions are few and carefully chosen. Production elements are optional, but if used, should also be few and carefully chosen. Providing students with a checklist, such as the one provided in Figure 4, will help guide them through the steps necessary in preparing for a performance. A reproducible version of this form can be found in Appendix C.

Discussing the Conventions of Readers Theatre

Before beginning to develop the performance, it is essential to discuss the purpose and style of Readers Theatre performances and their dramatic elements so that the time needed for the completion of vocal performances and staging the performance is more easily understood. Remind students that Readers Theatre emphasizes the oral performance of a text. The conventions of Readers Theatre require that the performers read from a text, even though they may be so familiar with the material that it is memorized. The physical presence of the text or script visually reinforces that the performance is centered in the text, and the performance is a reading of the text. The performers through their expressive reading, posture, limited actions, and carefully selected production elements are suggesting and enhancing meaning and creating pictures. The audience is also a partner in making and visualizing meaning from the same text

Figure 4. Student Preparation Checklist

Reminders
- Readers Theatre scripts don't need to be memorized. They are a dramatic reading of a piece of writing. This does not mean, though, that you can read your scripts word for word. You need to practice them enough to make the reading interesting for your audience.
- Use your voice and movements to make your scripts more entertaining.
- Remember the audience. The audience needs to understand the story you are trying to tell.
- When performing, don't stand with your back to the audience. It makes it difficult to hear you—not to mention difficult to see your face.

To-Do List
- ☐ As a group, decide which text will be the best choice for Readers Theatre.
- ☐ Read through the text once again. This time, make a note of the number of characters you will need to tell the story. Remember to include the narrator(s).
- ☐ Help each other to read and adapt the script. You may want a narrator to describe the setting and establish characters in your script. Your script should take between 5 and 10 minutes to read. Anything longer may be difficult for your audience to follow. Focus on important events.
- ☐ While you read your script, make sure you also discuss different voices and movements that will improve the quality of your performance.
- ☐ Feel free to add a part for your audience—the audience members will love it! You can create a cue card for them to read from.
- ☐ Be sure to plan how you will introduce your text to the audience. You should share your names, the name of the story, and the characters that you will play. If you choose to include your audience in the act, you may want to explain what you want to them to do or say during this time.
- ☐ Once the script is complete, discuss any small costume pieces or props that could be used to help your audience follow your story. Really consider this if you are reading more than one part.
- ☐ When you are finished, you should decide as a group how you want to share the script with each other. Is the written copy neat enough for everyone to read? Could each of you type a section of it at home and bring it in Friday? Is someone willing to type it for the group while others create costume pieces or props? Once your decisions are made, please know that you need enough copies of the script for everyone in your group to have one. (If you give a copy to [teacher's name] she can make copies for everyone.) [Teacher's name] needs a copy as well. You will hand it in with a copy of the original myth by [due date].

as the performers. It is as if the performers were sending partial images and meaning to a screen situated at a point in space between the performers and the audience; in other words, they are meeting in space to create a picture together. The performers cast partial images, sounds, and meanings on this screen, and the audience completes those images, sounds, and meanings on that screen with their own interpretation of the reading. It takes the text, the performer, and the audience to make complete meaning from the performance text, and it is this combination that brings the text alive.

Choosing the Performance Space

The space used for preparation for performance is the classroom. Each group works in an area that allows for discussion and script reading. There should be some distance between groups. Students will need to be reminded to keep their voice levels low enough so they do not disturb other groups. The dress rehearsal should take place in the setting for the actual performance.

The space needed for performance is simply an open space in a room large enough to separate the performance area from audience seating. The performance area is arranged to provide a visual focal point and enough room for four to five performers to stand, sit, and move in precise but limited ways. The audience should be close enough to see facial expression and actions without the need for stage lighting or make-up. The audience must also be able to easily hear the performers' dialogue. It is counter-productive to spend a large amount of preparation time rehearsing how to project voices in a large auditorium. A section of the classroom can be rearranged to look and feel different from its daily class setting. For example, one seventh-grade teacher pushed desks together to create tables for four to six students, covered each "table" with a tablecloth, and placed a vase of flowers on each table. She transformed her classroom space into a coffee house for poetry presentations. Other possible performance locations could be an open space in a library, cafeteria, or closed section of a gym.

Choosing the Audience

There are many possibilities when choosing an audience for a Readers Theatre performance. The simplest and most appropriate audience, particularly for the first experience with Readers Theatre, is members of the class itself. Because the students have been working in groups separately, they will benefit greatly from the opportunity to see their classmates' performances, particularly if the groups used different text for their scripts.

> "It was fun to watch other people perform."
> MIDDLE SCHOOL STUDENT

However, ideally, each class would have several invited audience members. Selected others (principals, counselors, other teachers for the same students, other staff who were used as consultants, other school personnel) might also be invited to view specific class performances. Depending on school scheduling and size of performance space, the teacher can have his or her classes perform for each other (e.g., a first-period class could perform for the third-period class). Another possibility is performing the pieces for another grade level. A seventh-grade class that gave a Readers Theatre performance of Native American creation myths first performed for their own class and then performed for a selected third-grade class. If students have successfully and comfortably performed for their own class or other classes, they may be ready to create a program of Readers Theatre for parents' night, open house, a community library, and so forth. Finally, the performances can be videotaped, replayed, and enjoyed by both the student performers and other selected audiences.

There are two additional aspects to consider when choosing an audience. The first is audience knowledge of the content, genre, and context of the script to be performed. The introduction and conclusion are developed to provide background information for the audience to understand and to become engaged with the performance.

Second, a student audience may need explanation or reminders of what, as one seventh-grade teacher stated, is a "polite" audience. Students are likely to be more accustomed to viewing films, videos, and TV programs, which do not require courteous behavior. Students may also have had little or no experience as audience members of live performances. The teacher will need to explain before the performance that a polite audience respects the performers and their work. The audience members listen and watch attentively; they do not talk with each other or to the performers, work on their own performance, write notes, or move out of their seats. If something is intentionally funny, audience members laugh; if the something funny is the result of a mistake, audience members do not laugh or comment. Finally, polite audience members show their appreciation by clapping at the end of a performance.

> "I like watching people perform and hearing the different stories and poems."
> MIDDLE SCHOOL STUDENT

Performance Time

In order to work effectively in Readers Theatre, the teacher must know his or her students' needs, interests, and abilities. Because students should also have had some experiences with group work and with the text used in the performance, the best time to plan a Readers Theatre performance is usually in the winter or spring semester of the school year. The length of each group's performance should be between 5 to 12 minutes. This time is determined by considering the length of the class period, the number of students in the class, and the need for short texts that can be understood and performed with limited rehearsal time.

The time scheduled for performance can be either the normal length of a class period or a specially scheduled time within the school day (such as a double period with two classes meeting together). If the performance is scheduled for a single class period, the time needed for each performance group can be easily estimated. If there are 50-minute periods and five performance groups, each group's performance can run between 5 to 7 minutes for 35 minutes total. Because production elements are simple and easily set up, each group should take no more than 2 minutes for setting up and removing their visuals and props, making the performance a maximum total of 10 minutes. This leaves 5 minutes for seating the audience prior to the performance. This is only an estimate of time needed; in the final stages of rehearsal and in the dress rehearsal, it will be easier to more accurately determine the time needed for performance. Students need to know at the beginning of the preparation process the performance date and schedule for rehearsal.

It is essential for both teacher and students to begin the process with a tentative or ideal schedule which can be modified if necessary. In planning, consider a flex day for the unexpected events or delay that are often a part of a change in school schedule, or a need for more time on certain aspects of the project. Figures 5, 6, and 7 provide suggested schedules for creating and performing Readers Theatre. When using either of the first two schedules (Figures 5 and 6)—a two-day schedule or a five-day schedule—text selections are simple and have been primarily teacher-developed. When using the third schedule (Figure 7)—a ten-day schedule—text selections may be more complex, and students have more opportunities to adapt and develop the scripts and related production elements. Rehearsal days (optional) do not need to be consecutive, except for the dress rehearsal, which should be the day prior to the performance.

A two-day schedule demands that students have full content and emotional understandings of the performance script material (see chapter 2, pages 27–29), time for repeated readings, and very simple (probably teacher-directed) staging by the end of the first day. A fable, folk tale, or short poem

Figure 5. Two-Day Schedule

Teacher direction with limited level of student suggestions for understanding and performance

Day 1	**Introduction to Readers Theatre Project**
Teacher	• Describes performance style, space, script content and context, schedule.
	• Assigns groups (tasks and performance roles) and scripts (already developed and labeled for each performer).
	• Explains necessary content and context of script material to each group.
	• Gives each group basic staging direction and describes performance space.
	• Observes groups and answers questions.
Students	• Work on vocal performance by reading through script silently and out loud.
	• Work on staging, postures, and actions.
Day 2	**Performance and Celebration**
Teacher	• Assigns performance order.
	• Sets up performance space.
	• Seats audience.
	• Arranges celebration.
Students	• Reread scripts silently.
	• Perform scripts and serve as an audience to other performers.

Figure 6. Five-Day Schedule

Teacher direction with limited to moderate level of student suggestions for understanding and performance

Day 1   **Introduction to Readers Theatre Project**

Teacher
- Describes performance style, space, script content and context, schedule.
- Assigns groups members tasks and performance roles and assigns scripts. (Scripts are already developed and labeled for each performer; students may develop introduction and conclusion from teacher-provided materials.)
- Explains necessary content and context of script material to each group.

Students
- Select group roles with some teacher suggestions, if needed.
- Read, analyze, and discuss script for meaning (content and emotions).

Day 2   **Rehearsal**

Teacher
- Describes performance space.
- Observes groups, answers questions, clarifies meaning, and makes suggestions for casting if needed.

Students
- Assign roles.
- Analyze script for meaning and emotions.
- Read and rehearse vocal performances.

Day 3   **Rehearsal**

Teacher
- Explains and models staging.
- Discusses how to develop and use props, costume pieces, sound, and visuals.
- Observes groups, answers questions, clarifies meaning, and makes suggestions.

Students
- Plan and create or find props and other production elements.
- Rehearse vocal performance and add staging elements.
- Complete their additions to script (introductions, conclusions).

Day 4   **Dress Rehearsal**

Teacher
- Sets up performance space.
- Assigns performance order.
- Observes groups, answers questions, offers suggestions.

Students
- Rehearse in work area.
- Rehearse in performance space.
- Finish props and sound.

Day 5   **Performance and Celebration**

Teacher
- Reviews performance order.
- Sets up performance space.
- Seats audience.
- Arranges celebration.

Students
- Reread scripts silently.
- Perform scripts and serve as an audience for other performers.

Note. Students may use their free periods, study hall, and time before or after school to work on production elements or as additional rehearsal times for their individual performances. All students should also be encouraged to spend some time at home or out of class reading their parts aloud.

Figure 7. Ten-Day Schedule

Limited teacher direction with moderate to high level of student suggestions for meaning and performance

Day 1   **Introduction to Readers Theatre Project**

Teacher
- Describes performance style, space, script content and context, schedule.
- Provides a simple text for the whole class to analyze and read parts aloud.
- Gives the whole class a set of selections to read and asks them to rank order in terms of their personal choice for performance.
- Supplies information needed for students to understand main ideas in material provided for performance choices.
- Gives deadlines for submission of top two or three choices.

Students
- Analyze and read simple text.
- Read and select top two or three choices for performance.

Day 2   **Rehearsal**

Teacher
- Assigns groups members their tasks and performance roles and assigns scripts (scripts already developed and labeled for each performer or students may develop; students may also develop introduction and conclusion from teacher-provided materials).
- Explains necessary content and context of script material to each group.
- Observes groups, answers questions, clarifies meaning, and makes suggestions.

Students
- Select group roles (director, recorder, etc.) with some teacher suggestions, if needed.
- Read, analyze, and discuss script for meaning (content and emotions).
- Mark and divide scripts into sections, if appropriate.

Day 3   **Rehearsal**

Teacher
- Describes performance space.
- Observes groups, answers questions, clarifies meaning, and makes suggestions for casting, if needed.

Students
- Assign performance roles.
- Analyze scripts for meaning and emotions.
- Read and rehearse vocal performances.

Days 4–8   **Rehearsals**

Teacher
- Explains and models staging.
- Discusses how to develop and use props, costume pieces, sound, and visuals.
- Observes groups, answers questions, clarifies meaning, and makes suggestions.

Students
- Plan and create or find props, costume pieces, sound, and visuals.
- Rehearse vocal performance and add staging elements.
- Complete their additions to script (introductions, conclusions).

Day 9   **Dress Rehearsal**

Teacher
- Sets up performance space.
- Assigns performance order.
- Observes groups, answers questions, offers suggestions.

(continued)

Figure 7. Ten-Day Schedule (continued)

Students	• Rehearse in work area.
	• Rehearse in performance space.
	• Finish props, sound, and other production elements.
Day 10	**Performance and Celebration**
Teacher	• Reviews performance order.
	• Sets up performance space.
	• Seats audience.
	• Arranges celebration.
Students	• Reread scripts silently.
	• Perform scripts and serve as an audience to other performers.

Note. Students may use their free periods, study hall, and time before or after school to work on production elements or as additional rehearsal times for their individual performances. For the creation of production elements, some group members may spend part or all of a class period in the art room, library, or computer lab. The classroom teacher arranges time outside of class with each group and the appropriate school personnel. All students should also be encouraged to spend some time at home or out of class reading their parts aloud.

would work best with this schedule. A five-day schedule is best suited for work with more complex materials, which need opportunities for extended discussion of content and emotional understandings, multiple repeated readings, opportunities for more complex staging, and creation and use of simple production elements. The ten-day schedule allows for more complex materials, staging, and production elements, and more student opportunities to create portions of a script (i.e., introductions, conclusions, transitions, divisions into speaker roles) as well as staging.

Practicing Vocal Performance Through Repeated Reading

Repeated readings of the scripts involve developing and practicing vocal performance of the text to convey the ideas and the emotions found in the performance piece (see Figure 8). Repeated, purposeful readings of the script enhance the student readers' comprehension, fluency, and expressiveness. This is a process based on the previous script analysis for content and emotional understanding (see chapter 2, pages 27–29). As one seventh-grade teacher stated, "You are not simply reading the poem, you are bringing it to life." Through repeated readings, the words of the text come alive initially for the performers and later for their audience. In Readers Theatre, rehearsing is especially important because it allows for repeated reading of the script.

Reading for Meaning and Fluency

During Readers Theatre performances, the emphasis is on the spoken word. (Performance elements discussed later should enhance but not detract or distract from the oral performance.) Readers Theatre performances should clearly communicate the main ideas, information, and feelings previously identified in the text. At this stage, readers should have already highlighted and studied the whole script and their own parts in the script, reviewed unfamiliar vocabulary words for meaning, and achieved an understanding of the content and emotions in order to give meaningful expression to their parts. Now, performers should read their parts silently to themselves or softly to a partner. It may be helpful for a reader to underline or bracket units of meaning, circle words for particular emphasis, or write a pronunciation guide above new vocabulary words.

Struggling readers or ELLs can perform successfully and enjoy Readers Theatre activities but may need additional time and support for practicing reading aloud. To produce fluent reading, it may be necessary to work with students alone and outside of class to mark scripts for units of meaning and correct pronunciation of words. These students may also need a reading teacher, special education teacher, classroom teacher, teacher aide, or older student as a coach to develop fluency and the expressive vocal variety (rate, tone, quality, dialect). It may also be helpful to model these vocal changes and perhaps tape-record them for the student to hear, repeat, and replay when working outside of class time. Students may also tape record their own readings and listen to and evaluate them.

After reading individually, the whole group should read their parts out loud, listen to one another, and provide constructive comments on the meaning and feelings they hear in the performance. The teacher needs to visit each group and note what aspects of the performance are working well, and what needs attention, answer students' questions, and offer specific suggestions on how to improve the reading performance. Students may initially focus their readings on either content or character feelings and motivation, but both need to be part of the final performance.

Improving Vocal Expression

Once the readings become somewhat fluent and expressive, the group begins to fine-tune the vocal expression. The teacher may choose to work with each group or with the whole class to explore how to communicate with voice and demonstrate how to use vocal volume and variation (rate of speaking, tone, dialect) to express both content and feeling within the text. Rate is more centrally connected to meaning and is key for audience understanding of text. Rate combined with tone and vocal quality provides clues to understanding the feeling within the text. For instance, in Little Red Riding Hood, Little Red's voice might be described as a faster rate (she is excited or frightened), higher pitched (she is a child and smaller), and the normal vocal quality of the reader. The Wolf in disguise as the ill Grandmother could have low volume with a slower rate (pretending to be sick), a forced high pitch, quavering tone (pretending to be sick and old), and a breathy, cooing voice quality (pretending to be sweet and loving). When the Wolf reveals his true identity, the volume and rate would greatly increase, the pitch would be low, and the voice quality would become coarse and harsh. Groups can analyze and try vocal variations to more clearly communicate the feelings of the speakers in the text.

Volume. Volume relates to the clear production of sound that can be easily heard and produced. Volume is needed in order for performers to be comfortably heard and understood by the audience. In order to easily produce effective sound, students need to know how to stand. Students should stand tall, with shoulders back and chin parallel to the floor, holding their scripts high. This posture allows for the taking of complete breaths with no obstructions to the flow of air over the vocal chords. When reading, many students will hold the book or paper too low, tilting their head down, cutting off their air supply and movement of air over the vocal chords. Shallow breathing also creates poor movement of air over the vocal chords. Students usually take shallow breaths, so they may need to work on taking full breaths.

Volume also communicates the feelings underlying the text. Loud volume may indicate anger or confidence; soft volume can indicate illness or shyness.

Many students—due to inappropriate sound production, shyness, or habit—speak softly and do not know what it feels like to produce louder voices. It will seem strange and uncomfortable for them to change their habits, and they will need both practice and reassurance from the group and the teacher to make a change for performance. Depending on the scale of your performance, you may even invite a teacher of singing or speech to work with the whole class for one 15- or 20-minute session on voice production.

Rate of Speaking. All students will need to be sure that they are speaking slowly enough for the audience to understand and relate to unfamiliar text performed. For most performers, nervousness will speed up the rate of speaking, so it is important to make students aware of this. In the rehearsal process, set the rate of speaking so that it will become automatic. The rate of speaking can also provide a sense of the speaker's feelings. A very slow rate of speaking might suggest a character who is impressed with himself; a very fast rate of speaking might suggest a character who is excited or frightened.

Tone. Tone is the level of the voice (high, medium, low). A high-pitched voice might suggest a character that is a child or who is small, weak, or uncertain. A low-pitched voice might suggest a character that is fully grown, very large, strong, and confident. The quality of the voice refers to the sound of the vowels. Voice quality might be described as nasal, shrill, flat, whiny, melodious, hoarse, guttural, and breathy. A nasal, shrill tone could indicate a person who dislikes others, always finds something wrong, complains, and is very dissatisfied with a situation or other people. A breathy quality to the voice can indicate anxiousness or fatigue.

Dialect. Dialect refers to particular regional or national ways of producing vowels and some consonants. For example, Southern U.S. dialects elongate and sing high and low tones for vowel sounds (e.g., I/Aaah am/aaaam so/sooooo tired /tiaaahd) and drop consonant endings (e.g., John/Jaaahn is/eeeez hiding/hidin over/ovah there/theah). In most work with students, it is best to focus on volume, rate, tone, and voice quality rather than attempting dialect, although some students do have both the ear and the ability to produce very good dialects.

Staging the Script Reading

Staging includes the visual aspects of the Readers Theatre performance. Although the performance emphasis is on the spoken word, the visual aspects need to create and express the content of the text. However, it is important to remember that visual elements are meant to emphasize but not overshadow the meaning of and the engagement with the spoken text. The visual aspects create the "whole picture," including where the performers sit and stand as well as a focal point or background for the performance; using specific postures, gestures, and actions during the performance; and creating and using production elements (costume pieces, props, background visuals, and sound or music). The details of the performance space include the seating placement and arrangement of the audience; the size and shape of the performance area; entrances and exits for the performers; and placement of the production elements before, during, and after the performance.

In order to begin staging, students need to know what the physical arrangement of the performance space will be. This arrangement can be explained in detail when the groups begin to work on expression of meaning and their visualization of the performance piece.

Creating the Whole Picture

The "whole picture" is the element of staging that determines the visual positioning of the performers (where the performers stand, sit, face, move) and the focal point or background for the performance. At this stage the teacher and students create the floor plan for the performance. All of the performers need to be in view for the entire performance. They may be standing or seated in a semicircle or line; they may face the audience full front, in profile, or turn their backs to the audience. They may step or move forward when speaking and return to their position when finished. There may be a space closer to the audience in the left, center, or right for specific actions or interactions. The whole picture should allow for physically emphasizing a performer or performers while the remaining performers add to the visualization but are not a focal point. Above all, it should be a simple visual and one that allows for an easy flow of movement in and out of focus. This positioning also needs to dictate ways for the performers to enter and exit the performance space, signaling the beginning and end of the performance.

Using Postures and Actions

Postures and actions of the performers suggest and reinforce content from the text and the feelings and emotions of the characters. Posture is necessary for performers to communicate clearly with the audience, so performers must have scripts that are easily read (large type or printing and clearly marked with their parts) and that are easily held or placed on music stands. In a Readers Theatre performance, each performer holds his or her script. The printed script can be mounted on large index cards or heavy, sturdy construction paper. Pages should be clearly numbered. Students must hold the script so that they can easily see it, make some eye contact with the audience, and position themselves so they do not lower their heads and cut off their air supply while reading.

Posture also suggests character. One way to examine posture is to think of the speaker as a statue and determine what pose would be most representative of a character at a particular moment in a text. For example, the Wolf in Little Red Riding Hood would try to be as thin as possible by turning sideways to the audience, taking a deep breath, and standing on his toes to suggest hiding behind a tree. As Grandmother, the Wolf could sit on a stool, double over, and peer over the top of his hands.

Actions are also important in conveying meaning. Actions include facial expressions, hand or arm movements or gestures, and physical movements, large and small. Hand or arm movements include waving, pointing, and writing. Larger physical movements include running, hopping, stomping, and skipping. Actions may also be stopped or frozen, which creates a stature or a frozen posture. For the most part, actions are performed where the reader is standing and do not move through the performance area. The Wolf as Grandmother might bend forward and smile sweetly but with closed lips when looking at Little Red Riding Hood's basket of food. Larger actions can be added to the performance. The Wolf as Grandmother can mime pulling a blanket up to his chin, blowing his nose in a handkerchief, and fluffing up the pillows on the bed.

Actions may also be used to emphasize or extend character or content of a performance text. The speaker may mime the action in place and move through the space, or another member of the group may mime the action as the speaker reads the text. For example, Little Red Riding Hood skips through the forest carrying her basket while the narrator describes the action. After the Wolf growls, "The better to eat you with my dear," he jumps from the bed and chases Little Red Riding Hood around the room. For all of these actions, the two performers remain in place, but they may turn toward or away from each other or the audience. Finally, postures and actions are used to highlight and emphasize the spoken words of the text and should not become the focus of the performance. (See the scripts in chapters 4, 5, and 6 for illustrations of postures and actions.)

Creating and Using Production Elements

Production elements comprise costume pieces, props or objects used, background visuals, and music or sounds. Selection, creation, and use of any of these elements will depend upon students' interests and abilities, performance space, and particularly how much time the teacher desires to devote to Readers Theatre (e.g., teachers using a two-day schedule would likely only use minimal production elements). These elements should be easily made or found and used by the performers. For examples of production elements used in performances, see the Production Elements sections in chapters 4, 5, and 6.

The production elements are intended only to enhance and supplement meaning and contribute to characterization and visualization of the content, so it is not imperative to use them. Production elements should not dominate or distract from the performance. Excellent performances can exist having only an established performance area with a strong focal point, meaningful reading and vocal performances, and effective posture and actions conveyed by the performers—all that is needed to effectively communicate the performance text. It is also possible to select only one element or any combination of elements to emphasize an aspect of the performance text.

Costume Pieces. Costume pieces identify the speaker as well as specific character attributes. In Little Red Riding Hood, the Grandmother might wear a night cap and a pair of glasses; the Wolf might wear a large pair of ears and as Grandmother a night cap with ears hidden; Little Red Riding Hood might wear a red cape or an apron. Costume pieces may also help student performers to more clearly connect to the characters. The costume piece becomes a kind of mask to hide behind and to more easily "become" someone else. They can be as simple as all performers wearing matching colored shirts or hats or coats.

Costumes are partial pieces of clothing (hats, coats, skirts, ties, jewelry) that can be easily put on and removed. They can be borrowed from a theater group, students' closets, or created with simple pieces of fabric, pins, glue, and construction paper. For developing costume pieces, students could collaborate with an art teacher or family. The artist in the performance group is responsible for making, collecting, and listing the costume pieces; other group members can also be assigned to assist the artist.

> "You can express your emotions with costumes and gestures."
>
> MIDDLE SCHOOL STUDENT

Props. Props are objects that are used and handled rather than mimed and imagined. In Little Red Riding Hood, Grandmother and the Wolf might be seated on a high stool and use a piece of fabric as blanket. Little Red Riding Hood might hold a small basket covered with a piece of fabric. The Woodcutter would have an ax. The props should be simple, used to convey both the character and the character's essential actions in the story. The art teacher or theater director may be a source of making and finding props. The artist is responsible for listing, finding, or creating props.

Visuals. Visuals are used to create a strong focal point. Because the performances are short (only 5 to 12 minutes per group), a single setting is the best plan. It is necessary to provide a focal point or a background for the performance space. This background could be a large piece of material stretched and hung between two poles or attached to a bulletin board or wall. It might be as simple as a neutral or colorful piece of fabric used as a backdrop.

Visuals can also be used to suggest a setting or a mood. These would be large murals that are easily moved and mounted on the rear wall of the performance area. In Little Red Riding Hood, a realistic or abstract forest scene could provide a focal point. Slides or computer graphics might also be used and projected onto a screen. Projections should be placed to the left or right of the performance area so that the performers are not moving through the images. The group's artist could collaborate with the art teacher to create a visual focal point for their performance. The development of the visuals is the responsibility of the artist.

Music or Sound. Music or sound can be used to introduce and end the performance. The piece of music or sound effect should suggest and anticipate the mood of the performance piece or provide a kind of emotional conclusion. Music seems to work best with poetry. For example, students who performed "Casey at the Bat" (see page 22) chose to introduce it with the theme music from *Star Wars*. They added the sounds of cheering and booing during the reading and ended not with sound but with a long silence and a tableau of Casey striking out. Whatever sound is used before, during, and after the reading should be short, yet long enough to establish the mood without dominating the performance. Personal recorders or computers can be used to play music. The music or sound should be added only if it adds to the meaning of the performance and is easily found, recorded, and used.

When creating music or sound, it is necessary for the group to identify the key emotion in the text. Once this emotion is identified, the sound creator may work with other group members to find, create, and record music or sounds. If the sound creator needs suggestions or opportunities to listen to music or sounds, a librarian or music teacher could be asked to help search for music that reflects that emotion. The sound system should be easily set up and easy to run during the performance.

Dress Rehearsal

Dress rehearsal is when the reading and staging of the texts are combined and performed as if there were an audience watching. Dress rehearsals are optional and, like most performance elements in this chapter, dependent upon how much time is being devoted to Readers Theatre. Classrooms using the five-day schedule and ten-day schedule, of course, can run a dress rehearsal (see pages 39 and 40). Because students have been working in groups with the teacher monitoring and advising, the dress rehearsal should also operate in the same way. The teacher should remind students about the details of performance space (e.g., classroom desks will be placed in long rows facing the side board; we will be in the open space in the library or cafeteria with chairs set up in this pattern). Ideally, the dress rehearsal takes place in the performance space, but because this is not always possible there needs to be a brief whole-class discussion on how the performers will move to the performance area.

At the beginning of the dress rehearsal, the group should focus on working with their production elements—costume pieces, props, visuals, and music or sound. Once this is completed, the students should have time to run through their whole performance at least two or three times. The teacher needs to see at least one performance of each group and comment on what is working well and what needs attention. It may be necessary to have more than one dress rehearsal, but a final dress rehearsal should take place the day before the performance for an audience.

> "At first I felt uneasy about speaking in front of everyone, but once I practiced it in front of everyone, I was fine."
>
> MIDDLE SCHOOL STUDENT

Performance Celebration

The performance is the culmination of the students' work; it is intended to be a demonstration and a celebration of what the students have created. It is not designed to be a perfect or professional theatrical performance, directed by a knowledgeable adult reader or performer. The emphasis is on the process and on the development of the students as readers and communicators. Most importantly, the performance is the students' work, not the teacher's or director's work. The performance should include recognition of work well done (applause and teacher feedback) and some type of party to celebrate the students' work (punch and cookies for performers and audience).

PART II

Exploring Genres Through Readers Theatre

This section provides a practical application of the steps outlined in the previous chapters by demonstrating the development of performance scripts from three literature genres: fiction, nonfiction, and poetry. Chapter 4, "From Script to Performance: Fiction," presents scripts and performance elements developed from the fable "The Tortoise and the Hare," the folk tale "The Blind Men and the Elephant," and a chapter from the young adult novel *The True Confessions of Charlotte Doyle*. Chapter 5, "From Script to Performance: Nonfiction," demonstrates scripts and performances based on The Diary of Lucy Medora Walker, September 1862; oral history and interviews from Ellis Island; and *The Universal Declaration of Human Rights*. Chapter 6, "From Script to Performance: Poetry," presents scripts and performances developed from "Casey at the Bat," Walt Whitman's poetry on Abraham Lincoln, and "In Beauty May I Walk." In each chapter, the scripts progress from a more basic sample from the genre to the more complex text materials, staging, and production elements.

CHAPTER 4

From Script to Performance: Fiction

There are several considerations that must be made when developing a script. The first consideration is the students' experience with the genre and their interests. Students have most likely had many experiences with reading, telling, and writing fiction. The purpose of fiction or story is to share an experience with readers by drawing them into the action and connecting them with the characters. Stories are found in a variety of forms suitable for performance: fables, folk tales, myths, legends, short stories, and novels. The following examples were selected because they are forms most middle school students have previously read and because the humor, determination, sense of adventure, and suspense would appeal to most middle school students. Each also examines a different time period and culture, which may also add to student engagement with the text. The three selected texts for scripts are "The Tortoise and the Hare," a fable adapted from Aesop (Lynch, 2000); "The Blind Men and the Elephant," adapted from an Indian folk tale (Forest, 1996); and chapter 6 of the young adult novel *The True Confessions of Charlotte Doyle* (Avi, 1990). Each selected text is developed in two sections: Adapting the Material to a Script and Staging the Script Reading.

"The Tortoise and the Hare"

Fiction Subgenre: Fable   **Group Dynamics:** Individual groups

Adapting the Material to a Script

Essential Reader Information

The tale of "The Tortoise and the Hare" is a fable. Students need to know that in this subgenre of fiction, animals talk and assume human characteristics. The action in all fables is intended to educate the listener about human behavior. Every fable closes with a direct statement of that lesson or a moral usually stated in a short, simple sentence. The content is direct, simple, and needs no additional explanation. Unknown or unfamiliar vocabulary words are identified and defined and pronounced at this time, but in "The Tortoise and the Hare," there is no vocabulary that needs to be identified.

Dividing the Text for Script Adaptation

Next, the script is divided into speakers' roles. There are four speaker roles: the hare (H), the hare narrator (N1), the tortoise (T), and the tortoise narrator (N2). Because "The Tortoise and the Hare" is a relatively simple story to adapt, the teacher may need only to explain that for each of the main characters—the Tortoise and the Hare—one speaker can narrate the actions and another speaker can read the direct dialogue. (See "The Tortoise and the Hare" script beginning on page 56 for division of roles.)

Necessary Script Additions

In "The Tortoise and the Hare," there is no need for any transitions. The tale itself provides a conclusion in the statement of the lesson. The only necessary addition is an introduction, which may be developed by the teacher or by the performance group. Teacher or students could develop an introduction with only a small amount of preparation time due to the story's simplicity.

> **Sample Introduction**
>
> "The Tortoise and the Hare" is a fable adapted from Aesop. Aesop was a Greek slave who lived in 6th-century BC. He told many wise and entertaining tales about animals. Through animal characters, he could safely comment on human nature and the Greek society. It is believed that Aesop was granted his freedom because of the power and art of his stories.

Staging the Script Reading

Creating the Whole Picture

In "The Tortoise and the Hare," the focal point is a simple backdrop hung behind the performance area—a large piece of fabric or a curtain attached to the back wall of the performance area or a screen or portable chalkboard. The material is a solid color (blue, white, black, or tan). There are two positions for the performers: one for the introduction and one for the story (see the floor plans within the script).

Using Postures and Actions

Because this tale is simple, staging is minimal. Actions are stated directly in the script, and the performers can develop postures and actions themselves (see Figure 9). In the script, there is a mime or a slow movement into a posture or "statue." This statue suggests that the action is continuing without the

Figure 9. Group Exploring Simple Postures and Actions

movement. For example, the Tortoise begins to slowly run and then becomes still in that pose—a statue of a runner. The Hare runs, yawns, drops head, and becomes a sleeping statue. Both the Tortoise and the Hare also mime selected actions (see "The Tortoise and the Hare" script).

Creating and Using Production Elements

"The Tortoise and the Hare" is an example of the most basic use of production elements. There is no plan for the use of props, visual background other than focal point, or music or sound. There are two ways to use costume pieces. The first is to have the Tortoise and the Tortoise Narrator (N2) dress in green shirts; the Hare and the Hare Narrator (N1) could dress in tan or brown shirts. The second choice is to add a sandwich board shell for the Tortoise and a baseball hat with ears for the Hare (with all performers still wearing the colored shirts).

"THE TORTOISE AND THE HARE"

Speakers' Roles
N1—Narrator Hare actions
N2—Narrator Tortoise actions
H—Hare dialogue
T—Tortoise dialogue

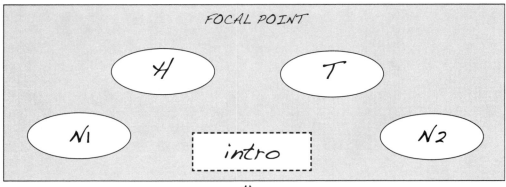

N1

moves to intro block - when finished returns to position

[Introduction for "The Tortoise and the Hare"]

[The Tortoise and the Hare is a fable adapted from Aesop. Aesop was a Greek slave who lived in 6th-century BC. He told many wise and entertaining tales about animals. Through the animal characters, he could safely comment on human nature and Greek society. It is believed that Aesop was granted his freedom because of the power and art of his stories.]

T → ["The Tortoise] [and the Hare"] ← *H*

N1 → [One day a Hare was teasing a Tortoise for being so slow on his feet.]

T → ["Hold on there," *N2* [said the Tortoise.] ["I'll bet if we had a race I would win!"] ← *T*

H → ["You've got to be kidding!" *N1* [laughed the Hare.] ["Okay slowpoke, let's go!"] ← *H*

(H laughs)

N1 + [They both started off at the same time,] [but very soon the Hare was so far ← *N1*
N2 *H+T* ahead of the Tortoise that he thought he might as well rest for a bit. Before
H
he knew it, he had fallen fast asleep.] [All the while, the Tortoise continued ← *N2*
H *T*
to move slowly along. Mile after mile he crept, and in time he reached the

finish line.] [Eventually the Hare <u>awoke</u> and <u>jumped up</u> to continue as fast
as he could. But he reached the finish line only to find] [that the Tortoise
had arrived before him and <u>won the race</u>.]

N1 (arrow pointing to "finish line")

H (above "finish line" second line)

T + H (below "won the race") *N2* (arrow)

All ———→ [**So remember! Slow and steady wins the race.**]

Postures and Actions

"<u>started off</u>"—*H runs fast in place (freeze or statue)*

 T walks slowly in place until reaches finish line
 (freeze or statue)

"<u>rest for a bit</u>"—*H stops, stretches, yawns, drops head, closes*
 eyes

"<u>awoke</u>"—*H opens eyes, jumps, runs fast in place (freeze or*
 statue)

"<u>won the race</u>"—*T has winner's posture (hands in fist over*
 head; freeze or statue)
 H pants, drops head (defeat; freeze or statue)

Adapting the Material to a Script

Essential Reader Information

In "The Blind Men and the Elephant," the subgenre is that of a folk tale, which is similar to a fable in that its purpose is to teach a lesson. However, it is different from a fable because the elephant does not assume human characteristics or speech, and humans are a part of the story. Further, there is not a directly stated moral or lesson as a conclusion. In this folk tale, the ending has been set in a poetic form, which is not a characteristic of the genre but a special feature of this adaptation.

Although the content is easy to understand, the context may need a few details added. India's climate is warm and tropical, and the setting for this story is a jungle, which includes many large and small plants as well as many birds and animals. A verbal and visual description of India's plant life, jungle, and walled gardens may be useful to the performers. A picture of an elephant with a person standing next to it may also be useful in order for students to understand the relationship of the size of the elephant to a human as well as to see the size and shape of an elephant's tail, leg, and ear.

Generally, the vocabulary is within the range of the students. There are some words that will need explanation because they relate to actions, postures, and vocal performance. These words are *trumpeted*, *posterior*, *girth*, *pillar*, *billowing*, *bellowing*, and *undefined*.

Dividing the Text for Script Adaptation

In "The Blind Men and the Elephant," there are five speaker roles. There is a narrator for the actions of the elephant (N1) and a narrator for the actions of the Blind Men (N2). Each of the Blind Men (B1, B2, B3) reads the dialogue and the dialogue tags for each one. The closing poem is split between N1 and N2. (See the division of roles in "The Blind Men and the Elephant" script beginning on page 60.) These role divisions may be suggested by the teacher or developed by the group members.

Necessary Script Additions

"The Blind Men and the Elephant" requires no transition. An introduction is needed, and a conclusion may or may not be added. These can be developed by the teacher or by the group depending upon the abilities of the students and the time planned for script development.

Sample Introduction

"There are not people a thousand years old, but there are words a thousand years old" (Forest, 1996, n.p.). "The Blind Men and the Elephant" is an ancient tale from India adapted from Jalal Al-din Rum's volume of poems, *Masnavi*.

Sample Conclusion

We hope the seed of this performance has taken root in your minds and hearts and will grow into a flower of understanding.

Staging the Script Reading

Creating the Whole Picture

For "The Blind Men and the Elephant," the focal point is a backdrop hung behind the performance space. The performers remain in the same positions, with one speaker moving into the center area for the introduction and conclusion. (See the floor plan within the script.)

Using Postures and Actions

In this tale, the postures and actions are suggested by the words in the text. They can be a combination of freezes or statues and mime of specific actions. Students can develop these actions once they have a clear idea of the size of an elephant and the specific shapes of tail, ear, and leg. Speakers remain in place but may use body turns for emphasis in the section that repeats "A rope! A rug! A pillar!" The script provides a description of the postures and actions in the performance.

Creating and Using Production Elements

Because this is a short, simple tale, preparation time will allow for the creation of a few production elements. Costume pieces and props are not good choices because they would be difficult to make (turbans, elephant ears) or would be better suggested in mimed actions. Performers can all wear tropical or brightly colored shirts. The visual element is an aspect that is selected for additional development. The backdrop could be painted to represent a literal or symbolic lush tropical garden, then becoming the focal point for the whole picture. A short piece of Indian music might be used before the introduction and after the conclusion.

"THE BLIND MEN AND THE ELEPHANT"

Speakers' Roles
N1—Narrator elephant actions
N2—Narrator actions of 3 blind men
B1—Blind man 1
B2—Blind man 2
B3—Blind man 3

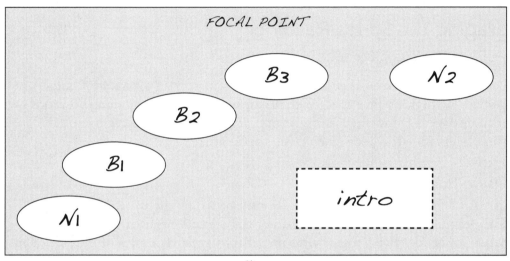

FOCAL POINT

B3   N2

B2

B1

intro

N1

audience

From WISDOM TALES FROM
AROUND THE WORLD by
Heather Forest, copyright 1996
by Heather Forest. Reprinted by
permission of Marian Reiner on
behalf of August House
Publishers, Inc.

*N2 moves to
intro block +
when finished
returns to
original position*

[~~Introduction for " The Blind Men and the Elephant~~ "]

"*There are not people a thousand years old, but there are
words a thousand years old*" (~~Forest, 1996, n.p.~~). [*The Blind Men
and the Elephant is an ancient tale from India adapted from
Jalal Al-din Rum's volume of poems, Masnavi.*] ← N2

B1
B2 ⟩→ [The Blind Men] [and the Elephant] ← N1
B3

N1 →[A large, gray elephant stood eating the lush greenery in an ancient, walled
garden. It paused for a moment and trumpeted loudly.] [Just then, three
blind men came along.] ← N2

B1 →["What made that sound?" asked the first man.]

B2 →[The second man replied knowingly, "That sound was made by an
elephant."]

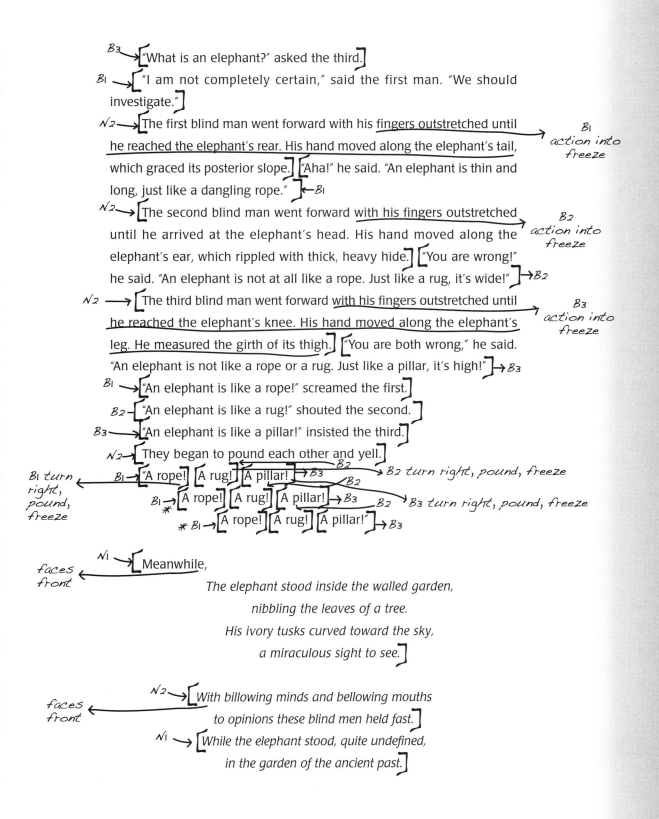

B3 → "What is an elephant?" asked the third.

B1 → "I am not completely certain," said the first man. "We should investigate."

N2 → The first blind man went forward with his <u>fingers outstretched until he reached the elephant's rear. His hand moved along the elephant's tail,</u> which graced its posterior slope. "Aha!" he said. "An elephant is thin and long, just like a dangling rope." ← B1

B1 action into freeze

N2 → The second blind man went forward <u>with his fingers outstretched until he arrived at the elephant's head. His hand moved along the elephant's ear, which rippled with thick, heavy hide.</u> "You are wrong!" he said. "An elephant is not at all like a rope. Just like a rug, it's wide!" → B2

B2 action into freeze

N2 → The third blind man went forward <u>with his fingers outstretched until he reached the elephant's knee. His hand moved along the elephant's leg. He measured the girth of its thigh.</u> "You are both wrong," he said. "An elephant is not like a rope or a rug. Just like a pillar, it's high!" → B3

B3 action into freeze

B1 → "An elephant is like a rope!" screamed the first.

B2 → "An elephant is like a rug!" shouted the second.

B3 → "An elephant is like a pillar!" insisted the third.

N2 → They began to pound each other and yell.

B1 turn right, pound, freeze ← B1 → "A rope!" "A rug!" "A pillar!" → B3 —B2 → *B2 turn right, pound, freeze*

B1 *→ "A rope!" "A rug!" "A pillar!" → B3 —B2 → *B3 turn right, pound, freeze*

* B1 → "A rope!" "A rug!" "A pillar!" → B3

faces front ← N1 → Meanwhile,

*The elephant stood inside the walled garden,
nibbling the leaves of a tree.
His ivory tusks curved toward the sky,
a miraculous sight to see.*

faces front ← N2 → *With billowing minds and bellowing mouths
to opinions these blind men held fast.*

N1 → *While the elephant stood, quite undefined,
in the garden of the ancient past.*

Postures and Actions
*on each repeat, speaker just pounds
" a rope"—B1 pounds and freezes
" a rug"—B2 pounds and freezes
" a pillar"—B3 pounds and freezes

Action Diagram—Pounds

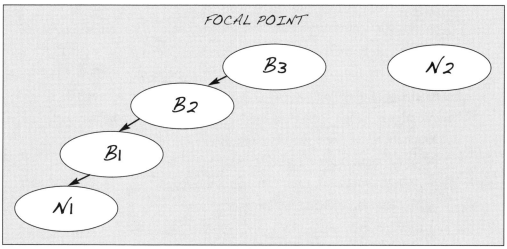

= "turns right"

audience

[~~Conclusion for " The Blind Men and the Elephant"~~]
[We hope the seed of this performance has taken root in your
minds and hearts and will grow into a flower of understanding.] N2

Adapting the Material to a Script

Essential Reader Information

The True Confessions of Charlotte Doyle is a novel. Students will have had many experiences with reading and responding to novels by the time they are in middle school. The whole text and each chapter presents a heroine, her supporters, her enemies, her trials, and her triumphs as she attempts to reach her goals. The chapter selected for performance presents one of the first glimpses of the dangers and difficulties that Charlotte will face on her voyage to America. The chapter ends with a dramatic recognition of the danger present on the ship.

The content is a clear line of action and reasonably direct; there are no subplots or complex characterizations. The context (time and place) may need some explanation for both performers and audience. The time period is 1832, and the custom for that time was for a young lady to travel with one or more adults (family members or others selected by her family). Because Charlotte does not have adult caretakers, she is anxious and frightened but determined to make the best of the situation. Another important aspect of the context is clothing and manner of dress. Young and old women alike always wore long dresses, which were tight at the waist, shoulders, arms, and wrists, and which had many petticoats filling out the long skirts. Shoes were more like short boots laced up the ankles to mid-calf. Movement was constricted. In contrast, the captain and the sailors had great freedom of movement. They wore variations of breeches, coats, shirts, belts, and boots or no shoes, which gave them the flexibility and protection needed to sail the ship, climb the rigging, move cargo, and endure the weather at sea.

The setting for the action also needs elaboration. Performers and audience need to be able to visualize a sailing ship and have a basic understanding of its structure—the levels of the ship, the deck, the hold, the cabins, the sails, and the masts. If the whole class is reading the text and performing a chapter, they will be familiar with these elements of context. If the text is not being read by the entire class, the teacher and the performance group will need to decide how much of the essential context information needs to be provided for the audience. This may be included briefly in the introduction or through the use of visuals. In the introduction for the sample script, the context information about the traveling arrangements for Charlotte is included. The audience must rely on their own knowledge and experience regarding clothing of the time period and structure of the sailing ship.

In this chapter of the novel, there is a variety of vocabulary words that will need to be defined and pronounced. There are two kinds of vocabulary: general words and words related to the ship's structure. The general vocabulary words are part of the setting description or character descriptions or feelings. These words include *sodden, decrepit, dexterous, forelock, beckoned, higgledy-piggledy, hasps, engrossed, sloshing,* and *impulsively*. Words related to the ship's structure are *forecastle deck, quarterdeck, braces, jigger gaff, shrouds, topgallant and royal yardmen, rigging, masts and spars, haul taut, sway, running lines and tackle, top steerage, winged hatch door, foreyard, foul bilge,* and *cargo deck*. The novel has two excellent drawing of sailing ships with labels for most of these words.

Unlike "The Tortoise and the Hare" and "The Blind Men and the Elephant," chapter 6 in *The True Confessions of Charlotte Doyle* needs to be edited because of the highly descriptive nature of the text, the unfamiliar terms, and the time limit for rehearsal and performance. Material that is deleted is considered nonessential to the development of the character relationships or the action of the story, or is too confusing or technical for the audience to grasp easily. All dialogue tags (such as "she shrieked") are also cut. The teacher does this editing because of the limited student preparation time and the complexity of the editing task. The need and rationale for editing sections are part of the teacher's discussions with the performance group (see *The True Confessions of Charlotte Doyle* script beginning on page 67 for examples of these deletions).

Dividing the Text for Script Adaptation

There are six speaker roles (see the script for the division of roles). Because the whole novel is framed as Charlotte's journal, there is a narrator (N) for the actions of Charlotte Doyle and the setting. The speaker for Charlotte Doyle (CD) reads the dialogue and her limited actions. The other speakers, Captain Jaggery (CAPT), Mr. Keetch (K), Mr. Hollybrass (H), and Barlow (B), read dialogue and character actions. Because of its complexity, the teacher should divide the text.

Necessary Script Additions

There is no need for a transition, and there is already a strong and dramatic conclusion at the end of the chapter. However, there is a need for an introduction to provide information about the context, to introduce the central character, and to summarize the action up to this point in the novel. In consideration of limited preparation time, the introduction would be better developed by the teacher.

Sample Introduction

The True Confessions of Charlotte Doyle by Avi is a diary that tells Charlotte's story of crossing the Atlantic in the sailing ship *The Seahawk*. In 1832, Charlotte Doyle, age 13, was traveling alone to join her family in Providence, Rhode Island. Charlotte's father had been recalled to Rhode Island for business after living in England for seven years. Charlotte's mother, brother, and sister returned to Rhode Island with her father. Her parents wanted her to finish the school year in England, so they made arrangements for Charlotte to sail to America in the early summer. She was supposed to travel with adult friends of the family, but these friends were not on board when the ship sailed. Alone from the moment she boards the ship, Charlotte meets with a series of unexpected and threatening attitudes and events. Her voyage tests her courage and her will to survive.

Staging the Script Reading

Creating the Whole Picture

For *The True Confessions of Charlotte Doyle*, the focal point is a backdrop hung behind the performance space. The performers remain in the same positions (see the script illustrations of this floor plan).

Using Postures and Actions

Because this text is complicated, there is little change in the postures, gestures, and actions of the performers. Charlotte, Captain Jaggery, Mr. Hollybrass, and Barlow turn to face each other several times. These same characters also mime one or two essential actions (for examples, see the staging of postures, gestures, and actions in the script). Because most of the preparation time for this script is spent on reading, the teacher selects the simple postures and actions used by the performers. Through discussion with the student performers, these postures and actions might be changed, but they should be limited to one or two per performer. The intent is not to mime every action or continually change postures but to select one or two key statues or movements to communicate meaning from text (see Figure 10).

Creating and Using Production Elements

The preparation and emphasis is on effective and expressive reading and not on the creation of production elements. Costume pieces would be difficult and time-consuming to make or find. Students may, however, choose to wear shirts or blouses that, through color or style, suggest something about their characters.

Props are also not appropriate for use in the performance of this text. The visual element, however, might be an easy and appropriate element to develop. Students could create a backdrop with a drawing, painting, or projection of a

sailing ship. The novel has a drawing of a ship in the appendix to use as a pattern. The background could also be expressive; for example, an abstract use of color to suggest the setting and mood of the chapter. Music or sound is not necessary; it might, however, provide a short introduction to the performance in place of a visual element. Because of the complexity of the material to be performed and the emphasis on the expressive reading, no more than one production element should be selected for use in performance.

THE TRUE CONFESSIONS OF CHARLOTTE DOYLE (CHAPTER 6)

Speakers' Roles
N—Narrator Charlotte Doyle actions and setting
CD—Charlotte Doyle dialogue
CAPT—Captain Jaggery dialogue and actions
K—Mr. Keetch dialogue and actions
H—Mr. Hollybrass dialogue and actions
B—Barlow dialogue and actions

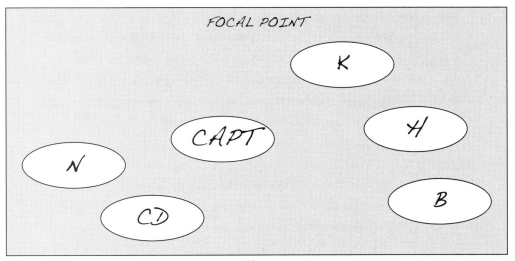

audience

intro
read in
place

[Introduction for The True Confessions of Charlotte Doyle]

B → [The True Confessions of Charlotte Doyle by Avi is a diary
which tells Charlotte's story of crossing the Atlantic in the
sailing ship The Seahawk. In 1832, Charlotte Doyle, age 13, was
traveling alone to join her family in Providence, Rhode Island.]

K → [Because of his business, her father had been recalled to
Rhode Island after living in England for seven years. Charlotte's
mother, younger brother, and sister returned to Rhode Island
with her father. Charlotte's parents wanted her to finish the
school year in England, so they made arrangements for
Charlotte to sail to America in the early summer.] [She would
travel with adult friends of the family, but these friends were ← CD

not on board when the ship sailed. From the moment she boards the ship, Charlotte is alone and meets with a series of unexpected and threatening attitudes and events. Her voyage tests her courage and her will to survive.

N →
The True Confessions of Charlotte Doyle
Chapter 6 by Avi

N → Never mind that my dress—having been worn for four days—was creased and misshapen, my white gloves a sodden gray. Never mind that my fine hair must have been hanging like a horse's tail, in almost complete disarray. With all eyes upon us as we crossed the ship's waist to the bowsprit and figurehead, I felt like a princess being led to her throne.

Not even the same lowering mist I'd observed when I first came from my cabin could dampen my soaring spirits. Captain Jaggery was a brilliant sun and I, a Juno moon, basked in reflected glory.

CD → "Captain Jaggery, sir," I said, "this ship seems to be moving so slowly."

CAPT → "You observe correctly," he replied, ever the perfect gentleman. "But if you look up there," he pointed beyond the mainmast, "you'll notice some movement. The cloud cover should be breaking soon and then we'll gain. There, you see," he exclaimed, "the sun I struggling to shine through."

CAPT points

N → As if by command a thin yellow disk began to appear where he pointed, though it soon faded again behind clotted clouds.

front

CD → From the forecastle deck we crossed to the quarterdeck and then to the helm. Foley, a lean, bearded man, was at the wheel. Mr. Keetch, as unsmiling as ever, stood by his side. The wheel itself was massive, with hand spikes for easier gripping.

When the captain and I approached, the two men stole fleeting glances in our direction but said nothing.

CAPT → Captain Jaggery released my arm and gazed up at the sails. At length he said, "Mr. Keetch."

The second mate turned to him. "Yes, sir." K

CAPT → "I believe," the captain said, "we shall soon have a blow."

Mr. Keetch seemed surprised. "Do you think so, sir?" ← K

CAPT → "I hardly would have said so otherwise, now would I, Mr. Keetch?"

K → [The man darted a glance] [at me as if I held the answer.] ~~All he said however was,~~ ["I suppose not, sir."] → K

CAPT → ["Thank you, Mr. Keetch. Now, I want to take advantage of it. Tighten all braces, and be ready with the jigger gaff."]

K → ["Aye, aye, sir."]

["And bring the studding sails to hand. We may want them to make up for lost time."] → CAPT

K → ["Aye, aye, sir."] [After another glance] [at me,] [Mr. Keetch marched quickly across the quarterdeck ~~and at the rail bellowed,~~ "All hands! All hands!"] ← K

N → [Within moments the entire crew assembled on deck.]

K → ["Topgallant and royal yardmen in the tops!"] ~~he cried.~~

N → [The next moment the crew scrambled into the shrouds and standing rigging, high amidst the masts and spars. Even as they ascended] [Mr. Keetch began to sing out] [~~a litany of commands~~] ["Man topgallant mast ropes! Haul taut! Sway and unfid!"] [that had men hauling on running lines and tackle until the desired sails were shifted and set. It was a grand show, but if the ship moved any faster for it, I didn't sense a change.] → N

~~The captain now turned to Foley. "One point south," he said.~~

~~"One point south," Foley echoed and shifted the wheel counterclockwise with both hands.~~

~~"Steady on," the captain said.~~

~~"Steady on," Foley repeated.~~

~~Now it was Mr. Hollybrass who approached the helm. The moment he did so Captain Jaggery hailed him.~~

CAPT → ["Mr. Hollybrass!"]

H → ["Sir!"]

CAPT → ["As convenient, Mr. Hollybrass, send Mr. Barlow to Miss Doyle. She needs to learn where her trunk was stowed."]

H → ["Yes, sir."]

CAPT → ["Miss Doyle," ~~the captain said to me,~~ "please be so good as to follow Mr. Hollybrass. I have enjoyed our conversation and look forward to many more."]

CAPT

capt extends right hand, bends over hand, kisses then releases hand

N → [Then and there—beneath the eyes of all the crew—he took my hand, bowed over it, and touched his lips to my fingers.] [I fairly glowed with pride. Finally I followed—perhaps floated is a better word—after Mr.

CD ← *extends left hand*

Action Diagram—CAPT kisses CD's hand

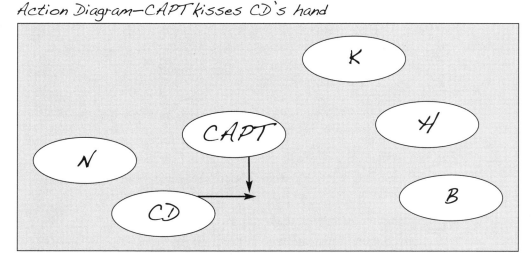

Note—hands do not touch, only extend in direction of speaker

Hollybrass.] [Barely concealing a look of disdain for the captain's farewell ← H to me, he made his way across the quarterdeck ~~and stood at the rail overlooking the ship's waist.~~ There he studied the men while they continued to adjust the rigging, now and again barking a command to work one rope or another.]

H → ["Mr. Barlow," ~~he called out at last.~~

B → ["Here, sir!" ~~came a response from on high.~~

N → [Some sixty feet above I saw the man.]

H → ["Get you down!" ~~Mr. Hollybrass cried.~~

B → [Despite his decrepit appearance, Barlow was as dexterous as a monkey. He clambered across the foreyard upon which he had been perched, reached the mast, then the rigging, and on this narrow thread of rope he seemed to actually run until he dropped upon the deck with little or no sound.]

B → ["Aye, aye, sir," ~~he said,~~ [← N no more out of breath than I—or rather less than I, for to see him at such heights moving at such speeds had taken *my* breath away.]

H → ["Mr. Barlow," ~~Hollybrass said.~~ "Miss Doyle needs her trunk. I understand you know where it is."]

B → ["I put it in top steerage, sir."

H → ["Be so good as to lead her to it."]

B ———→ "Yes, sir." Barlow had not yet looked ~~my way~~ *at Charlotte*. Now, with a shy nod,
and a touch to his forelock, he did so.] [I understood I was to follow.] ←—N

~~The normal entry to the cargo areas is through the hatchway~~
~~located in the center of the ship's waist. Since that was lashed down for~~
B ~~the voyage,~~ [Barlow ~~led me another way~~, *moved* to a ladder beneath the mates'
mess table—in steerage ~~just opposite my cabin door.~~

After setting aside the candle he'd brought along, he scrambled
under the mess table, then pulled open a winged hatch door that was
built flush into the floor. Once he had his candle lit,] [I saw him twist
about and drop partway down the hole.] ←— N

["If you please, miss,"] ~~he beckoned.~~ ——→ *B gestures right hand come down here*

Distasteful though it was, I had little choice in the matter. I crawled
N ——→ on hands and knees, backed into the hole, and climbed down twelve
rungs—a distance of about eight or nine feet.

B ——→ ["Here, miss," Barlow ~~said at my side, next to the ladder.~~ *was standing next to the ladder* "You don't
want to go down to the hold."]

N ——→ [I looked beneath me and saw that the ladder continued into what
appeared to be a black pit.]

B ——→ ["More cargo," ~~he explained laconically.~~ "Rats and roaches too. And
a foul bilge. That's where the brig is."

CD ——→ ["Brig?"]

["The ship's jail."] ←— B

CD ——→ ["A jail on a ship?"]

B ←— ["Captain Jaggery wouldn't sail without, miss."]

N ←— [I shuddered in disgust.]

B ——→ [Barlow held out one of his hard, gnarled hands.] [Reluctantly I took
it and did a little jump to the top cargo deck. Only then did I look about.]

B holds out right hand ↗
↙ *N*

CD holds
out left
hand—
jumps—
looks about

N ——→ It was a great, wood-ribbed cavern I had come to, which—because
Barlow's candlelight reached only so far—melted into blackness fore and
aft. ~~I recall being struck by the notion that I was Jonah-like in the~~
~~belly of a whale.~~ The air was heavy, with the pervasive stench of rot
that made me gag.

CD ←——→ ["What's that?"] [~~I asked, pointing~~ *I pointed* to a cylinder from which pipes ←— N
ran, and to which handles were attached.

B ——→ ["The pump," ~~he said.~~ "In case we take on sea."]

N ——→ In all directions I saw the kinds of bales, barrels, and boxes I had
seen upon the Liverpool docks. ~~The sight was not romantic now.~~ These

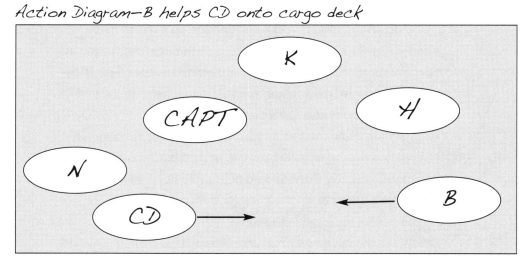

Action Diagram—B helps CD onto cargo deck

Note—hands do not touch, only extend in direction of speaker

goods were piled higgledy-piggledy one atop the other, braced and restrained here and there by ropes and wedges, but mostly held in place by their own bulk. The whole reminded me of a great tumble of toy blocks jammed into a box.

B → ["There's more below," ~~Barlow said, observing me look about.~~ "But your trunk's over there."] [Sure enough, I saw it up along the alleyway created by two stacks of cargo.]

CD → ["Would you open it, please," ~~I requested.~~]

B → [Barlow undid the hasps and flung open the top.] [There lay my clothing, wrapped in tissue paper and laid out beautifully.] ~~The school maids had done a fine job. A sigh escaped my lips at this glimpse of another world.~~

CD → ["I can't take everything," ~~I said.~~]

B → ["Well, miss," ~~Barlow said~~, "now that you know where it is, you could fetch things on your own."]

CD → ["That's true," ~~I said~~, and, kneeling, began to lift the layers carefully.]

B → ~~After a while Barlow said,~~ ["If it pleases, miss, might I have a word?"]

CD → ["You see I'm very busy Mr. Barlow," ~~I murmured.~~] *Pause*
~~For a moment the sailor said nothing, though I was conscious of his nervous presence behind me.~~

B → ["Miss," ~~he said unexpectedly~~, "you know I spoke out when you first arrived."]

B turns right, opens latches and pushes to, open — then turns fro — putting trunk in fron of him

Pause

CD turns left, kneels, goes through layers

CD "I have tried to forget it, Mr. Barlow," ~~I said with some severity.~~ "You shouldn't, miss. You shouldn't." | Pause | ~~His earnest, pleading tone made me pause.~~ "What do you mean?" *CD*

B "Just now, miss, the captain put us on display. All that hauling and pulling. It was to no account. Mocking us—"

CD "Mr. Barlow!" ~~I interrupted.~~

B "It's true, miss. He's abusing us. And you. Mark my words. No good will come of it."

N I pressed my hands to my ears. → *CD puts hands to ears*

B ~~After a moment the man said,~~ "All right, miss. I'll leave you with the candle. You won't go into the hold now, will you?"

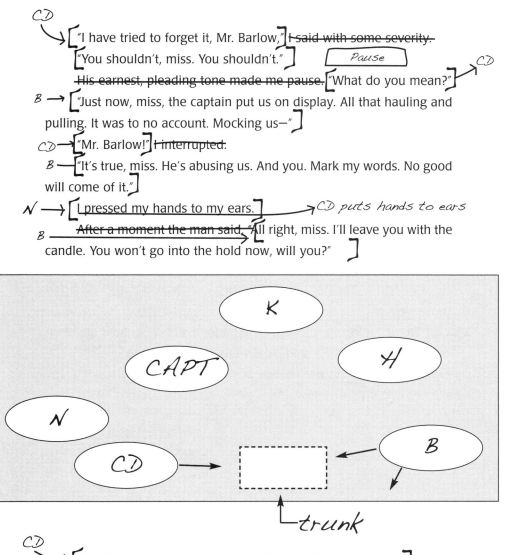

K

CAPT   H

N

CD → [ ] ← B

trunk

CD "I shall be fine, Mr. Barlow," ~~I declared.~~ "Please leave me."

N So engrossed was I in my explorations of my trunk that I ceased paying him any attention. ~~Only vaguely did I hear him retreat and ascend the ladder.~~ But when I was sure he was gone I did turn about. → *CD stands + faces front*
He had set the candle on the floor near where the ladder led further into the hold. Though the flame flickered in a draft, I was satisfied it would burn a while. I turned back to my trunk. → *CD turns left, kneels, goes through layers (same position as earlier)*

CD As I knelt there, ~~making the difficult but delicious choice between this petticoat and that—searching too for a book suitable for reading to the crew as the captain had suggested~~—the sensation crept upon me that there was something else hovering about, a *presence*, if you will, something I could not define.

N

At first I tried to ignore the feeling. But no matter how much I tried it could not be denied. Of course it was not exactly quiet down below. No place on a ship is. There were the everlasting creaks and groans. I could hear the sloshing of the bilge water in the hold, and the rustling of all I preferred not to put a name to—such as the rats Barlow had mentioned. But within moments I was absolutely certain—though how I knew I cannot tell—that it was a *person* who was watching me.

CD → As this realization took hold, <u>I froze in terror. Then slowly I lifted</u> my head and stared before me over the lid of the trunk. As far as I could see, no one was there.

CD freezes, lifts head, stares front

CD looks right — then left ←

N → <u>My eyes swept to the right</u>. No one. To the left. Again, nothing. There was but one other place to look, *behind*. Just the thought brought a prickle to the back of my neck until, with sudden panic, I whirled impulsively around.

→ CD stands quickly and turns front

N → There, jutting up from the hole through which the hold might be reached, was a grinning *head*, its eyes fixed right on me.

CD → I shrieked. The next moment the candle went out and I was plunged into utter darkness. *← N*

REFERENCES FOR SCRIPTS

Avi. (1990). *The true confessions of Charlotte Doyle* (pp. 52–59). New York: Scholastic.

Forest, H. (Ed.). (1996). *Wisdom tales from around the world* (n.p.). Little Rock, AR: August House.

Lynch, T. (2000). *Fables from Aesop* (p. 2). New York: Viking.

SUGGESTED FICTION MATERIALS FOR READERS THEATRE

Brown, D. (Ed.). (1993). *Folk tales of the Native American retold for our times*. New York: Henry Holt.

Crew, L. (1989). *Children of the river*. New York: Delacorte.

Curtis, C. (1999). *Bud, not Buddy*. New York: Delacorte.

Ehrlich, A. (Ed.). (2002). *When I was your age: Original stories about growing up*. Cambridge, MA: Candlewick.

Enzensberger, H.M. (1997). *The number devil: A mathematical adventure*. New York: Henry Holt.

Forest, H. (Ed.). (1996). *Wisdom tales from around the world*. Little Rock, AR: August House.

Gallo, D.R. (Ed.). (1987). *Visions: 19 short stories by outstanding writers for young adults*. New York: Bantam Doubleday Dell.

Gallo, D.R. (Ed.). (1989). *Connections: Short stories by outstanding writers for young adults*. New York: Bantam Doubleday Dell.

Gallo, D.R. (Ed.). (1997). *No easy answers: Short stories about teenagers making tough choices*. New York: Delacorte.

Hamilton, V. (1988). *In the beginning: Creation stories from around the world*. Orlando, FL: Harcourt Brace Jovanovich.

Hamilton, V. (1997). *A ring of tricksters: Animal tales from America, the West Indies, and Africa*. New York: Scholastic.

Hesse, K. (2001). *Witness*. New York: Scholastic.

Lynch, T. (2000). *Fables from Aesop*. New York: Viking.

Mazer, A. (1993). *America street: A multicultural anthology of stories*. New York: Persea.

Mazer, N.F. (1977). *Dear Bill, remember me? and other stories*. New York: Dell.

Myers, W.D. (2000). *145th Street: Short stories*. New York: Delacorte.

Myers, W.D. (2002). *Handbook for boys*. New York: HarperCollins.

Park, L.S. (2001). *A single shard*. New York: Clarion.

Paulsen, G. (1987). *Hatchet*. New York: Bradbury.

Paulsen, G. (1998). *A soldier's heart: A novel of the Civil War*. New York: Delacorte.

Rinaldi, A. (1999). *Amelia's war*. New York: Scholastic.

Soto, G. (1994). *Crazy weekend*. New York: Scholastic.

Spinelli, J. (1990). *Maniac Magee*. New York: Scholastic.

Weiss, M.J., & Weiss, A.S. (Eds.). (1997). *From one experience to another: Award-winning authors sharing real-life experiences through fiction*. New York: Tom Doherty Associates.

CHAPTER 5

From Script to Performance: Nonfiction

Before developing a script for nonfiction materials, it is useful to determine which materials are most suitable and adaptable for Readers Theatre performance. There are two types of materials that lend themselves most easily to performance. First, primary documents (such as oral histories and interviews, diaries and journals, and letters) are the simplest types to adapt. These materials capture human voices in writing and address particular audiences. The purpose is to communicate: to record, remember, describe, explain, question, and evaluate significant events in the life of the speaker or writer, events that give insight on a larger historical context. Second, biographies and autobiographies are easily adaptable to Readers Theatre performances, combining human voices with the plot elements of good stories.

Two other types of nonfiction are possibilities for script adaptation and development. Personal histories and biographies might be supplemented by the use of newspaper articles as introductions, transitions, conclusions, or a section of the full performance piece. The newspaper articles could provide additional information and different perspectives. Historical declarations (e.g., the Declaration of Independence, Magna Carta, or the Universal Declaration of Human Rights) might also be a portion of a script developed primarily from other nonfiction materials or become an entire script developed for a whole-class performance.

While considering the types of nonfiction materials, it is necessary to consider the students' experiences with and prior knowledge of the content, structure, and language of the nonfiction materials selected for performance. An effective way to examine and select nonfiction materials for performance is to connect to topics that are part of the social studies curriculum and to plan the performance with the social studies teacher as a content advisor. For example, the performance could be scheduled close to the end of a social studies unit. If students are studying the U.S. Civil War, a performance of the diaries and letters of Confederate and Union Soldiers would be rehearsed near the end of the unit and presented at the unit's conclusion. Students may also examine state or local historical events, documents, or a particular time period. A local or state historical association is an excellent source of suggestions and materials.

It is also possible that the content is related to other materials studied in the English language arts curriculum. *Anne Frank: The Diary of a Young Girl* (Frank & Pressler, 1995), for example, is often read in middle school classes. This historical text could provide further contextual information needed for the performance of diaries and letters of other adolescents who experienced the Holocaust and World War II. Performances based on nonfiction materials should provide an additional perspective to previously studied content. Performances are not intended to be the center of a unit of study but a culminating activity— a way of engaging students as performers and audience to connect and reflect on their prior knowledge and experiences.

In terms of the structure and language, most middle school students have written and read diaries, letters, and journals. They have also read biographical and autobiographical materials, as well as newspaper articles. The oral history interview format may be a new form for reading, but all students should be familiar with interviews from television. Only a brief explanation of that format is necessary. Depending upon both the context and specific content of these materials, the teacher may need to give more information about structure and language use. For example, if the Declaration of Independence is selected for performance, the teacher will need to explain its structure and language.

In this chapter, the following materials were selected for scripting: the 1862 diary of an adolescent girl from upstate New York (Walker, 1862); memories and information about Ellis Island (Coan, 1997; Lawlor, 1995; Levine, 1994; Pereg & Bober, 1995); and an adaptation for children of the Universal Declaration of Human Rights (Rocha & Roth, 1990). In both the diary and Ellis Island memories, the writers are adolescents during the events they describe or recall. (Levine's work provides information about Ellis Island and the immigrant experience but is not a first-person narrative.) These events may or may not be a part of students' prior knowledge. The experiences described are ones to which the students can relate because they involve relationships and daily life events that are familiar to students and with which they can empathize.

The third selection, an adaptation of the Universal Declaration of Human Rights, is written in simple, direct language rather than the concise but formal and more technical language of the original. The adaptation is easily understood by both reader and audience. The document is concrete and specific in what it describes as the essential rights that belong to all humans and that must be respected by all people. This content appeals to middle school students who are concerned with what is fair treatment for themselves and others in school, at home, in their community, in their state and country, and perhaps globally. They are beginning to assert their rights as students, family members, and citizens, and want to find out what their rights are. In short, they are developing their identities and their relationships with others and the world in which they live.

In this chapter, there are some detailed examples of script and performance development of nonfiction materials. These are not the only possibilities for approaching the selected materials. They are one set of choices that make understanding and developing other materials easier.

The Diary of Lucy Medora Walker, September 1862

Nonfiction Subgenre: Diary　　　**Group Dynamics:** Individual groups

Adapting the Material to a Script

Essential Reader Information

In the diary entries selected for performance, students need to know the style of writing is personal and informal. Dora, the writer, is a 13-year-old who lived in East Springfield, New York, USA. She uses her diary to record daily events such as the weather, visitors, and her activities at home, in school, at church, in the town shops, and on a hops farm. The language is direct and written in complete sentences. The use of complete sentences and lack of abbreviations is unlike many students' diaries today, whether handwritten in a journal or notebook or computer-generated in personal blogs or e-mails. Dora's entries are beautifully handwritten in a medium brown ink; there are few, if any, ink blots or words or phrases crossed out. It is interesting to note that the New York State Historical Association's Special Collections department has the actual diaries of Dora Walker. The diaries are in small, leather-bound books about 3¾ inches tall and 2½ inches wide. The paper is unlined, and each daily entry is headed by the day of the week, month, and date. It is like a modern-day book students might use. The size of Dora's diary makes it easy to fit into the pocket of an apron, dress, or coat or keep in a drawer or special hiding place.

Although the content is a straightforward description of and response to daily events in Dora's life, the context needs further explanation. First, it is important for the students to understand that Dora's diary is real and not a fictional account. Students may have previously read fiction set in a diary or journal format. It is a good idea to share information about where the actual diaries are located (New York State Historical Association, Special Collections, Cooperstown, New York, USA) and where the diary was found (in an area house). Offering information about the diary's appearance as well as any pictures of the diary adds more "real-world" details. Second, students need to understand the context of the diary entries. Students may have studied rural communities in the 1860s, but may need more specific information about upstate New York and small communities. A timeline for and brief description of the westward movement, the opening of the Erie Canal, the Albany turnpike, and the Civil War in upstate New York would be helpful. Information about Dora Walker, her family, her town, daily life, and hops crops need to be included in the script.

It will likely be necessary to provide an explanation of the growing, cultivating, and harvesting of hops. Hops were an important cash crop for the area, and everyone (the farmer and his family, members of the town and neighboring farms, and some traveling field workers) participated in the harvesting of the hops and connected social events. The money earned from the harvesting and sale of the hops provided all the workers with income. The price of this crop, however, fluctuated from season to season, as did the quality of the crop. The following sample text can be added to the script in order to provide this background about hops.

Sample Text Explaining Hops

In 1825, farmers in Springfield began to grow hops. By 1880, Otsego County was the largest producer of hops in New York and in America.

Hops were planted in lots or yards of 5 to 10 acres. The soil was carefully prepared and fertilized with manure from the neighboring dairy farms. The soil was then piled into hills, and each hill had at its center a 9-foot pole. Then the farmers cut runners from the previous year's hop vines and planted them next to the pole of each hill. The new vine's growth was then trained to climb the 9-foot pole.

In mid-August through mid-September, the hops were ready to pick. The flowers on the vines had changed from a light green to a deep yellow and felt hard when touched. The flowers were picked from the vines, placed in bags, and then taken to the hop house.

In the hop house, the flowers were dried, sweated, and baled like hay. At this point, the hop bales were ready to be sold.

Hop farmers hired townspeople including women and children to help with the harvest. People from outside the town were also hired as workers. During the harvest season, East Springfield was a busy place—filled with working, buying, selling, and transporting crops, and a variety of community social events and activities.

In September 1862, there was, according to an Otsego County newspaper *The Freeman's Journal*, an excellent harvest of hops. A note in the back of Dora's diary records her pay for the harvest and how she spent it.

There are some vocabulary words and phrases that will need additional definition and explanation. The words include *hops, turmoil, declamation, hopyard, The Freeman's Journal, gumarabic, worsted, merino, cornelian,* and *lozengers.*

Another possibility for script development in this text is the diary entries for the year of 1862, which include the topics of school, medicine, funerals, social events, and meetings about the Civil War. Any of these and related context information could be developed for and with other groups in the class. It would also be possible to add articles, features, letters from newspapers of that year, other diaries and letters of Dora's family or materials from Dora's later diaries, and related context information.

Dividing the Text for Script Adaptation

Because the diary has a single voice or writer and features additional context information, it is not immediately apparent how to divide the text. The text could be divided between diary writer and a narrator, but this choice gives an unequal opportunity for each reader to perform. It is, therefore, a better choice for the teacher to divide the entries into speaker roles. In the sample script, there are five speaker roles. Speaker 1 gives a general overview; Speaker 2 gives information about Dora herself; Speaker 3 is Dora; Speaker 4 provides information about Dora's family; and Speaker 5 provides general overview (see *Diary of Dora Walker* script).

Necessary Script Additions

The next and final part of scripting is to develop an introduction, transitions, and a conclusion. Context information, including setting and details of Dora's family life, is included in the introduction, as illustrated below.

Sample Introduction

In 1862, the United States is in a Civil War—the war between the states. In 1862, Lucy Medora Walker (Dora) is 13 years old. She lives in East Springfield, New York, in northern Otsego County. East Springfield was the first village in the northern end of Otsego Lake. In 1769, there were 10 families; in 1858, 20 houses; in 1870, 200 inhabitants.

Dora is an only child. Benjamin Walker and Hannah Seabrook Van Horne are her parents. Benjamin is a cabinet maker who makes different kinds of furniture and coffins. He also sharpens saws. In 1862, he has a good business. He is paid for his work, sometimes with money and sometimes with trade of goods or services.

Dora goes to a private school in East Springfield. She studies geometry, composition, Latin grammar, declamation, and French. She likes French better than Latin.

Dora writes almost every day in her diary. Her diary is a small leather-bound book with unlined paper. In this pocket-sized diary, she records her daily activities.

Dora's original diary is in the special collections at the New York State Historical Association in Cooperstown, New York.

Dora's diary begins...

The conclusion should contain information about Dora's education, family life, and date of her death. The following sample conclusion offers this information.

Sample Conclusion

Dora moved to Schenectady, New York, to finish her education and returned to East Springfield. On June 25, 1873, she married William Smith Guardenier. They lived in the house where Dora had lived with her family. They had nine children: Lucy Hotchkiss, Benjamin Walker, Blanche Ormiston, William H, Fred, Doane Sinclair, Edgar Van Horne, Anna, and Hannah Medora.

On February 16, 1916, Dora died at the age of 68. She is buried in Springfield. Some of her relatives are still living in East Springfield.

Staging the Script Reading

Creating the Whole Picture

In the diaries, the focal point is a simple backdrop hung behind the performance area, such as a large piece of fabric or curtain attached to the back wall of the performance area or to a screen or portable chalkboard. The material is a solid color (white, black, blue, or tan). There are two positions for the performers: one for the introduction and conclusion and one for the reading of the diary entries (see the floor plan within the script).

Using Postures and Actions

The emphasis in this performance is on the reading: the meaning and feelings and experiences created by the words in the text. The text does not suggest character conversations in which speakers might turn toward each other or specific actions for a speaker to perform. The readers face front in neutral postures. Speaker 3 (Dora) is seated on a small chair or stool with a small table in front of her. There is an open, diary-sized book on the table. Speaker 3 (Dora) holds a pen midpage, as if she is writing a journal entry. This is the only posture and movement for this performance, the emphasis instead being on the actions and images described in the text.

Creating and Using Production Elements

In the performance of the diaries, the production elements should be basic. Costume elements are helpful to students in assuming their roles. Performers could all wear white or light or dark blue shirts. For example, Speakers 1 and 5 could wear white, Speakers 2 and 3 light blue, and Speaker 4 dark blue. There are four suggested props: a small stool or chair, a small table, a book—diary size with lines or blank pages, and a pen. There is no need for visual elements beyond the backdrop. Music might be used as a brief bridge from the introduction or to the conclusion.

DIARY OF DORA WALKER

Speakers' Roles
1—General information
2—About Dora
3—Dora
4—About Dora's family
5—General information

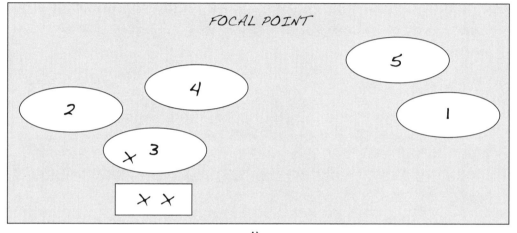

audience

Props

  X ⟶ *stool or small chair where Dora sits*

  XX ⟶ *small table with small open book (the diary) and*
     pen

Posture

  3 (Dora)—pen in hand, focus on diary as if frozen in the
  act of writing

Picture remains the same for the whole performance.

~~Introduction for the Diary of Dora Walker~~

[In 1862, the United States is in a Civil War—the war between
the states.]←₁

2 → [In 1862, Lucy Medora Walker (Dora) is 13 years old. She lives in East Springfield, New York, in northern Otsego County.] [East →5 Springfield was the first village in the northern end of Otsego Lake. In 1769, there were 10 families; in 1858, 20 houses; in 1870, 200 inhabitants.]

2 → [Dora is an only child.] [Benjamin Walker and Hannah Seabrook Van Horne are her parents. Benjamin is a cabinet maker who makes different kinds of furniture and coffins. He also sharpens saws. In 1862, he has a good business.] [He is paid for his work, sometimes with money and sometimes with trade of goods or services.]

2 → [Dora goes to a private school in East Springfield. She studies geometry, composition, Latin grammar, declamation, and French. She likes French better than Latin.]

3 → [Dora writes almost every day in her diary. Her diary is a small leather-bound book with unlined paper.] [In this pocket-sized diary, she records her daily activities.] ← 2

1 → [Dora's original diary is in the special collections at the New York State Historical Association in Cooperstown, New York.]

2 → [Dora's diary begins...]

2 → [Monday, September 1, 1862]
3 → [Anna and I went to the hopyard this morning. I picked 1 7/8 boxes it began to rain about four o'clock. Mother came up after dinner and fetched us some dinner she helped me some and Anna some. When it begun to rain Mother and Miss Ingalls came down as far as Mrs Hoyts and got an umbrella Aunt M & Anna stopped in the barn but I came home and was wet as a rat.]

2 → [Tuesday, September 2, 1862]
3 → [Oh! dear, dear me I don't have anything but trouble, trouble, trouble. This morning Charlie Van Horne came out after Anna and uncle William they got ready and went soon after dinner. Father and Mother went to Stark this afternoon. they fetched my book that Mr Fox gave me. Mary started for school to morrow. I expect Anna will have to stay over there all hop time we did not pick this morning Aunt Mary picked this afternoon]

2 → [Wednesday, September 3, 1862]

3 → [This morning it was so cold Mother thought she had better go to the hop
yard so I stayed home and done the work and then went up she helped
fill my box and then went home and got dinner and then came up in the
afternoon I got six eights by noon and picked two boxes in the afternoon
that made three boxes and a 1/4]

2 → [Thursday, September 4, 1862]

3 → [I went to the hop yard this morning Mother thought she would stay home.
I had a little start but got a box by noon she came up in the afternoon I
got a box and six eights. I couldn't get three boxes. the hopes were very
poor. Mr Ingalls was up most all day]

2 → [Friday, September 5, 1862]

3 → [I went this morning to the hop yard I got a box at noon Mother came up this
afternoon I picked two boxes that makes three boxes two day. Mr Ingalls
was up most all day. Miss Ingalls went home early she was very tired.
Warner Shecher came to tend our box today. I was in hopes it would rain to
day but no such thing it won't rain]

2 → [Saturday, September 6, 1862]

3 → [Mother came up this afternoon I had a box this forenoon then we picked a
box and six eights. We went home quite early to night because it was
Saturday night.]

~~About hops~~

1 → [In 1825, farmers in Springfield began to grow hops.] [By 1880,
Otsego County was the largest producer of hops in New York
and in America.] ← 5

1 → [Hops were planted in lots or yards of 5 to 10 acres. The soil
was carefully prepared and fertilized with manure from the
neighboring dairy farms. The soil was then piled into hills, and
each hill had at its center a 9-foot pole.] [Then the farmers 5
cut runners from the previous year's hop vines and planted
them next to the pole of each hill. The new vine's growth was
then trained to climb the 9-foot pole.]

1 → [In mid-August through mid-September, the hops were ready to pick. The flowers on the vines had changed from a light green to a deep yellow and felt hard when touched.] [The ← 2 & 4 flowers were picked from the vines, placed in bags, and then taken to the hop house.]

1 & 5 → [In the hop house, the flowers were dried, sweated, and baled like hay. At this point, the hop bales were ready to be sold.]

1 → [Hop farmers hired townspeople including women and children   2 & 4 to help with the harvest.] [People from outside the town were also hired as workers. During the harvest season, East Springfield was a busy place—filled with working, buying, selling, and transporting crops, and a variety of community social events and activities.]

5 → [In September 1862, there was, according to an Otsego County newspaper The Freeman's Journal, an excellent harvest of hops.] [A note in the back of Dora's diary records her pay for the harvest and how she spent it.] →²

2 → [Memorandum from the back of Dora's diary]

MEMORANDA

3 → [I received $18.85 picking hops and have spent it as follows,]　　　2

For a Cross	1.50
" clasp	37
" 3 collars	24
" Ruffle	7
" Paper of Needles	3
" 1 pair of gloves	20
" 1 " " stockings	14
" 1 yard of Rubber	6
" 3 sticks of Gum	3
" 6 " " Candy	6
" 3 cts woth Soap	3
" 1 Spool of Thread	3
" 1 Buckskin Purse	17
" 7 pen	01
" 3 cts Gumarabic	03
" Spool thread	04

1 Calico dress	1.48
1 ounce worsted	18
1 1/8 yd of Merino. 1.10	1.24
13 cts worth lozengers	13
10 cts worth candy	10
1 Bottle perfumery	20
1 birdseed pt	02
2 sticks liquorice	16
1 cornelian ring	06
2 balls cotton crotchet	08
3 skeins silk	06
Chain	5.50

2 →
3 →
3

Conclusion

2 → [Dora moved to Schenectady, New York, USA, to finish her education and returned to East Springfield. On June 25, 1873, she married 3 William Smith Guardenier.][They lived in the house where Dora had lived with her family. They had nine children:][Lucy
1 →Hotchkiss][Benjamin Walker,][Blanche Ormiston,][William H,] 5
4 →[Fred,][Doane Sinclair,][Edgar Van Horne,][Anna, and][Hannah Medora.] 4

5 →[On February 16, 1916, Dora died at the age of 68. She is buried in Springfield. Some of her relatives are still living in East Springfield.]

Adapting the Material to a Script

Essential Reader Information

The script is primarily composed of interviews with people who immigrated to Ellis Island between the years of 1911 and 1929. The introduction and conclusion are part of a text about Ellis Island and immigration (Levine, 1994). Students need to understand that the interviews (Lawlor, 1995; Pereg & Bober, 1995; and Coan, 1997, respectively) are fragments of conversations with an interviewer. These conversations are the speakers' memories of their experiences arriving at Ellis Island, staying at Ellis Island, and their hopes and fears about coming to a new country. Students also need to know that these interviews were videotaped or audiotaped and then transcribed. The interviews were also edited for themes or topics but words were not changed. The interviews were published as a collection of experiences connected to Ellis Island.

The content of the interviews is easy to understand. Students have some prior knowledge about immigration from their social studies courses. A brief description of the passage across the Atlantic would provide another connection with the immigrants. Students most likely have no idea how long it took to cross the Atlantic Ocean and what the living conditions were aboard ships. The vocabulary is within the range of the students, but the terms *Traveler's Aid* and *ringworm* will need explanation.

Unlike the previous text example, this script is a composite of multiple interviews and information about Ellis Island taken from several sources. When using materials from a variety of sources, it is necessary to copy selected sections of the text, cut and paste the selections in the appropriate order, and then recopy the newly compiled materials. Materials can also be scanned into a computer word-processing program, and the cutting, pasting, and enlarging can be done in the electronic files.

Interviews were selected for the performance based on the aspect of Ellis Island described (the food, the waiting, the first view), the age of the immigrant upon arrival, his or her native country, and his or her gender. There was an attempt to balance these elements and to present a snapshot of the immigrants' experience. The teacher would need to select which interviews to use; in some examples, it will be necessary to add a tag that states the immigrant's country of origin, age upon arrival, and year of arrival. This information is found in the text from which the interview has been selected.

Dividing the Texts for Script Adaptation

In the Immigrant Voices unit, there are five speaker roles. The divisions of these roles are based on the particular speaker (Mr. C., Lois, etc.), a need for balance (one reader does not read significantly more than the others), and the placement of the reader (voices should vary in direction and tone). See the Immigrant Voices script beginning on page 91 for divisions of speaker roles. Because of the multiple selections and different voices in the text materials, the teacher develops the divisions into speaker roles.

Necessary Script Additions

An introduction is needed to give information about the content of the interviews, Ellis Island, how the interviews were collected, and the time period between 1909 and 1929. Within the script at the end of each oral history, the age and country of origin for each speaker is provided (e.g., Helen Cohen, Poland, age 10). If this piece is performed in connection with a social studies unit on immigration, students could develop the introduction. The conclusion is already a part of the performance text. If not performed in connection with a social studies unit, the complexity of the text material necessitates that the teacher develop the introduction and select materials or labels to provide the transitions and conclusion.

> **Sample Introduction**
>
> Our performance describes the experiences of immigrants coming to America—specifically those who passed through Ellis Island between 1909 and 1929. These are oral histories collected through personal interviews and videotaped or audio recorded. These immigrants were between 4 and 25 years old when they came through Ellis Island. Their own words describe their arrival; their experiences going through Ellis Island; and their hopes, dreams, and fears about coming to America.

Staging the Script Reading

Creating the Whole Picture

In this performance piece, the focal point is a backdrop hung behind the performance space. The performers remain in the same positions, with one speaker moving to front center for the introduction (see the floor plan within the script).

Using Postures and Actions

The performers face the audience for the entire performance. The emphasis is not on the action but on the voices of the performers and the images and experiences they create for the audience.

Creating and Using Production Elements

Production elements are limited. Costume pieces could be one article of clothing selected for two or three readers (a suit coat, a shawl, a man's hat, a long skirt, a coat). Props would be used for the two or three readers who do not wear a costume piece. These props might include a small suitcase, a large bundle of clothing, food packages, quilts, and pillows. These items would be placed in front of or to one side of the performer. Performers would have either a costume piece or a prop, not both.

The visual element is not needed with the addition of props and costume pieces. If the emphasis is on the visual aspect, the props and costume pieces would not be used. *Ellis Island: The Immigrants' Experience* (www.jackdaw.com) provides a series of enlarged black-and-white photographs of the buildings on Ellis Island and the people who entered those buildings. These posters could be used as the focal point for performance. Figure 11 demonstrates students creating a simple backdrop for a performance.

Figure 11. Students Collaborating to Create a Simple Backdrop for a Performance

IMMIGRANT VOICES: MEMORIES OF ELLIS ISLAND

Speakers' Roles
1—"Ellis Island was," GP (with Mr. C), Mrs. K, Vartan
2—Intro, "Before Ellis Island," Mr. C, Theodore, "In 1954"
3—Intro, "Most people," Lois, Helen
4—Intro, Celia, Alvin, "In 1965"
5—Intro, Ann, David, GP (with Mrs. K), Lazarus, "In the summer"

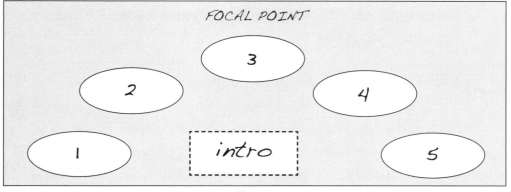

FOCAL POINT

3

2   4

1   intro   5

audience

Floor plan remains the same for the whole performance.

~~Introduction to "Immigrant Voices: Memories of Ellis Island"~~

5 → [Our performance describes the experiences of immigrants coming to America—specifically those who passed through Ellis Island between 1909 and 1929.] [These are oral histories collected 3 through personal interviews and video or audio recorded.] [These ← 2 immigrants were between 4 and 25 years old when they came through Ellis Island.] [Their own words describe their arrival; 4 their experiences going through Ellis Island; and their hopes, dreams, and fears about coming to America.]

5 → [**What was Ellis Island?**]
1 → [Ellis Island was an immigration center located in New York Harbor. Millions of newcomers passed through its gates and were examined by doctors and legal inspectors. Some were allowed to enter the United States right away, some were detained (held for a while), and some were deported (rejected and sent back).]

From ...IF YOUR NAME WAS CHANGED AT ELLIS ISLAND by Ellen Levine, copyright 1993 by Ellen Levine. Reprinted by permission of Scholastic, Inc.

2 → Before Ellis Island opened, immigrants had been examined at Castle Garden at the tip of Manhattan Island. At one time Castle Garden had been a fort, then a concert hall. In 1855 it was turned into an immigration center. Thirty-five years later, it was no longer big enough to handle the thousands of new immigrants arriving daily.

4 → **What impressions did immigrants have of Ellis Island?**

3 → Most people were excited by the adventure of coming to a new country. But as they approached Ellis Island, many were nervous and afraid. The place was called "Island of Tears" by many immigrants.

4 → *"I never saw such a big building [Ellis Island]—the size of it. I think the size of it got me. According to the houses I left in my town, this was like a whole city in one, in one building. It was an enormous thing to see, I tell you. I almost felt smaller than I am to see that beautiful [building], it looked beautiful.*

"My basket, my little basket, that's all I had with me. There was hardly any things. My mother gave me the sorah [a kind of sandwich], and I had one change of clothes. That's what I brought from Europe."

Celia Adler

Russia

Arrived in 1914 • Age 12

5 → *"There's just so much confusion.... We had interpreters and most of them were the Traveler's Aid. Let me tell you, they're wonderful. They helped us out every way they could and reassured us, which we needed very badly. Especially, like when we were getting off of Ellis Island, we had all sorts of tags on us—now that I think of it, we must have looked like marked-down merchandise in Gimbel's basement store or something. 'Where are you going, who's waiting for you?' and all that and then we were put in groups and our group was going to the Erie Railroad station in Jersey City."*

Ann Vida

Hungary

Arrived in 1921 • Age 10

1 →  Do you remember your passage to Ellis Island?]

2 → Mr. C. When I arrived at Ellis Island, my older brother was supposed to wait for me and lead me out. There were a lot of people, herds, really, and the inspectors were pushing some to one side and others to another side. Nobody understood what was happening. Suddenly, I saw an inspector making a cross on my sleeve. I was wearing a coat, a blue overcoat; I saw that on me he had made a cross, but on someone else, no cross, and they were pushing the ones with a cross to one side and the rest to the other. I didn't know why he had put this cross on me, so I took off my coat and I put it over my arm and I kept going.]

1 → GP: You didn't know what this cross meant?]

2 → Mr. C. No, I didn't know what it was. All I saw was that those with the cross went to one side and those with no cross went to another. And me, I preferred to go where those who didn't have a cross were going. I went there, found my brother, and he took me to his house.]

1 → GP. And that's all?]

Mr. C That's all. That same week, I got my identification papers and I
2 → found a job in Brownsville, near Brooklyn.

2 → [Baruch Chasimov
Russia
Arrived 1909
Age 25]

3 → LOIS. Anyway, when the boat docked, my father came on board before we were taken to Ellis Island because he was trying to get us off. I was so happy, because like any little girl I worshiped my father, and my father really was very handsome. He had blond hair and blue eyes and he was striking-looking. As a matter of fact, he had joined the theater here, you know, as a hobby. He was with the Jewish theater. And we were overjoyed. I mean, there was no question. I remember that very clearly. I remember the excitement. Do you remember that?]

4 → ALVIN: Sort of.]
DAVID: I was ecstatic to see my father.] ← 5

Originally published in French as RÉCITS D'ELLIS ISLAND: HISTOIRES D'ERRANCE ET D'ESPOIT by P.O.L. éditeur, Paris, France, copyright 1994 P.O.L. éditeur. English translations by Harry Mathews and Hessica Blatt copyright 1995 by The New Press. Reprinted with the permission of The New Press.

Copyright 1997 by Peter Morton Coan. Reprinted with permission of the Carol Mann Agency.

4 → ALVIN: Speak louder. What did you say?

DAVID: I was ecstatic... I cried and all. ← 5

3 → LOIS: Then, when we had to be detained, it was like a shock. They examined us on the boat and that's when they found that Alvin had a ringworm on his head, and that's why Papa couldn't take us directly from the boat home, and we were transported to Ellis Island.

4 → ALVIN: The ringworm was considered very contagious at that time. Why they kept the rest of the family there six weeks I don't know. But they kept me at the hospital on Ellis Island.

3 → LOIS: I remember going to see you in the hospital.

4 → ALVIN: They came to see me every day. And the nurses were crazy about me because I was a...

3 → LOIS: ...Cute little boy. I remember being in the hospital running up and down in the wards, and everybody being good to me. I had a wonderful time. From the nurses, I learned how to speak English very quickly. By the time we left there, Alvin was speaking like a native American.

4 → ALVIN: When I left Ellis Island people couldn't believe that I wasn't born American... The bad part was they took off my hair by electrolysis, and they told my mother, "Your son will never have hair again." And to this day I have a bald spot. My hair has been the same way for sixty years. It hasn't changed.

5 → *David, Lois, Alvin Garrett* ← 4 ←3

Poland ← 3

5 → *Arrived 1929*

Ages
David—11—legally deaf ← 5

Lois—7 ← 3

4 → *Alvin—4*

5 → *In the dining hall*

GP: Do you remember these windows? ← 5

1 → Mrs. K.: I remember, yes. It was the only place we could look out. We couldn't go outside, you know, not even to get some fresh air or see the light. Only through these windows. We weren't allowed in the yard...(...) When they let us leave, we were happy, I can tell

you that.... Every day, every day we cried. Every day we saw people leaving, but not us. People would stay one day, two days, and then they could go. But we never got called. Every time they would come for the roll call and they called those who could leave and they didn't call us, my mother would start crying and crying and crying. But then when they did call us, we couldn't believe it; we took a couple of the suitcases and we had to come back for the trunks a week later.

GP: Do you remember this dining hall? ← 5

Mrs. K: Of course. But there were a lot of tables, you know. Now it's empty. There were tables everywhere. You would go get your own dish, there weren't any waitresses to serve you, and over there was this sort of little table with dishes and they would give you food and then you went to sit and eat. Not that the food was very good, but we ate.

GP: What kind of food did they give you? ← 5

Mrs. K: Potatoes, a lot of potatoes, not much meat. Sometimes stew. You know, stew—oh yes, stew, we had that about four times a week. On Sundays they gave us chicken.

1 → *Mrs. Kakis*
Italy
Arrived in 1924
Age 13

2 → Everybody was hungry, and they started examinations on Ellis Island. I had twenty-five dollars in my pocket. I knew to bring money, otherwise they keep you there. They wouldn't let you go to shore without money. Because if you were hungry, you might steal. And I was alongside Gus, and I noticed he had a chalk mark on his back. I couldn't reach or see my back, so I asked him, "Do I have a chalk mark on the back?" So he looked, he say, "No." I say, "You've got one. Your father, too." And I'm thinking, either they go back to Greece or I go back to Greece. So what happened, the one with the chalk mark went back to Greece. Gus and his father had to go back. I don't know why.

I just thank God. To this day, I pray, dear Lord, and thank God, that I was admitted to the United States, that they didn't put a chalk mark on my back.

2 → Theodore Spako
Greece
Arrived 1911
Age 16

1 → *"Coming to America had meaning. I was a kid of seven and in contrast to what I had gone through, Ellis Island was like not a haven, but a heaven. I don't remember any fright when I got to Ellis Island.*

"My father's dream and prayer always was 'I must get my family to America.' ...America was paradise, the streets were covered with gold. And when we arrived here, and when we landed from Ellis Island and [went] to Buffalo, it was as if God's great promise had been fulfilled that we would eventually find freedom."

Vartan Hartunian
Turkey (Armenian)
Arrived in 1922 • Age 7

5 → *"I feel like I had two lives. You plant something in the ground, it has its roots, and then you transplant it where it stays permanently. That's what happened to me. You put an end...and forget about your childhood; I became a man here. All of a sudden, I started life new, amongst people whose language I didn't understand.... [It was a] different life; everything was different...but I never despaired, I was optimistic.*

"And this is the only country where you're not a stranger, because we are all strangers. It's only a matter of time who got here first."

Lazarus Salamon
Hungary
Arrived in 1920 • Age 16

3 → *"When I was about 10 years old I said, 'I have to go to America.' Because my uncles were here already, and it kind of got me that I want to go to America, too....I was dreaming about it. I was writing to my uncles, I said I wish one day I'll be in America. I was dreaming to come to America....And*

I was dreaming, and my dream came true. When I came here, I was in a different world. It was so peaceful. It was quiet. You were not afraid to go out in the middle of the night....I'm free. I'm just like a bird. You can fly and land on any tree and you're free."

Helen Cohen

Poland

Arrived in 1920 • Age 20

~~Buildings, not used, began to decay. Weeds rapidly spread.~~ In 1954, Ellis Island, the place of so much happiness and so many tears, was finally closed. ←2

4 → In 1965 the island was turned over to the National Park Service. Seventeen years later, workers began to restore the main building to what it had looked like when thousands had passed through its halls daily. In the summer of 1990, Ellis Island reopened as an immigration museum.

From ...IF YOUR NAME WAS CHANGED AT ELLIS ISLAND by Ellen Levine, copyright 1993 by Ellen Levine. Reprinted by permission of Scholastic, Inc.

The Universal Declaration of Human Rights

Nonfiction Subgenre: Historical document   **Group Dynamics:** Whole class

Adapting the Material to a Script

Essential Reader Information

The Universal Declaration of Human Rights excerpt (Rocha & Roth, 1990) used for the script is actually an adaptation of the original document itself. The adaptation simplifies the language of the original and explains in greater detail its concepts. Students need to know that a declaration is "not a treaty and lacks any enforcement provisions. Rather it is a statement of intent, a set of principles to which United Nations member states commit themselves in an effort to provide all people a life of human dignity" (Flowers, 1998, p. 4). Students also need to know the history of the declaration as well as the shift in language and tone from complex and formal in the original to more direct and informal in the script prepared for performance.

The teacher should also prepare the students for the differences between their typical small-group performances and a whole-class performance. This whole-class performance is more like a choral reading. Most students will be familiar with choral style, but it may be helpful to work with the whole class on a short choral reading before beginning work on this script.

Dividing the Text for Script Adaptation

Because this is a whole-class performance, the teacher determines the division of speakers' roles. This division is based on meaning units and involves placing students in groups of five. Within each meaning unit, there are sections that are read by all five students, and sections that are read by each individual student. Sections at the beginning and end are read by the entire class. The groups are labeled A, B, C, D, and E, with five students in each group. Within each group, each student reader has a number (A1, A2, A3, A4, A5). (See *The Universal Declaration of Human Rights* script beginning on page 100 for an illustration of these script divisions.)

Necessary Script Additions

The script adaptation of *The Universal Declaration of Human Rights* needs an introduction that describes what a declaration is, what human rights are, and when and how the document was developed, as in the sample introduction below. The teacher should create this introduction. Transitions and a conclusion are included in the text to be performed.

Sample Introduction

Our performance is an adaptation of *The Universal Declaration of Human Rights*. The language is simpler and easier to understand when you hear it read aloud. The declaration was adopted by the United Nations on December 10, 1948, just after World War II. The declaration is a set of guidelines which describe the rights of all humans and declares that the United Nations will make every effort to see that those rights are respected. "The document sets the standard for how human beings should behave towards one another so that everyone's human dignity is respected" (Flowers, 1998, p. 39).

Staging the Script Reading

Creating the Whole Picture

In *The Universal Declaration of Human Rights*, the focal point is a backdrop hung behind the performance space. The performers remain in the same positions, with two speakers moving to the front area for the introduction (see the floor plan within the script).

Using Postures and Actions

In this performance, the emphasis is completely on the voice, the meaning of the words, and the sound of the language. All that is necessary is simply good posture that allows for maximum sound production and gives the audience a clear view of the performers' faces.

Creating and Using Production Elements

Costume pieces could be solid color shirts; each of the groups would have the same color shirts (group A white; group B blue). The type of clothing also should have a more formal look (no shorts or sweatshirts). There are no props needed. The visual element should be a simple backdrop of a neutral color. There is also no need for music. The emphasis is on vocal sound and meaning with little concern for visualization.

THE UNIVERSAL DECLARATION OF HUMAN RIGHTS

Speakers' Roles
5 Voices Per Group
A group—A1, A2, A3, A4, A5
B group—B1, B2, B3, B4, B5
C group—C1, C2, C3, C4, C5
D group—D1, D2, D3, D4, D5
E group—E1, E2, E3, E4, E5
ABCDE—Whole class

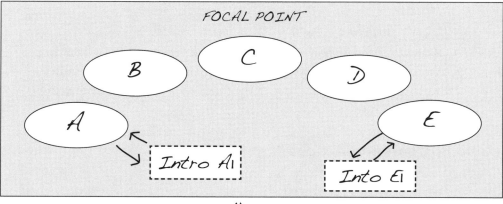

A1 moves
into Block

~~[Introduction to the Universal Declaration of Human Rights]~~

A1 → [Our performance is an adaptation of the Universal Declaration of Human Rights. The language is simpler and easier to understand when you hear it read aloud. The declaration was adopted by the United Nations on December 10, 1948, just after World War II.] [The declaration is a set of guidelines which describe the rights of all humans and declares that the United Nations will make every effort to see that those rights are respected." The document sets the standard for how human beings should behave toward one another so that everyone's human dignity is respected" (~~Flowers, 1998, p. 39~~).] ← E1

A1 goes to
position

E1 moves
forward—when
finished returns to position

universal Declaration of Human Rights

[One day, a large number of people gathered together.] ← *ABCDE*

From THE UNIVERSAL DECLARATION OF HUMAN RIGHTS: AN ADAPTATION FOR CHILDREN by R. Rocha and O. Roth, copyright 1989. Reprinted with the permission of United Nations Publications.

A_1 → [They came from different places][and they were quite different from *A2* one another.] [Some were men and some were women.] ← A_3 *Begin section group A*

A_4 → [Their skin, their hair and their eyes were different colours.]

A_5 → [Their bodies and faces were different shapes.]

A_1 → [They came from rich countries and poor countries,][from hot places and *A2* cold places.] [Some came from kingdoms][and some came from republics.] *A4* [They spoke many different languages. They worshipped different gods.] ← *All A's [A1, A2, A3, A4, A5]* *A3*

A_1 → [Some of the countries they represented had just come out of a terrible war that had left many cities destroyed and an enormous number of people killed.] [Many people had lost their homes and their families.] *A2*

A_3 ⟋ [Many people had been hurt or killed because of their religion, their race or their political opinions.]

A_4 → [What brought those people together was the wish that there should be no more war,][that nobody should ever be hurt again][and that people who *A5* hadn't done other people any harm should never be punished again.] *A4*

All A's → [So, all together, they wrote a document.][In this document they tried to *A1* make a list of the rights that every human being has, and that everyone else should respect.]

All A's → [This document is called the universal declaration of human rights; and this is what it says:] *End section group A*

Begin section group B

All B's → [All people are born free.][All people are born equal and have equal rights.] B_2 [People can think for themselves and understand what's going on around *B1* them.][Everyone should act as brothers and sisters.] *B3*

B_4 → [It doesn't matter what race you are.][It doesn't matter whether you're a *B5* man or a woman.][It doesn't matter what language you speak, what your *B1* religion is, what your political opinions are, what country you come from or who your family is.][It doesn't matter whether you're rich or poor.][It *B2* doesn't matter what part of the world you come from; whether your *B3* country is a kingdom or republic.] [These rights and freedoms are meant to be enjoyed by everyone.]

B2

B1 → [Everyone has the right to live,] [the right to be free] [and the right to ←— B3
B4 — personal safety.] [No one can be someone else's slave.] [No one is to be hurt or to be punished in cruel or humiliating ways.] ←—B5

All B's → [The law must be the same for everyone. The law must protect everyone. People have the right to be protected by the courts, so that their rights are respected.]

End section group B

Begin section group C

C1 → [People cannot be arrested, or sent away from their country,] [unless it's ✓ C2
for a very serious reason.] [Everyone has the right to a fair trial.] ←— C3

C4 → [No one has the right to interfere in peoples private lives, in their families, in their homes, or in their correspondence.]

C5 → [People have the right of free movement within their country.] [People have C2
the right to leave any country, even their own, and then return.]

All C's → [No person or people shall have their nationality taken away from them.]
C1 → [This means everyone has the right to belong to a nation.] [And they also C2
have the right to change their nationality, if they want to.]

All C's → [All men and women have the right to get married and start a family, once they've reached a certain age.] [It doesn't matter what race, C3
nationality or religion they are.] [A man and a woman can only get married if they both want to.] ←—C4

C5 → [Everyone has the right to own property.] [Anything that belongs to a C1
person can't be taken away from him or her unless there's a fair reason.]

C2 → [Everyone has the right to think the way they like.] [People have the right C3
to hold opinions] [and to tell other people what their opinions are.] [And C4
they have the right to practice their religion in private or in public.] C5

All C's → [All people have the right to meet together and to form associations.]
C1 → [But no one can be forced to join an association if he or she doesn't want to.]

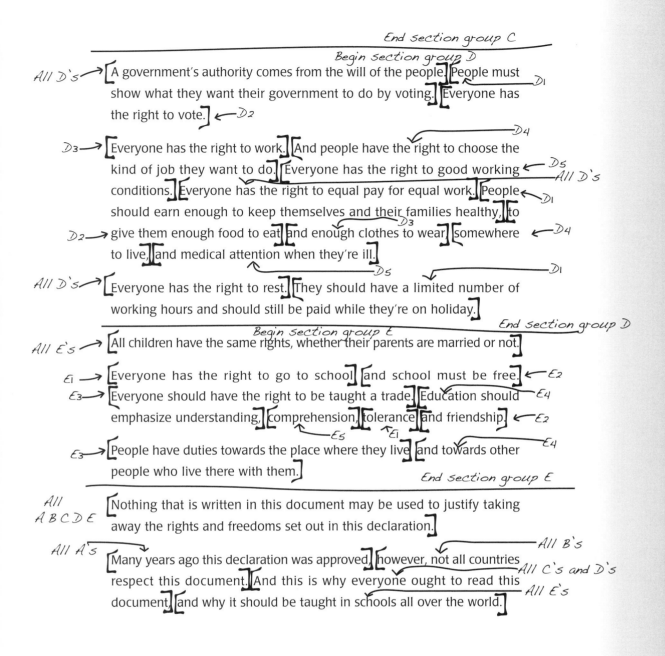

End section group C

Begin section group D

All D's → [A government's authority comes from the will of the people.] [People must show what they want their government to do by voting.] [Everyone has the right to vote.] ←D2 ·D1

D3 → [Everyone has the right to work.] [And people have the right to choose the kind of job they want to do.] [Everyone has the right to good working conditions.] [Everyone has the right to equal pay for equal work.] [People should earn enough to keep themselves and their families healthy,] to give them enough food to eat] [and enough clothes to wear] [somewhere to live,] [and medical attention when they're ill.] ←D4 ·D5 ·All D's ·D1 ·D3 ·D4

D2 →

All D's → [Everyone has the right to rest.] [They should have a limited number of working hours and should still be paid while they're on holiday.] ·D5 ·D1

End section group D

Begin section group E

All E's → [All children have the same rights, whether their parents are married or not.]

E1 → [Everyone has the right to go to school] [and school must be free.] ←E2

E3 → [Everyone should have the right to be taught a trade.] [Education should emphasize understanding,] [comprehension,] [tolerance] [and friendship.] ←E2 ·E4 ·E5 ·E1 ·E4

E3 → [People have duties towards the place where they live] [and towards other people who live there with them.]

End section group E

All ABCDE [Nothing that is written in this document may be used to justify taking away the rights and freedoms set out in this declaration.]

All A's [Many years ago this declaration was approved,] [however, not all countries respect this document.] [And this is why everyone ought to read this document] [and why it should be taught in schools all over the world.] All B's · All C's and D's · All E's

REFERENCES FOR SAMPLE SCRIPTS

Coan, P.M. (1997). *Ellis Island interviews: In their own words* (pp. 164–165, 278). New York: Facts on File.

Lawlor, V. (Ed.). (1995). *I was dreaming to come to America: Memories from the Ellis Island Oral History Project* (pp. 14, 16, 20, 22, 32). New York: Penguin.

Levine, E. (1994). *...If your name was changed at Ellis Island* (pp. 8–9, 62, 79). New York: Scholastic.

Pereg, G., & Bober, R. (1995). *Ellis Island* (pp. 116, 146–147). New York: The New Press.

Rocha, R., & Roth, O. (1990). *The Universal Declaration of Human Rights: An adaptation for children*. New York: United Nations Publications.

Walker, D. (1862). *Papers of Dora Walker of East Springfield, New York, January 1862–December 1862*. Cooperstown, NY: New York State Historical Association, Special Collections, 1, 2, 67, 68, 69, 73, 91.

REFERENCES

Flowers, N. (Ed.). (1998). *Human rights here and now: Celebrating the Universal Declaration of Human Rights*. New York: Amnesty International.

Frank, O.H., & Pressler, M. (Eds.). (1995). *Anne Frank: The Diary of a Young Girl*. New York: Doubleday.

SUGGESTED REFERENCES FOR SCRIPT ADAPTATION

Adler, D.A. (1989). *We remember the Holocaust*. New York: Henry Holt.

Auerbacher, I. (1986). *I am a child of the Holocaust*. New York: Puffin.

Beals, M.P. (1994). *Warriors don't cry: A searing memoir of the battle to integrate Little Rock's Central High*. New York: Archway.

Bode, J. (1991). *New kids in town: Oral histories of immigrant teens*. New York: Scholastic.

Budhos, M. (1999). *Remix: Conversations with immigrant teens*. New York: Henry Holt.

Cha, D. (1996). *Dia's story cloth: The Hmong people's journey of freedom*. New York: Lee & Low.

Fradin, D.B. (2000). *Bound for the North Star: True stories of fugitive slaves*. New York: Clarion.

Frank, O., & Pressler, M. (Eds.). (1995). *Anne Frank: The Diary of a Young Girl*. New York: Doubleday.

Freedman, R. (1983). *Children of the Wild West*. New York: Clarion.

Freedman, R. (1994). *Kids at work: Lewis Hine and the crusade against child labor*. New York: Clarion.

Greene, J.M., & Kumar, S. (2000). *Witness: Voices from the Holocaust*. New York: Simon & Schuster.

Hirschfelder, A.B., & Singer, B. (Eds.). (1992). *Rising voices: Writings of young Native Americans*. New York: Macmillan.

Hunter, L. (1992). *The diary of Latoya Hunter: My first year in junior high*. New York: Random House.

Jackson, E. (1998). *Turn of the century*. Watertown, MA: Charlesbridge.

Kuklin, S. (1998). *Igbal Masik and the crusaders against child slavery*. New York: Henry Holt.

Levine, E. (1993). *Freedom's children: Young Civil Rights activists tell their own stories*. New York: Putnam.

Levine, E. (2000). *Darkness over Denmark: The Danish resistance and the rescue of the Jews*. New York: Holiday House.

Masters, A. (1997). *True survival stories*. New York: Sterling.

Murphy, J. (1990). *The boys' war: Confederate and Union soldiers talk about the Civil War*. New York: Clarion.

Murphy, J. (2000). *Blizzard: The storm that changed America*. New York: Scholastic.

Myers, W.D. (2001). *Bad boy: A memoir*. New York: HarperCollins.

Ousseimi, M. (1995). *Caught in the crossfire: Growing up in a war zone*. New York: Walker.

Stanley, J. (1994). *I am an American: A true story of Japanese internment*. New York: Scholastic.

Strom, Y. (1996). *Quilted landscapes: Conversations with young immigrants*. New York: Simon & Schuster.

Tunnel, M.O., & Chilcoat, G.W. (1996). *The children of Topaz: The story of a Japanese-American internment camp based on a classroom diary*. New York: Holiday House.

Warren, A. (1996). *Orphan train rider: One boy's true story*. New York: Houghton Mifflin.

From Script to Performance: Poetry

Before developing a script, it is useful to consider the nature and the language of poetry. Though it is important that we teach students to find and clarify meaning in poetry, we need to take care not to convey the message that poetry is by its very nature hard to understand, a puzzle to solve, or something designed for only a few excellent and expert readers. In our efforts to make meaning from poetry, we should try to remember that poetry is "natural, primal expressions...it is primal, it is personal, very subjective form, belonging to the inarticulate as well as the eloquent, the illiterate as well as the educated" (Rubin, 1993, p. xv) in our efforts to make meaning from poetry. It is important that students who read, listen to, and speak poetry understand that a poet speaks of remembered and universal feelings and experiences.

An aspect of poetry that is often overlooked is poetry's sound and music and the enjoyment in hearing that sound and music. It is essential to remember and demonstrate that

> Certain poems come alive when read out loud. They may wait quietly on the printed page, dressed neatly in rhymes and stanzas, sheltering modestly beneath clever titles. But when read aloud they explode with life and color and fervor. Poetry was a way of speaking before it was a way of writing; it was language arranged memorably, given pattern and form so it would not vanish into empty air—so it could be passed along. (Rubin, 1993, p. 4)

The language of poetry is selected to contribute to both the meaning and the music or sound of the poems. The reader of poetry (whether the reader reads aloud or to himself or herself) needs to take the time to understand and discover how the poem's language works. It is also essential to remember that

> Poetry is not a different language, it is *our* language—only stretched, purged of certain habits, intensified by careful choice, made memorable by pattern and rhythm. It is language taken away from its familiar business and made to work more slowly, more exactly. You need not be an expert to enjoy it. Certainly, knowing a little about how poems work can help.... (Rubin, 1993, p. 5)

In order for students to understand, enjoy, read aloud, and bring poems to life, there are certain features of the language they need to understand. Using poetry in Readers Theatre allows students to discover in an enjoyable way features that are connected to both the meaning and the sound of the poem.

Features connected to the meaning are allusion, antithesis, hyperbole, imagery, metaphor, paradox, personification, simile, symbolism, and tone. The elements connected to the sound are alliteration, assonance, onomatopoeia, rhyme scheme, and refrain. All of these elements do not need to be emphasized at once, but they should be addressed based upon the poems to be presented. These terms explain the ways in which poets make their feelings, meanings, and experiences accessible to their readers and listeners. In order to understand and perform poetry, students need to know how these specific features (e.g., metaphor, allusion) underline and emphasize the content and feelings in a poem. The use of the specific terms provides students with labels and ways of identifying the poet's intentions.

Furthermore, it is also necessary to consider students' experience with the genre of poetry and their interests. The following poems were selected for script development because they are simple and direct, and use language the students can understand easily. The first, "Casey at the Bat" (Thayer, 1993), is a narrative poem that uses subject matter that is already a part of students' prior information and experiences. The second set of poems, "O Captain! My Captain!" "Hush'd Be the Camps To-day," and "This Dust Was Once the Man," are Whitman's (1992) responses to the death of Abraham Lincoln. Lincoln's death and its surrounding events are also subjects that the students have previously encountered. Whereas the Thayer and Whitman poems describe or respond to events imagined and real, the third poem, "In Beauty May I Walk," is different in style, more abstract, and part of a different culture. Although these differences are part of understanding a more complex poem, students can relate to the description of nature and the wish for a peaceful and beautiful old age or life after death. Moreover, each topic—the baseball game, the responses to an important event in American history, and the strong connection with nature—can appeal to middle school students.

Because understanding and creating scripts from poetry can be a more complex process than prose, Figure 12 provides a checklist and Figure 13 offers a set of guidelines for students as they begin creating scripts based on poetry. Reproducible versions of these forms can be found in Appendix C.

In this chapter, there are detailed approaches to and possibilities for the script development and staging of poetry performances. These are not the only way that these poems can be developed; the intent is to provide patterns and examples for creating and developing Readers Theatre performances with students.

Figure 12. Readers Theatre Poetry Project Checklist

☐ With your group, choose the poem you would like to work with.

☐ Let [teacher's name] know which poem you have chosen so that [teacher's name] can make copies for you.

☐ As a group, break your poem into parts. Don't forget to decide who will

    ☐ Introduce the poem and poet.

    ☐ Introduce the people in your group.

    ☐ Share information about your poet.

    ☐ Give an explanation of the poem that you will perform.

☐ Practice, practice, practice!

☐ Write a summary of your section of the poem to share with your group.

☐ Practice, practice, practice again!

☐ Share your summaries and combine them to create one complete interpretation of your poem to share during your presentation.

☐ Practice, practice, practice some more!

☐ Decide on any small props that you might make or bring in for the presentations to add to your performance. Remember—the most important tools your group has are your voices and gestures. Any additional props should be used to clarify parts of the poem for the audience, or possibly to invite the audience to participate.

Figure 13. Readers Theatre Poetry Project Guidelines

Readers Theatre Poetry Presentations
Presentation Date: _____
Dress Rehearsal Date: _____

Introduction
Include the following:
• Group members' names
• Name of poem
• Author
• Explanation of mural

Script
• Your script should be well rehearsed.
• Your script should be read with emotion.
• Appropriate use of expression is expected.

Music
• Background music only
• Appropriate for the poem
• Instrumental only, if possible

Murals
• Two team members responsible: _____
    _____
• Should illustrate your interpretation of the poem
• Should show images from the poem

Costumes
• Should represent interpretation of the poem
• Groups may choose to have "uniform" costumes (for example, all dressed in a particular color)

"Casey at the Bat"

Poetry Subgenre: Narrative poem   **Group Dynamics:** Individual groups

Adapting the Material to a Script

Essential Reader Information

It would be helpful to inform students that "Casey at the Bat" is a narrative poem—a poem that tells a complete story and that has both a central figure and a conflict that is resolved at the end. The features of this poem that connect to meaning are metaphor, simile, and tone. Metaphors include comparing the batting of Flynn and Casey to a "pudding" and a "fake" and comparing the sound of the crowd to "five thousand tongues applauded." Similes, such as "death like silence" and "went up a muffled roar, Like the beating of the storm waves on a stern and distant shore," are also used to describe the crowd's response. The narrative perspective is that of a sportscaster describing the action of a baseball game and the crowd's excitement and sorrow at the performance of the home team. The sound features are connected to the dialogue ("strike one," "kill him, kill the umpire," "strike two," "fraud," and Casey's "haint"). The rhyme scheme is a part of reading for meaning, and it should not be overemphasized.

Many vocabulary words will need explanation because they are closely connected to setting the scene and to the actions and reactions of the speakers. These words include *pallor, stricken, dell, writhing, hurtling, unheeded, visage, tumult,* and *sneer.* There are also some phrases that will need clarification: *doffed his hat, tore the cover off the ball, leather-covered sphere, haughty grandeur, smile of Christian charity, spheroid flew,* and *pounds with cruel vengeance.*

Dividing the Text for Script Adaptation

Because poetry is more complex and condensed than prose, the teacher will need to work closely with students to select sections for speakers. Alternatively, the teacher may divide the poem into sections and explain these divisions. Students could divide text independently, but it might take more time and effort and detract from the emphasis on the performance.

In "Casey at the Bat," there are five speaker roles. Speaker 1 describes the setting, game actions, crowd's responses, and catcher's actions; Speaker 2 describes the crowd's actions and responses; Speaker 3 describes players' actions, the pitcher, crowd's responses, and intro; Speaker 4 describes the players' actions, the umpire, and crowd responses. Speaker C reads the dialogue and actions for Casey. The "Casey at the Bat" script beginning on page 111 illustrates these divisions of speakers' roles.

Necessary Script Additions

In "Casey at the Bat," there is no need for transitions, and the poem provides a clear conclusion. Therefore, the only necessary addition is an introduction, which may be created by the teacher or the performance group. Because students are familiar with baseball, they could develop an introduction with a limited amount of preparation time.

Sample Introduction

This poem, "Casey at the Bat," is a story about a baseball game. The baseball game is an important one, and Casey, a strong hitter, is at bat and can make the game-winning run.

Staging the Script Reading

Creating the Whole Picture

In "Casey at the Bat," the focal point is a backdrop attached to the back wall of the performance area, a screen, or a portable chalkboard (see the "Mural" activity in chapter 7, page 132, for further instruction on creating such a backdrop). The material is a solid color (dark blue, black, gray, tan, or white). There are two positions for the performers: one for the introduction and one for the poem (see the floor plans within the script).

Using Postures and Actions

Because most students are familiar with baseball games, the performers can develop the postures and actions themselves. In "Casey at the Bat," the performers face front in neutral postures; the emphasis is on the reading. The actions and postures change in the pitch, bat, strike sequences in the poem (see Figure 14). In these sections, Speaker 3 turns to Speaker C and pitches. Speaker 4 kneels in the umpire posture, and 1 goes to the catcher position (see Figure 15). Speaker C follows all the actions and postures described in the script; these include posture for batting, signaling to pitcher and crowd, doffing hat, and so on. In order to demonstrate how the postures and actions could work, more detailed directions should be written in margins of the script (see the "Casey at the Bat" script).

Creating and Using Production Elements

In "Casey at the Bat," performers speak and mime the actions while speaking; therefore, costume pieces need to be basic. Speaker C, Speaker 3, and Speaker 4 could each wear baseball hats; Speakers 1 and 2 could wear visors or sunglasses. Props might be too difficult to handle along with miming, simultaneous reading, and holding the script. The postures and actions developed in the sample script preclude the use of props (bats, baseball gloves).

Figure 14. Demonstrating Changing Postures and Action for "Casey at the Bat"

Figure 15. Students Performing "Casey at the Bat"

The visual element, however, might be further developed. A background mural could be created as a literal presentation of a baseball field or symbolic presentation through the use of color to suggest the emotions of the crowd and players. Sound might also be used to introduce the poem; this could include crowd sounds at a game or the song "Take Me Out to the Ball Game." In one seventh-grade performance of this poem, the group used the theme from *Star Wars* to introduce their performance—a surprising choice, but an expressive and appropriate one.

"CASEY AT THE BAT"

Speakers' Roles
1—Setting, game actions, crowd responses, catcher actions
2—Crowd actions and responses
3—Player actions, pitcher actions, crowd responses, intro
4—Player actions, umpire actions and dialogue, crowd responses
C—Casey actions and dialogue

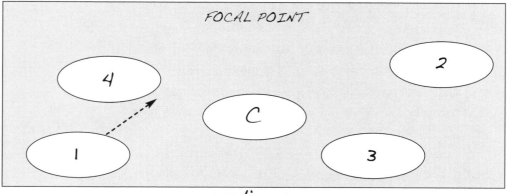

Performers remain in these positions. In the pitch, bat, and strike sequences, 3 turns in to pitch, 4 kneels in umpire position, 1 moves to catcher, and C angles to 3 to hit. Depending on C's swing, 3 pitches ball above or below C (right or left hitter).

~~Introduction~~

3 → [*This poem, "Casey at the Bat," is a story about a baseball game. The baseball game is an important one, and Casey, a strong hitter, is at bat and can make the game-winning run.*]

C → Casey at the Bat
Ernest Lawrence Thayer

1 → It looked extremely rocky for the Mudville nine that day;
The score stood two to four with but one inning left to play.
So, when Cooney died at second, and Burrows did the same,
A pallor wreathed the features of the patrons of the game.

2 →

A straggling few got up to go, leaving there the rest,
With that hope which springs eternal within the human breast.
For they thought: "If only Casey could get a whack at that,"
They'd put even money now, with Casey at the bat.

3 →
But Flynn preceded Casey, and likewise so did Blake,
And the former was a pudd'n and the latter was a fake.

4 →
So on that stricken multitude a death-like silence sat;
For there seemed but little chance of Casey's getting to the bat.

3 →
But Flynn let drive a "single," to the wonderment of all.
And the much despised Blakey "tore the cover off the ball."

2 →
And when the dust had lifted, and they saw what had occurred,

4 →
There was Blakey safe on second, and Flynn a-huggin' third.

shift in positions

1, 2, 3, 4 →
Then from the gladdened multitude went up a joyous yell—

1 →
It bounded from the mountaintops, it rattled in the dell;

2 →
It struck upon the hillside and rebounded on the flat;

1+2 →
For Casey, mighty Casey, was advancing to the bat.

3 & 4 take pitcher & umpire postures—each face C
1 moves in front of 4-catcher position

C →
There was ease in Casey's manner as he stepped into his place.
There was pride in Casey's bearing and a smile on Casey's face;
And when responding to the cheers he lightly doffed his hat,
No stranger in the crowd could doubt, 'twas Casey at the bat.

C steps in, smiles, doffs hat, holds bat position at home plate facing 3

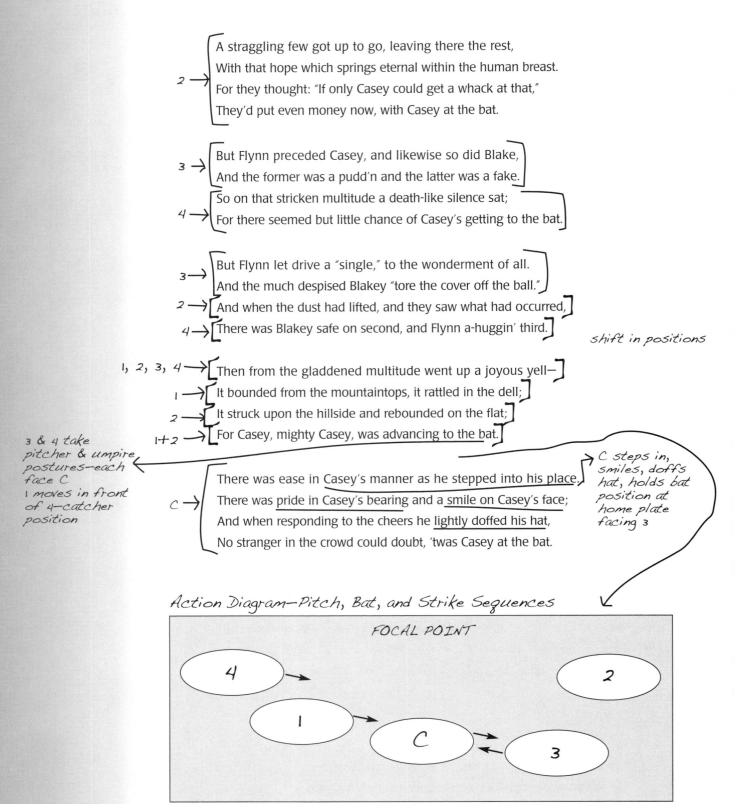

Action Diagram—Pitch, Bat, and Strike Sequences

FOCAL POINT

audience

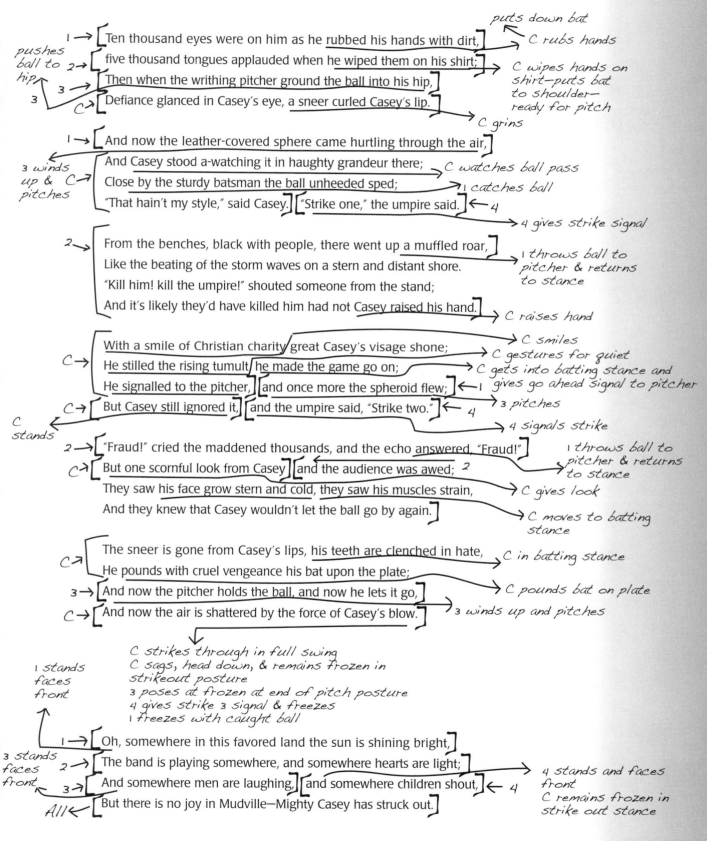

pushes
ball to
hip.

1 → Ten thousand eyes were on him as he rubbed his hands with dirt,

puts down bat
C rubs hands

2 → five thousand tongues applauded when he wiped them on his shirt;

C wipes hands on shirt—puts bat to shoulder—ready for pitch

3 → Then when the writhing pitcher ground the ball into his hip,

3 C → Defiance glanced in Casey's eye, a sneer curled Casey's lip.

C grins

1 → And now the leather-covered sphere came hurtling through the air,

3 winds up & C → And Casey stood a-watching it in haughty grandeur there;

C watches ball pass

Close by the sturdy batsman the ball unheeded sped;

1 catches ball

"That hain't my style," said Casey. "Strike one," the umpire said. ← 4

4 gives strike signal

2 → From the benches, black with people, there went up a muffled roar,

1 throws ball to pitcher & returns to stance

Like the beating of the storm waves on a stern and distant shore.

"Kill him! kill the umpire!" shouted someone from the stand;

And it's likely they'd have killed him had not Casey raised his hand.

C raises hand

C → With a smile of Christian charity great Casey's visage shone;

C smiles
C gestures for quiet

He stilled the rising tumult, he made the game go on;

C gets into batting stance and gives go ahead signal to pitcher

He signalled to the pitcher, and once more the spheroid flew; ← 1

C → But Casey still ignored it, and the umpire said, "Strike two." ← 4

3 pitches

C stands

4 signals strike

2 → "Fraud!" cried the maddened thousands, and the echo answered, "Fraud!"

1 throws ball to pitcher & returns to stance

C → But one scornful look from Casey and the audience was awed; 2

They saw his face grow stern and cold, they saw his muscles strain,

C gives look

And they knew that Casey wouldn't let the ball go by again.

C moves to batting stance

C → The sneer is gone from Casey's lips, his teeth are clenched in hate,

C in batting stance

He pounds with cruel vengeance his bat upon the plate;

3 → And now the pitcher holds the ball, and now he lets it go,

C pounds bat on plate

C → And now the air is shattered by the force of Casey's blow.

3 winds up and pitches

C strikes through in full swing
C sags, head down, & remains frozen in strikeout posture
3 poses at frozen at end of pitch posture
4 gives strike 3 signal & freezes
1 freezes with caught ball

1 stands
faces
front

1 → Oh, somewhere in this favored land the sun is shining bright,

3 stands
faces
front

2 → The band is playing somewhere, and somewhere hearts are light;

4 stands and faces front

3 → And somewhere men are laughing, and somewhere children shout, ← 4

C remains frozen in strike out stance

All ← But there is no joy in Mudville—Mighty Casey has struck out.

Walt Whitman's Poetry on Abraham Lincoln—
"O Captain! My Captain!"
"Hush'd Be the Camps To-day [May 4, 1865]"
"This Dust Was Once the Man"

Poetry Subgenre: Elegy   **Group Dynamics:** Individual groups

Adapting the Material to a Script

Essential Reader Information

These three poems are a response to particular events—the assassination and funeral of Abraham Lincoln. The poems are descriptive and present two perspectives (the citizens' and the soldiers') and their responses to Lincoln's death. The form is an elegy—a lament over the death of Lincoln. The content is easy to understand; the context may need some elaboration. For example, students need to recall how, when, and why Lincoln was assassinated. Further, they need to know in what ways the country (civilians and soldiers) mourned his death. Students should have previously studied this period, but summaries and visuals of the state ceremonies could be helpful in connecting with the poems.

The features of this set of poems that connect to meaning are metaphor, allusion, and tone. In "O Captain! My Captain!" the metaphor of President Lincoln as captain of a ship is used throughout the poem. Students need to be able to define what a captain does, his relationships with officers and crew, the sailing of the ship, and the ship's voyage, and connect that to the role of President. Allusion is present in the third poem—"this dust that once was man" echoes the phrase from the Bible "for dust thou art and unto dust shalt thou return" (Genesis 3:19–20). Because all three poems are elegies, the tone is sad and sorrowful yet also laudatory and hopeful in the second and third poems.

The only sound features of the three poems to be considered are in "O Captain! My Captain!" There is repetition of long-vowel sounds in the phrase "O Captain! My Captain!" This poem also has ending-word rhyme patterns; these do not need to be emphasized but are part of the fluent and expressive reading of the poems.

The vocabulary is not difficult; there are only a few words that will need definition and explanation. These words include *rack, keel, trills, exult, tread, invault,* and *resolute.* In the poem, "Hush'd Be the Camps To-day," there is one word and a few phrases that need clarification. Students need to understand that the word *camp* is used in reference to a military site and not a recreational area, and the following phrases—*drape our war-worn weapons, musing soul, invault the coffin*, and *close the doors of earth upon him*—also need explanation. In "This Dust Was Once the Man," the phrase *the foulest crime in history* also needs a description.

Dividing the Texts for Script Adaptation

There are five speaker roles in the Whitman poems. The division of roles in these poems is based not on content but on varying the patterns and directions of the voices. (The script for the Whitman poems on Lincoln beginning on page 117 illustrates the division of roles in the three poems.) Each performer speaks either an entire line or a whole thought. In these poems, there are also several times when all of the performers are speaking in unison. The pattern of narrator and characters is not well-defined in these poems, so the divisions of roles are best determined by the teacher.

Necessary Script Additions

The introduction needs to establish the time and characters and the events that provide the setting for these poems. The teacher or the group members could gather information through research on Walt Whitman. There also needs to be a transition to the second and third piece, a simple statement about who is speaking. The third poem provides a conclusion in its final line.

Sample Introduction

The poems in our performance were written by Walt Whitman. Whitman, known as the first great American poet, was born in Long Island, New York, in 1819. During the Civil War, he volunteered to nurse the wounded soldiers in the military hospitals. The three poems are elegies, sorrowful responses to the death of President Abraham Lincoln. The first poem, "O Captain! My Captain!" describes how the people felt when their leader, the captain of their government, was assassinated.

Sample Transitions

The second poem, "Hush'd Be the Camps To-day," shows how the army felt when their leader was killed.

The third poem, "This Dust Was Once the Man," reminds all who read or hear it who Abraham Lincoln was and what he accomplished.

Staging the Script Reading

Creating the Whole Picture

In these three poems, the focal point is a backdrop hung behind the performance space. The performers are in the same positions for "This Dust Was Once the Man," but there is a shift in position for "O Captain! My Captain!" and "Hush'd Be the Camps To-day." For the first and third poem, the positions are of mourners standing around a coffin. The positions for the second poem suggest soldiers standing at attention behind a coffin (see the floor plans within the script).

Using Postures and Actions

In the first and third poems, the postures are those of grief, sadness, and mourning. The performers face front with heads and eyes tilted down, looking at the imaginary coffin placed between Speakers 1 and 5. This slight tilt of the head should not cut off the performers' air supply. The intention is to provide a contrast with the posture in the second poem. In the second poem, the postures are erect, standing at attention with head and eyes forward. There are no specific actions (see the script markings for postures and actions).

Creating and Using Production Elements

Because the shifts in whole picture and postures are somewhat elaborate, the production elements need to be simple. Costume pieces are the most effective way to add a single element to emphasize both the meaning and feeling of the three poems. Performers can wear black shirts or white or gray shirts with black crepe paper arm bands. There is no need for props. The visual element should also be a simple black, white, or gray background. Sound also is not an essential or important part of this presentation and might even be a distraction. It is important to select only one or two production elements to emphasize the meaning, mood, or action of the poems.

WHITMAN POEMS ON LINCOLN

Speakers' Roles
5 speakers—1, 2, 3, 4, 5

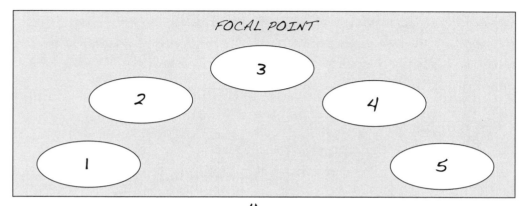

FOCAL POINT

audience

~~Introduction~~

5 → [The poems in our performance were written by Walt Whitman. Whitman, known as the first great American poet, was born in Long Island, New York, in 1819.] [During the Civil War, he → 4 volunteered to nurse the wounded soldiers in the military hospitals.] [The three poems are elegies, sorrowful responses → 3 to the death of President Abraham Lincoln.] [The first poem → 2 "O Captain! My Captain!" describes how the people felt when their leader, the captain of their government, was assassinated.]

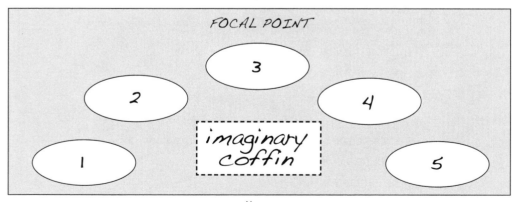

FOCAL POINT

imaginary coffin

audience

Movement—As each performer speaks line in first stanza, they move closer together as if surrounding the imaginary coffin and looking down at it.

Posture suggestions—Sad, crying, hands to eyes; holding flowers or prayer books. Help each performer find an individual mourning statue posture. Be sure posture does not hide face or make vocal projection difficult.

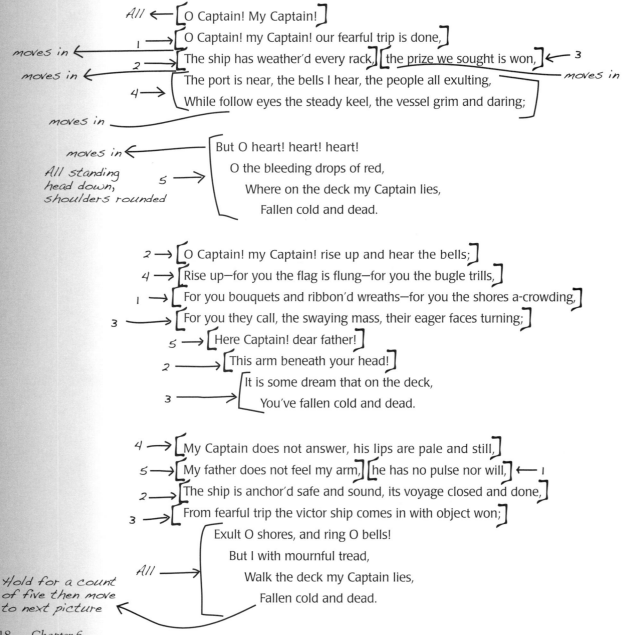

All ← [O Captain! My Captain!]

1 → [O Captain! my Captain! our fearful trip is done,]

moves in ← 2 → [The ship has weather'd every rack,] [the prize we sought is won,] ← 3 moves in

moves in ← 4 → The port is near, the bells I hear, the people all exulting,

While follow eyes the steady keel, the vessel grim and daring;

moves in

moves in ←
All standing head down, shoulders rounded

5 → But O heart! heart! heart!
O the bleeding drops of red,
Where on the deck my Captain lies,
Fallen cold and dead.

2 → [O Captain! my Captain! rise up and hear the bells;]

4 → [Rise up—for you the flag is flung—for you the bugle trills,]

1 → [For you bouquets and ribbon'd wreaths—for you the shores a-crowding,]

3 → [For you they call, the swaying mass, their eager faces turning;]

5 → [Here Captain! dear father!]

2 → [This arm beneath your head!]

3 → It is some dream that on the deck,
You've fallen cold and dead.

4 → [My Captain does not answer, his lips are pale and still,]

5 → [My father does not feel my arm,] [he has no pulse nor will,] ← 1

2 → [The ship is anchor'd safe and sound, its voyage closed and done,]

3 → [From fearful trip the victor ship comes in with object won;]

All → Exult O shores, and ring O bells!
But I with mournful tread,
Walk the deck my Captain lies,
Fallen cold and dead.

Hold for a count of five then move to next picture ←

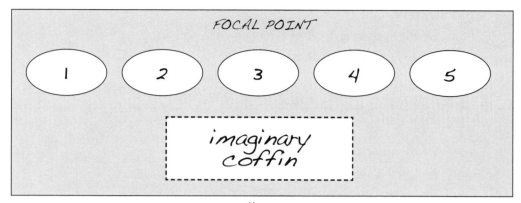

FOCAL POINT

1   2   3   4   5

imaginary coffin

audience

<u>*Move to picture before introduction*</u>

~~Transition~~

1 → [The second poem," Hush'd Be the Camps To-Day [May 4, 1865]," shows how the army felt when their leader was killed.]

↳ Posture —Military, salute at attention behind coffin; assume posture after introduction.

Begins after shift in whole picture

All → [Hush'd Be the Camps To-Day [May 4, 1865]]

1 → [Hush'd be the camps to-day,]
[And soldiers let us drape our war-worn weapons,]

2 → [And each with musing soul retire to celebrate,
Our dear commander's death.

3 → [No more for him life's stormy conflicts,]
4 → [Nor victory, nor defeat] — [no more time's dark events,
Charging like ceaseless clouds across the sky.] ← 5

All → [But sing poet in our name,
Sing of the love we bore him—because you, dweller in camps, know it truly.

3 → [As they invault the coffin there,]

All [Sing—as they close the doors of earth upon him—one verse,
For the heavy hearts of soldiers.

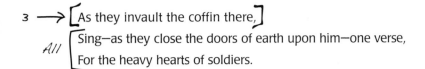

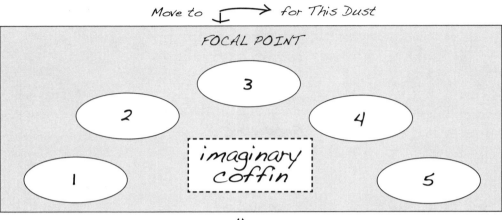

audience

Hold previous position for a count of five—then return to positions for first poem as illustrated above. (Move before transition for last poem "This Dust Was Once the Man.") Same postures as "O Captain, My Captain!"

~~Transition~~

[The third poem "This Dust Was Once the Man," reminds all who read or hear it who Abraham Lincoln was and what he accomplished.]

3 → [This Dust Was Once the Man]

2 → [This dust was once the man,]

4 → [Gentle, plain, just and resolute,][under whose cautious hand,] ← 5

1 → [Against the foulest crime in history known in any land or age,]

[Was saved the Union of these States.] — *All*

Posture—All face front, raise heads—erect posture.

Hold for a count of 5 and exit.

Adapting the Material to a Script

Essential Reader Information

"In Beauty May I Walk" is a poem that describes nature, a wish, and a vision of a path or journey. It is also lyrical in nature, specifically more like a chant or prayer. Performers follow a call-and-response pattern. This poem also reflects Navajo culture and tradition, which includes the love of and respect for nature, the vision of an elder living again in beauty, and the group chanting and response pattern. The meaning of the poem is simple and direct. The refrain "may I walk" is repeated with the same rhythm and emphasis each time it is said. There are no vocabulary words that need explanation.

Dividing the Text for Script Adaptation

The division of roles is based on the pitch or level of the reader's voices. It is possible to use six students for this poem; two readers with high voices, two with medium voices, two with low voices. It is also possible to perform this poem with a larger number of students or a whole class. In a whole-class activity, the performance becomes more like a song sung by a choir. The sample script is designed for six speakers in which the high voices are labeled H1 and H2, the medium voices are labeled M1 and M2, and the low voices are labeled L1 and L2. (See the "In Beauty May I Walk" script on page 123 for the division of these roles.) Because role assignment is based on voice quality, meaning, and the direction of the sound, it should be chosen by the teacher. The performers will need to spend preparation time on the effective and expressive reading of the poem.

Necessary Script Additions

The poem needs an introduction to describe the tradition and style of the poem as well as its connection to the Navajo culture. It would be best for the teacher to develop this introduction, incorporating suggestions from the performance group. If the group has been studying Native American tribes and their cultures, they could contribute additional information. There is no need for transitions or a conclusion.

Sample Introduction

"In Beauty May I Walk" is a poem. It describes nature, a wish for all humans, and a vision of the path or journey of life and beyond. The poem has been translated from the Navajo and shows a Navajo's love and respect for nature, the elders' vision and path, and the circle of life.

Staging the Script Reading

Creating the Whole Picture

For "In Beauty May I Walk," the focal point is a backdrop hung behind the performance space. The performers remain in the same positions (see the floor plan within the script).

Using Postures and Actions

There are no changes in posture or actions. The emphasis is specifically on the voices of the performers and the images those words and voices create in the minds of the audience.

Creating and Using Production Elements

Production elements should be carefully selected and minimal. Costume pieces could be white shirts or shirts in forest and meadow colors (greens, yellows, pinks, blues, or purples) or colors of the seasons (green, gold, red, or white). The costume pieces help the performers move more easily into the poem and do not distract from the music of the poem. There are no props needed. A visual element could be an abstract mural painted with colors suggesting the seasons but for this poem, little or no additional visuals are needed because a visual background could be a distraction rather than a complement to the poem.

"IN BEAUTY MAY I WALK"

Speakers' Roles
H1 and H2—Higher pitch
M1 and M2—Medium pitch
L1 and L2—Lower pitch

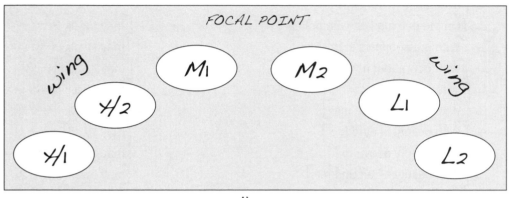

FOCAL POINT

M1   M2

wing   wing

H2   L1

H1   L2

audience

Picture remains the same for the whole poem—total emphasis on sound

Postures and Actions—postures straight, relaxed for good sound production; no action

~~Introduction~~

M1 → ["In Beauty May I Walk" is a poem. It describes nature, a wish for all humans, and a vision of the path or journey of life and beyond. The poem has been translated from the Navajo and shows a Navajo's love and respect for nature, the elders' vision and path, and the circle of life.]

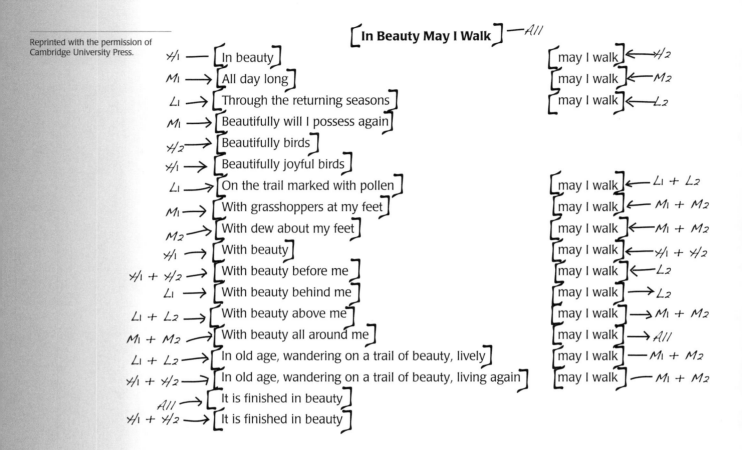

In Beauty May I Walk — *All*

H_1 — [In beauty] [may I walk] ← H_2

M_1 → [All day long] [may I walk] ← M_2

L_1 → [Through the returning seasons] [may I walk] ← L_2

M_1 → [Beautifully will I possess again]

H_2 → [Beautifully birds]

H_1 → [Beautifully joyful birds]

L_1 → [On the trail marked with pollen] [may I walk] ← $L_1 + L_2$

M_1 → [With grasshoppers at my feet] [may I walk] ← $M_1 + M_2$

M_2 → [With dew about my feet] [may I walk] ← $M_1 + M_2$

H_1 → [With beauty] [may I walk] ← $H_1 + H_2$

$H_1 + H_2$ → [With beauty before me] [may I walk] ← L_2

L_1 → [With beauty behind me] [may I walk] → L_2

$L_1 + L_2$ → [With beauty above me] [may I walk] → $M_1 + M_2$

$M_1 + M_2$ → [With beauty all around me] [may I walk] → *All*

$L_1 + L_2$ → [In old age, wandering on a trail of beauty, lively] [may I walk] — $M_1 + M_2$

$H_1 + H_2$ → [In old age, wandering on a trail of beauty, living again] [may I walk] — $M_1 + M_2$

All → [It is finished in beauty]

$H_1 + H_2$ → [It is finished in beauty]

Anon

From the Navajo (trans. Jerome K. Rothenberg)

REFERENCES FOR SAMPLE SCRIPTS

Anonymous. (1990). In beauty may I walk (J.K. Rothenberg, Trans.). In P. Abbs & J. Richardson (Eds.), *The forms of poetry: A practical guide* (p. 59). New York: Cambridge University Press.

Thayer, E.L. (1993). Casey at the bat. In R.A. Rubin (Ed.), *Poetry out loud* (pp. 44–47). Chapel Hill, NC: Algonquin.

Whitman, W. (1992). *Leaves of grass: The deathbed edition* (pp. 251–253). New York: Simon & Schuster.

REFERENCES

Rubin, R.A. (Ed.). (1993). *Poetry out loud* (pp. xv, 4–5). Chapel Hill, NC: Algonquin.

SUGGESTED REFERENCES FOR SCRIPT ADAPTATION

Adoff, A. (1995). *Street music: City poems*. New York: HarperCollins.

Adoff, A. (Ed.). (1997). *I am the darker brother: An anthology of modern poems by African Americans*. New York: Simon & Schuster.

Bolin, F.S. (Ed.). (1995). *Poetry for young people: Carl Sandburg*. New York: Sterling.

Bruchac, J., & Locker, T. (1995). *The earth under the Sky Bear's feet: Native American poems of the land*. New York: Philomel.

Carlson, L.M. (Ed.). (1994). *Cool salsa: Bilingual poems on growing up Latino in the United States*. New York: Henry Holt.

Collins, B. (2005). *The trouble with poetry and other poems*. New York: Random House.

Dillon, L., & Dillon, D. (1998). *To everything there is a season*. New York: Blue Sky.

Fletcher, R. (1994). *I am wings*. New York: Atheneum.

Franco, B. (2000). *You hear me? Poems and writings by teenage boys*. Cambridge, MA: Candlewick.

Goldstein, B.S. (1992). *Inner chimes: Poems on poetry*. Honesdale, PA: Boyds Mills Press.

Hesse, K. (1997). *Out of the dust*. New York: Scholastic.

Hopkins, L.B., & Alcorn, S. (2000). *My America: A poetry atlas of the United States*. New York: Simon & Schuster.

Hughes, L. (1995). *The block*. New York: Knopf.

Hughes, L. (1996). *The dream keeper and other poems*. New York: Knopf.

Lathem, E.C. (Ed.). (1979). *The poetry of Robert Frost*. New York: Henry Holt.

Masters, E.L. (1996). *Spoon River anthology*. New York: Tom Doherty Associates.

Nye, N.S. (1992). *The same sky: A collection of poems from around the world*. New York: Simon & Schuster.

Nye, N.S. (1998). *The space between our footsteps: Poems and paintings from the Middle East*. New York: Simon & Schuster.

Panzer, N. (Ed.). (1994). *Celebrate America: In poetry and art*. New York: Hyperion.

Philip, N. (Comp.). (1996). *Earth always endures: Native American poems*. New York: Viking.

Rosenberg, L. (Ed.). (1996). *The invisible ladder: An anthology of contemporary American poems for young readers*. New York: Henry Holt.

Rottmann, L. (1993). *Voices from the Ho Chi Minh Trail: Poetry of America and Vietnam, 1965–1993*. Desert Hot Springs, CA: Event Horizon.

Rubin, A.R. (Ed.). (1993). *Poetry out loud*. Chapel Hill, NC: Algonquin.

Schmidt, G.D. (Ed.). (1994). *Poetry for young people: Robert Frost*. New York: Sterling.

Seeley, V. (1994). *Latino poetry*. Paramus, NJ: Globe Fearon.

Serio, J.N. (Ed.). (2005). *Poetry for young people: The seasons*. New York: Sterling

Siebert, D. (2006). *Tour America: A journey through poems and art*. San Francisco, CA: Chronicle.

Soto, G. (1990). *A fire in my hands: A book of poems*. New York: Scholastic.

Soto, G. (1992). *Neighborhood odes*. San Diego, CA: Harcourt.

Turner, A., & Moser, B. (1993). *Grass songs: Poems of women's journeys west*. New York: Harcourt Brace.

Wilard, N., Provensen, A., & Provensen, M. (1981). *A visit to William Blake's inn: Poems for innocent and experienced travelers*. New York: Harcourt Brace.

PART III

Extending Readers Theatre Applications

One of the benefits of Readers Theatre is its service as a springboard to a variety of language arts activities. Chapter 7, "Supplementary Activities for Students," explores a variety of activities that extend the skills addressed by Readers Theatre, providing a skills focus, purpose, list of materials, procedures, and assessment for each activity. Readers Theatre is also easily adaptable to other grade and ability levels. Chapter 8, "Readers Theatre Beyond the Middle School Classroom," looks at specific adaptations of Readers Theatre in other grade levels—the elementary school classroom and the high school classroom—and students with varied abilities—ELLs, struggling readers, and gifted students. The particular aspects of Readers Theatre discussed for each adaptation include group dynamics, text selection and script adaptation, staging, rehearsal and performance, and assessment.

CHAPTER 7

Supplementary Activities for Students

This chapter briefly describes a number of activities that can augment the use of Readers Theatre in the classroom. Teachers should feel free to adapt any of these activities and to create their own. Each of the activities concentrates on a specific language arts skill or skills that derive from the use of a Readers Theatre script (with the exception of the activity "Real People, Real Stories" on page 140, which generates ideas for a Readers Theatre script). The main purpose of these activities is to increase student comprehension of the script and to enhance specific language arts skills.

Activities are organized into three sections by their final product: Writing Activities, Visual Activities, and Speaking Activities. Each activity described in this chapter is introduced with an indication of which of the following skills is targeted by that activity:

1. Critical thinking (the ability to interpret, analyze, and synthesize information)

2. Listening (developing comprehension of what is spoken)

3. Reading comprehension (understanding the meaning of what is read)

4. Reading fluency (reading with accuracy, expression, pacing, and phrasing for content meaning)

5. Speaking (developing oral language skills)

6. Vocabulary development (increasing word recognition and comprehension skills)

7. Writing (using language, both structure and vocabulary, to communicate in written form)

The purpose of each activity, the materials needed, the procedure, and the assessment of each activity are discussed. (For specific assessment criteria and instruments, see chapter 10, and for blank assessment instruments, see Appendix C.)

Writing Activities

Character Profile

Skills Developed: Critical Thinking, Reading Comprehension, Writing

Purpose: To facilitate students' reading for information about a specific character and to create a written description of that character.

Materials: Readers Theatre scripts, pens, paper

Procedure: A character profile is a written characterization that goes beyond the text. Students select or are assigned a character from their Readers Theatre script. Some of the ideas students could address in their writing include the following:

1. What does the character look like?
2. How does the character act?
3. Why does the character act this way?
4. What is the character thinking?
5. What part does the character play in the script?

Assessment: Assessment may take the form of a basic checklist or rubric, focusing on writing mechanics such as spelling, punctuation, and grammar, as well as each of the questions or ideas students were told to address in their writing.

Letter to the Character

Skills Developed: Critical Thinking, Reading Comprehension, Writing

Purpose: To facilitate students' understanding of a character through the writing of an informal letter, addressing specific questions or concerns.

Materials: Readers Theatre scripts, pens, paper

Procedure: Similar to the "Character Profile" activity (see above), this activity allows for a more personal connection to the character. Students select or are assigned a character—their own role or another's—and write a letter to that character. The letter uses the structure of informal correspondence (salutation, body, complimentary close) that the teacher may need to model. The body of the letter could include the following:

1. Describing the student who is writing the letter
2. Explaining why the student is writing the letter
3. Asking the character about his or her specific actions or dialogue
4. Sharing some concerns about the problem or ideas presented in the script

5. Proposing solutions to these problems

6. Asking the character for advice

Assessment: If the teacher provides students with a checklist of items the letter needs to address, that checklist may also serve as an assessment. An alternative assessment would be the teacher's use of a rubric to address each of the six components of the letter.

New Endings

Skills Developed: Listening, Reading Comprehension, Speaking, Vocabulary Development, Writing

Purpose: To work together as a group to create a viable ending to a script and to discuss and perform that script.

Materials: Short Readers Theatre script (e.g., short story, poem, or letter), pens, paper

Procedure: The class is divided into groups of four to six students, and each group is given the same short script (a short story, poem, or letter). Each group is asked to create their own ending to the script. A scribe in each group writes down this ending as others dictate it. The group then rehearses and performs this new ending to the script for the class. Discussion follows each performance, with the group providing a rationale for the new ending and answering questions from the teacher and their peers.

Assessment: This is a project that could provide both a group grade and an individual grade. A checklist concentrating on group dynamics, the written ending and its relevance to the script, students' performance, and their discussion could serve as the main assessment. The "Rubric for Readers Theatre" in chapter 10 (Figure 22; see page 175) provides a structure for both a group and an individual grade. In addition, the "Checklist for Assessing Script Adaptation" (Figure 30; see page 184) could be modified to focus on an appropriate ending.

Research Project

Skills Developed: Reading Comprehension, Vocabulary Development, Writing

Purpose: To provide background information through a research paper to enhance students' understanding of a topic.

Materials: Readers Theatre script, pens, paper, Internet access, trade books from the school and classroom library

Procedure: During script development, students are assigned or select a topic to investigate such as background information about the setting, plot incidents, or historical connections. This research often results in additional scripting or a separate short paper handed in to the teacher or shared at the final performance. An alternative would be to use the research project as an extension to Readers Theatre following the final performance.

Assessment: As with any written project, the research paper's directions may serve as the components of a checklist or rubric for the teacher's use. If the written project is shared at the final performance, that sharing may be evaluated as a part of the whole performance. In addition, a graphic organizer, such as the web discussed on page 182 in chapter 10, could be given to the students to complete, focusing on vocabulary or key elements of their paper. This abbreviated form of their paper could then be more easily assessed by the teacher.

Visual Activities

Inside the Character

Skills Developed: Critical Thinking, Reading Comprehension, Writing

Purpose: To make clear, through words and pictures, a character's thoughts and feelings.

Materials: Readers Theatre scripts, colored markers, pen, paper

Procedure: Similar to the "Character Profile" activity (see page 130) this art activity, adapted from "The Open-Mind Portrait" (Tompkins, 1998), focuses on what a character is thinking and feeling. Students draw a silhouette of a character from the script and, within that silhouette, express in pictures and keywords that character's thoughts and emotions. For example, if students are performing a script about the Underground Railroad, they might focus on Harriet Tubman. Her full-body silhouette could have the words *sore—so much running* within the silhouette of her feet, pictures of the North Star with the word *freedom* in her head, and the name *Moses* written near her hands, which are holding a staff.

Assessment: A checklist or rubric is an appropriate assessment for this activity. Its components should address the inclusion and relevance of both pictures and keywords, the number of pictures and keywords used (three to five of each is suggested), and the neatness or overall quality of the content.

Mural

Skills Developed: Critical Thinking, Reading Comprehension

Purpose: To create a backdrop or visual that makes clear the setting or the theme of the script.

Materials: Readers Theatre scripts, paint or markers, pencils, roll of paper

Procedure: Serving as an integrated art project and also as a possible backdrop for the final performance, the mural is created by students to provide a visual that may be factual, informative, and symbolic (see Figure 16). Relating specifically to the setting and theme as well as students' interpretation of the script, the mural could be a group project facilitated by the art teacher. For example, a mural depicting bleachers and a ball field could serve as a backdrop for the performance of "Casey at the Bat" (Thayer, 1993).

Assessment: The collaborative nature of this activity allows for both a group grade and an individual grade. The "Rubric for Readers Theatre" in Figure 22 on page 175 in chapter 10 provides the structure for both grades. Students could be assessed on their work within the group, the success of the mural as an informative visual, and the overall quality of the mural.

Poster

Skills Developed: Critical Thinking, Reading Comprehension, Writing

Purpose: To provide a visual that represents important elements of content or setting.

Materials: Readers Theatre script, markers or paint, posterboard or poster paper

Procedure: Each group or each student is responsible for a poster that provides facts about the author of the text adapted for Readers Theatre, about the

Figure 16. Students Creating a Mural for a Performance

setting, or about specific content. Students should use a graphic organizer (such as the web or other organizers described in chapter 10) to record notes about the adapted text or the author, which will become the inspiration for the art included in the poster. Teachers may also require students to create a works cited page while researching this information. Very similar to the "Mural" activity on page 132, the poster includes both illustrations and writing and may be shared with the audience as an introduction to the final performance.

Assessment: A to-do list given to students stating requirements for the poster may serve as an assessment tool and guide, with the teacher using those requirements as an assessment checklist as well (see Figure 17). This to-do list focuses on the author of the poem and offers an assessment focus of the poster as a clear representation of author information and the works cited as relevant to the final product. If the poster is used as a part of the final performance, consider whether the poster matches the students' verbal explanation or talk.

Puppetry

Skills Developed: Reading Fluency, Speaking

Purpose: To provide another venue for performance.

Materials: Readers Theatre script, puppets

Procedure: By adapting their Readers Theatre performance to a puppet show, students can often overcome their performance-related inhibitions and focus on

Figure 17. Poster To-Do List

☐ Research information about your poster topic and record that information on your graphic organizer. Complete a works cited page for the sources you use in your research.

☐ As a group, use your graphic organizer to create a rough draft of the poster. Review your graphic organizer as a group to make sure that your rough draft is complete. Remember, your final copy will be seen by lots of people! ☺

☐ Using poster paper, begin creating the final draft. Use pictures, markers, colored paper, and any other materials that you can think of to make your poster a clear and creative representation of all the work you have done. This is your opportunity to show us what you've learned!

☐ You may want to assign each other some homework here. You may want to type some of the information. Someone in your group may have a color printer at home that will make great pictures or decorations for your poster. Talk about it and plan what to do. Write down any tasks that you are supposed to complete on your own so that you don't forget.

☐ Check your works cited page. Make sure all of your resources have been listed. If any are missing, **neatly** write the resources on the page. Here is another guide for the citation of a book:

      Author's last name, First initial. <u>Title of book</u>. Date. Publishing Company: City/State/Country where published.

☐ Tape or glue the works cited page to the back of the poster.

☐ Make sure all of your names are on the back of the poster.

☐ Find a safe place for your poster so that it will be ready to hang up on [due date].

☐ Congratulate each other on a job well done!

their speaking skills, such as voice projection. Puppet shows are also great for performing for younger students.

It is important not to let the puppet show's staging overcome the production. Puppetry can be kept simple by making paper plate puppets (one face for each role); exploring garage sales and discount stores to purchase puppets; or borrowing puppets from sources such as libraries, school staff, and community members. Students need not be too concerned that the puppet match their character—for example, "Casey at the Bat" (Thayer, 1993) can be performed convincingly by female puppets or even by animal puppets. The puppets often become an extension of the individual and take on a life of their own—almost like the posture, facial expression, gesture, and movement discussed in chapter 3 as an integral part of a Readers Theatre performance.

Assessment: Because the most important skills incorporated into puppetry are reading fluency and speaking, any checklist or rubric (such as those in chapter 10) should focus on them. This activity may also be used for an extra-credit grade.

Setting the Scene

Skills Developed: Critical Thinking, Reading Comprehension, Writing

Purpose: To facilitate students' understanding of setting.

Materials: Readers Theatre script, markers or paint, poster paper

Procedure: Similar to the "Mural" activity (see page 132) and the "Poster" activity (see page 133), this activity allows students (individually or in small groups) to illustrate with pictures and keywords where and when the action in the script occurs. Such a visual representation may serve as a poster to introduce the final performance, as a mural and backdrop during the performance, or simply as a separate activity to facilitate students' understanding of setting.

Assessment: A handout that lists the requirements for this illustration can be adapted as a checklist to assess whether students have met those requirements. The focus should be on the relevance of the pictures and keywords used to denote time and place.

Story Sequence Strip

Skills Developed: Critical Thinking, Reading Comprehension

Purpose: To enable students to understand story sequence.

Materials: Readers Theatre script, pens or markers, paper

Procedure: To make the story sequence visible and clear, students create a story sequence strip by illustrating six major plot elements of the story. This strip is made by folding an 8.5- by 11-inch paper in half horizontally (the "hot dog fold"), then folded again into three panels to create six panels. Suggest that students illustrate the first panel with a plot element that begins the story and the last panel with the conclusion of the story. They then need to determine which of the story's many plot elements will fill the remaining four panels. Sharing the strip with peers can create some interesting discussions, as students talk about why they included specific plot elements.

Assessment: This activity may be peer reviewed by using a 3-point rating scale. A "3" indicates that the strip has a very clear sense of the story sequence and includes appropriate major plot elements. A "2" indicates that the strip is somewhat clear or that some of the major plot elements are missing. A "1" indicates that the strip is confusing and does not clearly illustrate the sequence of the story but does have at least two major plot elements. A "0" indicates that the strip does not illustrate the sequence of the story or has only one or no major plot elements.

Video Production

Skills Developed: Critical Thinking, Listening, Reading Comprehension, Speaking

Purpose: To allow students to view their own performance and critique it.

Materials: Readers Theatre script, video equipment or other technology with visual recording and playback capability

Procedure: Each of the final performances is videotaped. After groups view their own performance, they discuss what they liked about it and what improvements could be made. An alternative would be to have the whole class view and discuss each performance video. It is important, however, that the teacher model constructive criticism and facilitate the discussion. Videotaping, like the "Audiotape Recording" (see page 137) and "Radio Drama" speaking activities (see page 139), gives students the opportunity to view their performance and learn from it. If the videotapes are shown as a final product, they may be shared with other classes and grades, at open house, and during parent–teacher conferences. The video could also be an important addition to students' portfolios.

Assessment: This activity serves as an excellent introduction to the field of constructive criticism and as a final product of performance. Assessment could focus on students' performance, specifically their reading fluency and expression. The "Checklist for Assessing Staging" in Figure 31 on page 185 in chapter 10 could serve as a self-assessment for individuals or the group or as a peer assessment (the audience) for feedback.

Speaking Activities

Audiotape Recording

Skills Developed: Reading Fluency, Speaking

Purpose: To provide practice in expressive and fluent reading.

Materials: Readers Theatre script, microphone, audiotape recorder (or computer or other technology with audio-recording capability), tape

Procedure: Similar to the "Video Production" activity (see page 136) but without the visual aspect, "Audiotape Recording" may be done by one student or the whole group. This activity is especially helpful for shy or struggling readers who may lack confidence in reading aloud. Beginning readers who are audiotaped may listen to themselves and begin to see themselves as readers. Older students who struggle with reading can listen to how they read and, with feedback and discussion, evaluate their reading and understand what they need to practice. Audiotaping creates a product that can document students' progress in reading aloud. Audiotape recording can also be effective as a form of rehearsal, giving students practice in reading aloud and building their confidence.

Assessment: An audiotape created at the beginning and the end of the school year can be a powerful tool in documenting a student's reading growth. One assessment could be students responding critically to their own recording in a journal entry. Examples of possible prompts are noted in the "Reading Buddy" activity (see page 140).

Choral Reading

Skills Developed: Listening, Reading Fluency, Speaking

Purpose: To provide students practice reading expressively and fluently in unison.

Materials: Readers Theatre scripts or other written text

Procedure: Choral reading is an excellent way to introduce students to the concept of Readers Theatre and can be used regularly to introduce a new Readers Theatre script. "In Beauty May I Walk" (Anonymous, 1990) in chapter 6 is an example of choral reading. This type of reading is especially effective with poetry because poetry, like singing, encourages rhythm and a variety of tone and pitch. The teacher may group students in several ways for choral reading: the whole class reads the entire script, roles are divided into three or four groups that read the script, or a number of students are assigned to read each role. The key to choral reading is that all students read more than one line together. Reading in unison with others gives struggling readers a safe way to become more fluent. Initially, the teacher may need to model a fluent reading of each script.

Assessment: Teacher observation is important when there is no written product. This activity is a way to introduce students to Readers Theatre, and it does not need to be assessed. If necessary, the teacher could mark a student as "participating" or "not participating" and include that as part of a grade for the entire Readers Theatre process. The choral reading could be audiotaped or videotaped, and the class could critique it, as noted in the "Video Production" activity (see page 136) and the "Audiotape Recording" activity (see page 137).

Dialogue Practice

Skills Developed: Listening, Reading Comprehension, Reading Fluency, Speaking

Purpose: To provide practice in the oral reading of dialogue.

Materials: Reader theatre scripts or other dialogue-rich texts

Procedure: Prior to script development (see chapter 2 for information on script adaptation), the teacher has groups of students read from dialogue-rich text (picture books or short story excerpts work well here). Copies of the text are made for all students. Students are asked to highlight their roles with a marker and told to read only their character's words inside the quotation marks. One member of the group is assigned as narrator. The narrator reads all words not in quotation marks, which could include the speech tags of "he said" or "she said." After rehearsal, the groups can perform the reading for the whole class.

Assessment: As another speaking and listening activity, "Dialogue Practice" need not be assessed. However, students could be granted a participation grade, and the activity could be included in the assessment for the Readers Theatre process. Because the focus in this activity is on group interactions, students may be asked to grade one another or themselves on aspects such as cooperation, listening skills, reading fluency, and speaking skills.

The Family Connection

Skills Developed: Listening, Reading Fluency, Speaking

Purpose: To create family support for reading aloud both in and out of the classroom.

Materials: Readers Theatre scripts

Procedure: Scripts can be sent home with students with a request that family members assume different roles to help the student rehearse. Prior to the Readers Theatre activity, the teacher can ask family members to participate as listening aides during the Readers Theatre process and as audience members for the final performance. The student can work with another supportive adult if a relative is not available.

Assessment: A journal response from the student reflecting upon the importance of rehearsal and listening aides is an appropriate assessment for this activity.

Partnered Oral Reading

Skills Developed: Listening, Reading Fluency, Speaking

Purpose: To provide practice in expressive and fluent reading (reader) as well as listening with a purpose and constructive analysis of performance (listener).

Materials: Readers Theatre script

Procedure: Students pair up and take turns reading the script. One student reads first while the other listens and provides feedback. Then the students switch roles. This activity is initially modeled by the teacher, who facilitates the use of appropriate constructive criticism. The "Reading Fluency Checklist" on page 181 in chapter 10, focused on components of reading fluency and expression, may be used or adapted for the students to follow as they listen to their peers.

Assessment: An assessment for this activity could be an informal written reflection where each student addresses what went well and what needs work regarding his or her own reading. The "Reading Fluency Checklist" noted above could also be used as a form of assessment.

Radio Drama

Skills Developed: Listening Skills, Reading Fluency, Speaking, Vocabulary Development

Purpose: To focus on listening and speaking skills in an oral performance.

Materials: Readers Theatre script, tape recorder (or other technology with audiorecording options), tape, microphone, sound props

Procedure: Although very similar to the "Audiotape Recording" activity (see page 137), "Radio Drama" goes beyond the focus of expressive and fluent reading to enact a performance that is dependent solely upon sound. The teacher could introduce the students to classic radio shows of the past and allow them to experiment with sound, using their voices and sound props (i.e., a sheet of metal for lightning). Discussions as to what sounds or words replace gestures, actions, props, and costumes are helpful. Each group may record their oral performance. Audio recordings allow students to rewind and redo their oral performances, if necessary. Students may also be more comfortable reading their script because they are not seen. "Radio Drama" audio recordings could be shared with other classes and grades, sent home for families to hear, made available for open house or parent–teacher conferences, and added to students' portfolios.

Assessment: "Radio Drama" is a Readers Theatre performance that does not use visuals and focuses on sound. Any assessment should therefore concentrate on students' speaking skills (see chapter 10 for suggestions). A checklist highlighting the sounds and words students use to create setting, characterization, and other story elements would also be appropriate. Terminology for a checklist may also be found in the "Vocal Performance" section in chapter 3.

Real People, Real Stories

Skills Developed: Listening, Reading Comprehension, Speaking, Vocabulary Development

Purpose: To provide students access to real stories of real people.

Materials: Textbooks, trade books, magazine articles, Internet access

Procedure: Stories need not be fiction; they need only to involve the narrative shaping of any content area (Wilson, 2002). The book *Cosmos* (Sagan, 1980) is an excellent illustration of the use of story in a nonfiction science text. Such stories provide a wealth of content and allow students insight on the process of discovery and the lives of real people. A teacher could read story excerpts aloud, assign reading, or adapt such stories to scripts for Readers Theatre. Students could also be asked to find, read aloud, and share such stories, selected from a teacher-generated list of resources (see Appendix B for other ways to use stories with science or other content areas).

Assessment: This activity is an excellent extra-credit project for students. It could also easily become a written research project for advanced readers and writers. Figure 34 in Appendix B provides suggestions for the assessment of content areas used in Readers Theatre.

Reading Buddy

Skills Developed: Reading Fluency, Speaking

Purpose: To provide practice in expressive and fluent reading.

Materials: Readers Theatre script

Procedure: This activity is similar to the "Partnered Oral Reading" activity (see page 139) but instead focuses on the reader. After rereading and becoming comfortable with the Readers Theatre script, a student reads to a younger child. As the only reader, that student can use a variety of voices and expression. Because the reader has an audience of one and that audience is younger, the reader has an opportunity to be the expert. Excellent for building a reader's confidence, this activity helps the reader progress from an audience of one to a collaborative performance for a larger audience.

Assessment: A written journal response by the reader, serving as a self-assessment, could address a specific prompt. Some possible prompts include the following:

1. My reading was _____ because....

2. I was good at....

3. I need to work on....

4. I think my buddy really liked _____ because....

5. I had trouble....

6. What I liked best about this was _____ because....

7. This was hard for me because....

Role Playing

Skills Developed: Critical Thinking, Listening, Speaking

Purpose: To provide additional practice for students who are skilled at speaking and improvising.

Materials: Readers Theatre script, trade books

Procedure: Students are allowed to improvise through the activity of role playing. Each student or small group selects a character from the script and decides how that character would react in another setting, another situation, and with other characters. For example, if excerpts from *Maniac Magee* (Spinelli, 1990) were used in a Readers Theatre script, how would Maniac act as a member of the students' class? What would he be like if he were adopted into one student's family? If he were an adult, what kind of teacher would he be? How would he and Brian from *Hatchet* (Paulsen, 1987) get along? Once decisions have been made regarding a character's actions and talk, the individual or the group shares ideas with the class by role playing.

Assessment: A handout would guide students interested in this activity and could be used as a focus for the components of assessment. Because it is more complex, role playing may best serve those who are better readers and speakers. The "Checklist for Assessing Performance" in Figure 32 on page 186 can be adapted to use as an assessment for this activity.

Vocabulary Race

Skills Developed: Critical Thinking, Listening, Vocabulary Development, Speaking

Purpose: To increase students' vocabulary knowledge.

Materials: Readers Theatre scripts, pen, paper

Procedure: Students are paired, and the teacher selects a topic related to the script's theme, characters, or setting. When signaled, one partner names as many words as possible relating to that topic. For example, if the topic is *The True Confessions of Charlotte Doyle* (Avi, 1990), taken from the script in chapter 4, the first student could name characters in the script, elements of setting, or terms related to the sailing ship, such as *quarterdeck*, *shrouds*, and *spars*. The partner listens carefully, tracking the number of words spoken or even writing the actual words, and after 30 seconds or less (at a prearranged signal), he or she becomes the speaker, careful not to repeat what has already been said.

Assessment: The timed component makes this activity ideal for competition. Teams would compete for the most words or the most relevant words, but such an activity need not be graded.

Who Am I?

Skills Developed: Critical Thinking, Listening, Speaking

Purpose: To identify a specific character through dialogue and movement.

Materials: Readers Theatre script

Procedure: After the final performance, students divide into small groups. Each group selects a character's name from one of the scripts, not necessarily their own. This selection should be random and secret so that no one outside of the group learns that identity of the character. Without mentioning the character's name, group members then act the part of that character through dialogue and movement, and the class attempts to guess who the character is.

Assessment: This activity focuses on dialogue and movement so these two components should be the basis for any grading. Consider using this activity as an extra-credit grade for the group.

REFERENCES
Tompkins, G.E. (1998). *50 literacy strategies: Step by step*. Englewood Cliffs, NJ: Merrill.
Wilson, E.O. (2002). The power of story. *American Educator, 26*, 8–11.

LITERATURE CITED
Anonymous. (1990). In beauty may I walk (J.K. Rothenberg, Trans.). In P. Abbs & J. Richardson (Eds.), *The forms of poetry: A practical guide* (p. 59). New York: Cambridge University Press.
Avi. (1990). *The true confessions of Charlotte Doyle* (pp. 52–59). New York: Scholastic.
Paulsen, G. (1987). *Hatchet*. New York: Scholastic.
Sagan, C. (1980). *Cosmos*. New York: Random House.
Spinelli, J. (1990). *Maniac Magee*. New York: Scholastic.
Thayer, E.L. (1993). Casey at the bat. In R.A. Rubin (Ed.), *Poetry out loud* (pp. 44–47). Chapel Hill, NC: Algonquin.

Readers Theatre Beyond the Middle School Classroom

Readers Theatre is a language arts process focused on text and performance that enhances students' reading fluency and comprehension. It has great value to students at all grade levels, with adaptations easily made for elementary school, high school, ELLs and struggling readers, and gifted students.

Adaptations are easily made because Readers Theatre has the potential to incorporate each of the language arts components (reading, writing, speaking, listening, and viewing) and can address a multitude of learning styles. There is quality literature in the form of fiction, nonfiction, and poetry that is accessible to all ages and abilities—from classic folk tales to classic novels, from topics that address the five senses to the story of the atom, and from nursery rhymes to T.S. Eliot. Readers Theatre is flexible enough to use any and all of this literature. It offers individuals, pairs, small groups, or the whole class opportunities to perform roles of varying sizes and complexity and allows students to enhance the performance with visuals, music, and their own unique organizational skills.

Adaptations of the Readers Theatre process—including group dynamics, text selection and script adaptation, staging, rehearsal and performance, and assessment—will be addressed in this chapter.

Adaptations for Elementary Classrooms

Adapting Readers Theatre to the elementary classroom retains many of the components that make Readers Theatre so successful for middle school. Although beginning readers (Pre-K through grade 2) will benefit from repeated reading, the goal for these readers should be the building of reading fluency and confidence, the understanding of basic concepts of print, and the power and enjoyment of reading. Consequently, the patterns of predictable text that include repetition, rhyme and rhythm, sequential patterns, and cumulative sequence should play a major role in the selection of text and the adaptation of scripts for beginning readers. These patterns allow for reading success that will motivate beginning readers to keep reading. In addition, Readers Theatre provides an excellent venue in which to build primary students' sight word vocabulary. The adaptations for the elementary classroom will be discussed in this chapter with a focus on group dynamics, text selection and script adaptation, staging, rehearsal and performance, and assessment.

Group Dynamics

The entire class should be given a script that is either read aloud as a class with individual readers or as a choral reading (see chapter 7, "Choral Reading," on page 137) where all students or groups of students read specific roles. If this is a new activity for the class, the teacher may assign roles. For an initial Readers Theatre project, the teacher could break the class into several small groups and have each group rehearse and perform the same script. Once students become familiar with Readers Theatre, each group can have its own unique script to perform. When students are rereading their roles, older students or adult volunteers could serve as listeners or an audience of one. These listeners can model audience behavior, provide basic feedback ("I can't hear you, read louder"), and help readers gain confidence in their reading.

Before any staging is used, a teacher may want to have all students read the script together as a choral reading to create comfort and confidence. This could be done by putting the script on an overhead projector, allowing the class to focus on one part of the script at a time.

Text Selection and Script Adaptation

The most appropriate genre of text for elementary students is fiction because it is a familiar text structure that lends itself easily to scripting. Overall, text chosen for Readers Theatre in the elementary classroom should be easy and familiar to the students. This means that the text should be at an independent reading level and can be read without a lot of teacher guidance or at an instructional level with teacher support. It must be easily adapted to script with potential for a great deal of dialogue, and the text narration or concepts must be understood by students. The elementary grades are also a good place to introduce the language of story structure, such as setting, characters, plot, and theme, and to focus on reading with expression.

Quality picture books often provide appropriate material for scripts because they are written to be read aloud to children, and their language usually flows with a distinct rhythm. Fables are another good choice because they are short, can be easily adapted to script format, and have a moral that may be read as a whole-class chorus during the performance. An example would be using "The Tortoise and the Hare" (Lynch, 2000) as described in chapter 4. For primary grades, the material must be interesting and accessible to the beginning reader. If the audience or performers are very young, the script should be kept short with action or lines built in for all students.

If students are learning to write, the teacher may lead the creation of a collaborative class script with input from all students. Such a script should focus on the patterns of predictable text, most notably repetition and rhyme. Each student's role can be kept to one or two sentences that both the teacher and the student are confident the child can read. One or two words can be used as lines for students who are struggling. For example, in The Little Red Hen, selected children may simply respond, "Not I!" Even sounds such as "Bang!" or "Moo!" will provide student participation and a forum in which students may begin to connect spoken words with written symbols.

If a collaborative class script is too time-consuming or confusing, the teacher should create or adapt the script or use an existing script, keeping in mind that it must enable the highest and lowest level readers to be full participants. One way to do this is to provide narration of a higher reading level for the strong readers and include simple dialogue or a repetitive chorus for struggling readers. A repeating refrain, whether a moral, a line from the book, a phrase, or even a single word, can be used as a chorus that all students or a large group read.

For more advanced readers (grades 3 to 6), the focus may remain on fluency, confidence, and enjoyment, but should also expand to include reading comprehension and vocabulary development. Fables and well-known folktales or fairy tales are excellent sources because they have simple plots, specific settings, and several distinct characters. Students at this level may read or have read to them several versions of a story, then discuss the parts of the plot that remain constant throughout the different versions.

Staging

Once students are comfortable with the format of a script, the teacher should decide what aspects of staging will be used for the performance. At the elementary level, staging, including creating the whole picture; using postures and actions; and the use of production elements such as sound, props, costumes, and artwork (see chapter 3), should be kept to a minimum because too often students' energies are taken up with staging elements rather than reading. When students become familiar and proficient with Readers Theatre, staging may become more elaborate as long as the emphasis of rehearsal and performance remains on the expressive and fluent reading of the script.

Students, as a whole class or in small groups, need to discuss the "whole picture" aspect of staging, basically a consideration of what their performance will look like to the audience. This means they should address such issues as performer placement, movement, and eye contact with the audience. Postures and actions should be kept to a minimum and, if used, highlight key aspects of the script. For example, students may shake their heads, point, or run in place to indicate movement appropriate to their role.

A basic staging technique for elementary grades is to have the readers wear nametags of their characters or a simple prop or costume indicative of that character. For example, in *Caps for Sale* (Slobodkina, 1947), the peddler could wear a black hat and a jacket and all the monkeys could wear hats of different colors. Music stands help in keeping scripts organized and in keeping students' hands free to gesture.

Rehearsal and Performance

Rehearsal is especially important at the elementary level. It allows for rereadings of the script as well as instructional support and feedback from teacher and peers. Beginning readers often believe that reading at a rapid rate is "good reading." With teacher support and repeated readings, they begin to realize that good oral reading means understanding what is read, reading fluently, and bringing the text to life through expressive reading.

It is also during rehearsals that the teacher may present a group or whole-class minilesson to model or clarify something with which students struggle or that seems confusing. For example, a teacher may demonstrate how punctuation affects reading aloud or what a reader's reading rate and pacing conveys.

While rereading, students should not be encouraged to memorize. When students memorize, they often stop interpreting the text and their reading begins to lack expression.

An audience for the final performance is vital, especially at this grade level. As for middle school students, having an audience serves as an incentive for students to read and reread, and to read with expression and understanding. Students become the experts, and beginning readers gain much-needed confidence in their ability to read if they perform before an audience.

Assessment

The same assessment tools discussed in chapter 10 are appropriate for use in the elementary classroom. However, at the elementary level, the focus should be on students' reading fluency, phrasing, pacing or reading rate, and expressiveness as well as comprehension. Running records are especially helpful in monitoring beginning readers' progress and also to identify problems that may necessitate a one-on-one conference or a class or small-group minilesson.

RECOMMENDED EXTENSION ACTIVITIES

Audiotape Recording (page 137)

Choral Reading (page 137)

Dialogue Practice (page 138)

The Family Connection (page 138)

Inside the Character (page 132)

Puppetry (page 134)

Reading Buddy (page 140)

Story Sequence Strip (page 135)

Adaptations for High School Classrooms

As in middle school, Readers Theatre in a high school setting gives an immediate and concrete reason for reading and rereading a text—that of public performance. This performance aspect can provide not only motivation for reading but a deeper understanding of the text and opportunities for developing and discussing text from a number of viewpoints (character, director, potential audience, and personal experiences). As high school students develop their own unique worldview, this discussion allows for an exploration of viewpoints and builds confidence in grasping multiple meanings from a single text. Students' increased need to understand themselves and their place in the world combined with additional academic and personal experiences make the forum of Readers Theatre an ideal vehicle for exploration in the high school classroom.

Because high school students' experiences, understanding, and knowledge are more similar to middle school than the elementary-grade students' are, using Readers Theatre at the high school level closely follows the pattern this book has laid out for middle school. The main difference is the change in text and content and the expectations for higher level thinking and greater understanding.

As in all other grades, Readers Theatre should not be used at the beginning of the school year. Individual classroom teachers, as they come to know their students' abilities and interest, will make instructional decisions as to when and how Readers Theatre is used. Often, because the high school curriculum is so full and demanding, Readers Theatre itself is considered an extension activity with a primary emphasis on performance, or as in most middle school classrooms, is relegated to the English classroom and not considered for other content areas. The suggested adaptations for the high school classroom discussed in this chapter address group dynamics, text selection and script adaptation, staging, rehearsal and performance, and assessment.

Group Dynamics

At the high school level, it is assumed that students have experience working in groups. However, that experience may be tainted by past occasions where one group member did most of the work or another's lack of work impacted everyone's grade. It is important, therefore, that the teacher focus assessment on the group as well as the individual to ensure a balanced grade. Another viable option would be to not assign a grade.

Students' abilities are more developed at the high school level than at the middle school level, so the use of roles in Readers Theatre has the potential to motivate them and to create a forum for their success. As with other grade levels, it is necessary that the teacher clarify and explain the specific roles. High school groups may be given more responsibility and have more control over the process and performance of Readers Theatre, moving toward the concept of "student-directed performances" as discussed in chapter 2.

Text Selection and Script Adaptation

The main difference between Readers Theatre at the high school level and the middle school level is the increased complexity of materials, performance, and production elements. Texts adapted to Readers Theatre scripts at the high school level may be fiction, nonfiction, or poetry. Novels and short stories are excellent sources for scripts, as are primary documents such as diaries, journals, letters, newspaper articles, memoirs, historical documents, and biographies. The text used in Readers Theatre at the high school level is often employed to expand or illuminate specific content area knowledge.

The combination of fiction and nonfiction texts as a basis for a Readers Theatre production in a high school classroom is an example from the teaching field. Juniors in an urban high school were given the assignment to research, develop, and present information about the Romantic period in British Literature. Students developed a script and performance illustrated with a series of nature slides they had created in which they explained the concept of Romanticism. They selected poems by Shelley, Keats, Wordsworth, Tennyson, and Byron, and read these poems accompanied by jazz recordings they felt emphasized the theme and emotion of each poem. The visual background for the poetry reading was a series of shifting colored lights on a backdrop. The audience for the final performance consisted of students, school faculty and staff, parents, and community members.

Through this activity, students had a variety of opportunities for creating, elaborating, and revising meaning that was developed from a series of fiction, nonfiction, and poetry sources. It offered students a reason to research and reread and gave them a forum to work together to present their knowledge.

Having students self-select scripts may increase motivation. Allowing high school students to further develop an existing Readers Theatre script may create meaningful and more sophisticated chunks of language using both an author's words and their own. Scripting helps to develop organization, coherence, details, and sense of purpose as students write for an audience. Development of a script encourages frequent revision of text and stage directions based upon audience response as students reread, rewrite, and rehearse. Their adaptation or creation of a script may include a research component as well as visuals and sounds that emphasize important vocabulary, text meaning, emotion, content, and themes. The creation and development of promotional materials for a Readers Theatre performance also provides a different format and audience for authentic writing activities.

Staging

As discussed generally in chapter 3 and more specifically in chapters 4, 5, and 6, staging refers to the visual aspects of performance. Keeping in mind that the emphasis still remains on the text that is read, the use of postures and actions during the performance, and the creation and use of production elements such as costumes, props, and music provide high school students with a variety of roles and opportunities. Readers Theatre in the high school classroom may be more of a performance activity because student independence is stronger at this level. Therefore, due to visual aspects involved, staging is especially important at this level.

The discussion of staging for middle school is applicable for students in the high school classroom. Some minor adaptations may include the positioning of performers which may be more student-directed at this level. Also, the use of postures and actions may be more subtle or sarcastic, even larger and vaudevillian. The creation and use of production elements will be more sophisticated but should always supplement or enhance the script meaning and not dominate or distract from the performance.

Rehearsal and Performance

The discussion of rehearsal and performance for middle school serves the high school classroom as well. All aspects of staging need to be considered, and students' roles, especially that of director, are very important here. In the high school classroom, one or two students in each group are very capable of taking on this role.

Assessment

The same assessment tools discussed later in chapter 10 for the middle school classroom may be used with Readers Theatre in the high school classroom.

Adaptations may be made to better address high school students' capabilities and can even focus on specific content areas.

RECOMMENDED EXTENSION ACTIVITIES

New Endings (page 131)

Puppetry (page 134)

Radio Drama (page 139)

Reading Buddy (page 140)

Real People, Real Stories (page 140)

Video Production (page 136)

Vocabulary Race (page 141)

Adaptations for English-Language Learners and Struggling Readers

Because of today's increasingly diverse classrooms, more teachers are working with students who enter their room speaking a language other than English. These ELLs should be taught by the same principles that guide effective language and literacy instruction and learning in a first language. Struggling readers may have a reading disability or may not have developed basic decoding skills that allow them to read fluently and with comprehension. They may also be in need of developmental reading activities (e.g., strategies for reading nonfiction as opposed to fiction) or may lack necessary background knowledge to understand specific aspects of text or content. In other words, the language arts (reading, writing, speaking, listening, and viewing) taught in the primary grades should guide a teacher's instruction of ELLs (Echevarria & Graves, 1998).

Reading, writing, speaking, listening, and viewing are interrelated language processes, all of which are a part of Readers Theatre. Using these five components of language arts helps ELLs students and struggling readers to become more proficient language users. Readers Theatre allows these students to experience the thrill of performance and the joy of success in reading and in collaboration with their peers.

Useful for all levels of students needing refined skills in the spoken, written, and nonverbal aspects of language, Readers Theatre has been found to effectively teach reading as well as writing to ELLs and students with special needs (Goodman, 1978). Readers Theatre has the potential to help ELLs and struggling readers improve their oral language fluency and motivate them to read. It provides a visual and oral stimulus, drawing upon students' creative skills and allowing for success in reading. When ELLs and struggling readers participate in an activity such as Readers Theatre that requires the use of oral and written language, they learn content and language more easily. These students are also given the opportunity to interact with their peers and with adults who provide support, ideas, and feedback.

Before teachers begin any project such as Readers Theatre, it is vital that they realize the benefits of bilingualism and the abilities ELLs bring to the classroom. Their rich cultural heritage offers a different perspective and may serve as a door to folktales and stories well suited to Readers Theatre. In addition, recognition of an environment where "the teacher is not proficient in the student's language and the student is not proficient in the teacher's language" (Vacca, Vacca, Gove, Burkey, Lenhart, & McKeon, 2005, p. 336) will facilitate the teacher's use of basic script adaptations, staging, rehearsal and performance, and assessment. Finally, the teacher must recognize that ELLs students' social vocabulary is far more advanced than their academic vocabulary; the former usually attained within two years while it could take up to seven years to achieve a fluent academic vocabulary (Cummins, 1989). Teachers may use Readers Theatre to help develop their ELLs' academic vocabulary and to increase other struggling readers' vocabulary. In addition, the rereading inherent in Readers Theatre provides an opportunity for these students to hear and practice unfamiliar words.

Group Dynamics

Partner sharing and cooperative grouping are two strategies that support students by allowing student participation, enhancing student success, and making each group member feel valued (Slavin, 1987). The teacher may deliberately pair individuals of different academic strengths and backgrounds so they can learn from one another. Because only two students are involved, partner sharing helps to increase the ELL and struggling reader's comfort level and their active involvement. By allowing students to share with each other and work toward a common goal, cooperative grouping promotes problem solving and creates opportunities for scaffolding, where students may build on one another's knowledge.

Although consistent ability grouping is not recommended for ELLs and struggling readers, forming small groups of students with similar needs can be very productive because the teacher is able to more effectively teach and monitor students' comprehension and performance. The key is to continually change group structures to prevent stigmas associated with any one specific grouping (Echevarria & Graves, 1998).

Text Selection and Script Adaptation

The creation or selection of a script for Readers Theatre, as noted earlier, often falls to the teacher because of time constraints. It is recommended in classrooms with diverse learners that the teacher develop or select the script. It is also helpful for them to provide an outline, web, or summary of the original text prior to reading the complete text so that students have a sense of plot or key concepts. When developing the scripts, the teacher should use visual as well as verbal examples to clarify important terms or difficult vocabulary and to use repetition in words, phrases, and ideas throughout. Teachers should also use simple language in the script that rephrases information and use body movements (postures and actions) and objects (props or costumes) to support that information.

In classrooms with ELLs, teachers should focus on environmental print both in English and the students' first language. They may label objects in both languages, then shift this focus to the language used in the text. Certain words or refrains could be read in two languages (i.e., a growing number of children's picture books are in both English and Spanish). Teachers should also take advantage of the opportunity to include the students' native language and allow time for ELLs to share writing in their first language. When adapting a script, the teacher may solicit their help in using some of their writing or in having them translate English words into their first language, as long as the context provides a clear understanding of that word or words.

ELLs and struggling readers are also able to participate in Readers Theatre because certain roles or a chorus in the script can be adapted to their reading level. The repeated readings of a script will help them identify specific words. Their role, which should be highlighted with a marker, may be one word or a phrase; it may be in a student's first language with its English counterpart or it may be part of a group chorus. The teacher as director/producer should make these decisions based upon the individual student's comfort level and ability.

Staging

Staging with ELLs and struggling readers of any grade will use the same strategies as middle school students because it does not depend upon students reading but upon their visualization of the performance, their postures and actions, and their use of production elements. The Visual Activities on pages 132 through 136 in chapter 7 can be used to enhance ELLs' and struggling readers' comprehension of the script as well as the staging process of Readers Theatre. Staging is the part of Readers Theatre where nonverbal communication is most important. All students should be encouraged to use their body and face, gestures and actions, and any other means to get their ideas across. This focus on the whole body enables students who struggle with reading to be active participants in Readers Theatre. For example, students reading a line that asks a question may shrug their shoulders; they may scowl and clench their fists if their role expresses anger.

During staging, the teacher or peers may help the ELL and the struggling reader adapt written materials to pictorial representations or diagrams that serve as mnemonic devices. If production elements such as sound, props, costumes, or artwork are used, ELLs may be able to offer suggestions based upon their culture and background knowledge. This international voice has the potential to add a great deal to the Readers Theatre performance in both sight and sound.

Rehearsal and Performance

Rehearsal for ELLs and struggling readers during the Readers Theatre process offers a unique forum for feedback and support. It is during rehearsal that the teacher or peers can work with these students on their reading fluency and comprehension of text. Because they lack the experience of processing the words and meaning of a text written in English automatically and fluently, it is difficult for ELLs and struggling readers to monitor their own reading and determine when they are successful. They are often so focused on decoding that it is difficult for them to comprehend the text and, most importantly for Readers Theatre, they lack the knowledge of how it sounds to read fluently and expressively. Therefore, the modeling of fluent reading and guided repeated readings is very important for ELLs and struggling readers. This modeling and guidance can be done by the teacher, by knowledgeable peers, and by volunteers. It is at this stage in the Readers Theatre process that the teacher should connect with the families of ELLs and struggling readers. Families have a wealth of culture and knowledge to share and would be an excellent audience for the final performance. They may also serve as bilingual aides, reading models, or guides who listen to a student's rereading and who work with them on pronunciation, fluency, and comprehension.

The model or guide must ensure that the ELL and the struggling reader is comfortable with his or her role and allow that student time for rereading. The model or guide may want to coach these students during rehearsal by positioning himself or herself behind each student. When the student reads, the guide is there to whisper words or comments if needed, ensuring for a successful and expressive reading.

Assessment

The retelling strategy noted in chapter 10 (see page 181) is especially valuable for use with the ELL and the struggling reader. The students may initially draw several pictures to retell what they have heard or read. When the student is able, that visual retelling should shift to a verbal retelling and eventually to a written retelling.

In addition to the retelling strategy, the teacher should keep a record of the ELLs and the struggling reader's increase in fluency and comprehension. Students' comprehension can be assessed through running records, retellings, one-on-one conferencing, anecdotal records, and checklists. Teachers may assess fluency by creating a graph of the student's reading words per minute (WPM). See Table 2 on page 181 in chapter 10 for a fluency graph with average reading rates.

From scripting to assessment, teachers must allow the ELL and the struggling reader more time for processing information. They should also provide time for brainstorming, allowing all students—but especially these students—the opportunity to discuss and question the process. If the teacher is able to minimize teacher talk, students may be encouraged to express their understanding of the text as well as the process through their own talk, role-play, and pictures. (The Visual Activities in chapter 7 are especially helpful here.)

RECOMMENDED EXTENSION ACTIVITIES

Audiotape Recording (page 137)

Choral Reading (page 137)

Partnered Oral Reading (page 139)

Puppetry (page 134)

Radio Drama (page 139)

Reading Buddy (page 140)

Visual Activities (pages 132–136)

Adaptations for Gifted Students

In referring to gifted students, we are talking about those who are highly competent readers, reading fluently and with high degrees of comprehension. They are linguistically talented and able to use and manipulate verbal and written language easily.

There are several ways gifted students may benefit from Readers Theatre. First, they may select or create scripts for their peers or individual groups, using their written skills to adapt existing text. Second, they may serve in a directorial role, creating staged pictures (backdrops, actions, gestures, etc.) and acting as the teacher's assistant. Finally, they might serve as a reading coach for individual students, their own group, all groups, or the class as a whole prior to performance. This would entail listening, modeling expressive reading, giving constructive feedback, and helping students explore the intellectual and emotional meanings of words.

Too often the gifted students are not acknowledged and are expected to fulfill only the basic requirements. The adaptability of Readers Theatre provides unique opportunities for these students to shine. They may serve as reading models, listening aides, researchers, script writers, public relations people, and critics. They may offer to the class their own expertise, support the teacher in producer/director efforts, and be a supportive audience member. In short, there are many places for the gifted student in Readers Theatre. Where they best fit should be, as always, determined by the teacher who knows them and their strengths.

REFERENCES

Cummins, J. (1989). *Empowering minority students*. Sacramento: California Association for Bilingual Education.

Echevarria, J., & Graves, A. (1998). *Sheltered content construction: Teaching English-language learners with diverse abilities*. Boston: Allyn & Bacon.

Goodman, J.A. (1978). *Teaching the total language with Readers Theatre*. (ERIC Document Reproductive Service No. ED191321)

Slavin, R.E. (1987). Ability grouping and student achievement: A best-evidence synthesis. *Review of Educational Research, 60*, 471–500.

Vacca, J., Vacca, R., Gove, M.K., Burkey, L.C., Lenhart, L.A., & McKeon, C.A. (2005). *Reading and learning to read* (6th ed.). Boston: Allyn & Bacon.

LITERATURE CITED

Slobodkina, E. (1947). *Caps for sale*. Reading, MA: Addison-Wesley.

Lynch, T. (2000). *Fables from Aesop* (p. 2). New York: Viking.

Accountability

The current climate in education is one focused on accountability. Educators must ensure that their teaching practices are derived from and supported by content-specific standards, and they often must prove the success of their practices through assessment of their students' performance. Fortunately, Readers Theatre, with its flexibility and its emphasis upon the skills of reading, speaking, and listening, is the type of practice that enables teachers to address many standards. Chapter 9, "Meeting the Standards Through Readers Theatre," illustrates how Readers Theatre meets state and national standards for literacy, specifically the International Reading Association and National Council of Teachers of English Standards for the English Language Arts, the California English-Language Arts Content Standards for Grade 6, and the New York State English Language Arts Core Curriculum. The assessment methods and forms discussed in chapter 10, "Assessing Readers Theatre," are directly related to the skills and objectives outlined in these standards.

Meeting the Standards Through Readers Theatre

Standards are created and ideally used as guideposts for educators to ensure that all students have the opportunities and resources necessary to meet the challenges of the 21st century. The promotion of literacy, with a focus on reading, writing, speaking, listening, and viewing, is an ongoing task because an individual's literacy abilities develop over a lifetime. Built upon a knowledge base of current research and practice, standards for literacy have been created by professional organizations and many states.

The understanding of and adherence to these standards has become even more important today because of the current climate of accountability. Teachers need to make clear that their teaching practices are derived from and supported by content-specific standards. The use of Readers Theatre, with its flexibility and its emphasis upon the skills of reading, speaking, and listening, is the type of practice that enables the teachers to address many standards.

In this chapter, the following standards will be introduced, and specific ways in which Readers Theatre meets those standards will be addressed.

- International Reading Association and National Council of Teachers of English Standards for the English Language Arts (found online at www.reading.org/resources/issues/reports/learning_standards.html)

- The California English-Language Arts Content Standards for Grade 6 (found online at www.cde.ca.gov/be/st/ss/engmain.asp)

- The New York State English Language Arts Core Curriculum (found online at www.emsc.nysed.gov/ciai/ela.html)

These standards also appear in Appendix D. Three matrixes are included in this chapter, providing a more detailed look at how Readers Theatre addresses standards of literacy. First, on page 162, Figure 18 provides a comprehensive matrix of standards addressed by Readers Theatre. The second matrix in Figure 19 (see page 165) organizes the standards met by Readers Theatre according to the specific schedule chosen: Two-Day Schedule, Five-Day Schedule, or Ten-Day Schedule (see chapter 3). Finally, the matrix in Figure 20 (see page 170) illustrates the standards met by the supplementary activities to Readers Theatre provided in chapter 7.

International Reading Association and National Council of Teachers of English Standards for the English Language Arts

Created with the assumption that literacy begins before school and continues long after an individual may finish school, these standards are valid for all ages. In the eyes of a middle school educator, each of the 12 IRA/NCTE standards can be met through the use of Readers Theatre.

IRA/NCTE Standards for the English Language Arts

1. Students read a wide range of print and nonprint texts to build an understanding of texts, of themselves, and of the cultures of the United States and the world; to acquire new information; to respond to the needs and demands of society and the workplace; and for personal fulfillment. Among these texts are fiction and nonfiction, classic and contemporary works.

2. Students read a wide range of literature from many periods in many genres to build an understanding of the many dimensions (e.g., philosophical, ethical, aesthetic) of human experience.

3. Students apply a wide range of strategies to comprehend, interpret, evaluate, and appreciate texts. They draw on their prior experience, their interactions with other readers and writers, their knowledge of word meaning and of other texts, their word identification strategies, and their understanding of textual features (e.g., sound–letter correspondence, sentence structure, context, graphics).

4. Students adjust their use of spoken, written, and visual language (e.g., conventions, style, vocabulary) to communicate effectively with a variety of audiences and for different purposes.

5. Students employ a wide range of strategies as they write and use different writing process elements appropriately to communicate with different audiences for a variety of purposes.

6. Students apply knowledge of language structure, language conventions (e.g., spelling and punctuation), media techniques, figurative language, and genre to create, critique, and discuss print and nonprint texts.

7. Students conduct research on issues and interests by generating ideas and questions, and by posing problems. They gather, evaluate, and synthesize data from a variety of sources (e.g., print and nonprint texts, artifacts, people) to communicate their discoveries in ways that suit their purpose and audience.

8. Students use a variety of technological and information resources (e.g., libraries, databases, computer networks, video) to gather and synthesize information and to create and communicate knowledge.

9. Students develop an understanding of and respect for diversity in language use, patterns, and dialects across cultures, ethnic groups, geographic regions, and social roles.

10. Students whose first language is not English make use of their first language to develop competency in the English language arts and to develop understanding of content across the curriculum.

11. Students participate as knowledgeable, reflective, creative, and critical members of a variety of literacy communities.

12. Students use spoken, written, and visual language to accomplish their own purposes (e.g., for learning, enjoyment, persuasion, and the exchange of information). (International Reading Association & National Council of Teachers of English, 1996)

One of the most valuable aspects of Readers Theatre is the need for students to read and reread both silently and orally as they prepare for a performance. As noted previously, the practice of repeated reading has many positive benefits. It also provides teachers the opportunity to enact IRA/NCTE Standard 3 and Standard 10 in their classrooms (see Figure 18 for a matrix of the standards). Standard 3, with its focus on effective reading strategies, is especially important for struggling readers at any level, but especially at the middle school level. It has relevance for all students because it helps to make the unconscious processes of reading conscious. Standard 10 focuses on ELL students' use of their first language and serves as a bridge to understanding English. For example, a teacher may provide ELL students with materials to read in their first language for Readers Theatre, then require that their group incorporate the content as well as some of the non-English language into the performance, enabling students to also address Standard 9—an understanding and respect for diversity in language use.

In creating a script for Readers Theatre, students may use "a wide range of print and nonprint texts" (Standard 1) as well as "a wide range of literature from many periods in many genres" (Standard 2). Nonprint materials include the use of photographs, posters, and other visuals. Because of its adaptability, Readers Theatre may hone in on specific cultures, concepts, and information, allowing for integration in all content areas. A Readers Theatre project on immigration, for example, may be a full experience for students, beginning with researching the topic of immigration and using "a variety of technology and information resources" (Standard 8) to access the information they would need for their script.

Aside from the reading of text, students may also create scripts for Readers Theatre. It must be noted, however, that the creation of a script within the context of Readers Theatre is usually not the writing of a script but refers to the adapting and connecting necessary to bring existing text into script format. This is more of a cut-and-paste process. Student-adapted scripts address Standards 5, 6, 7, and 12; they "employ a wide range of strategies as they write" (Standard 5), they "apply knowledge of language structure, language conventions" (Standard 6), they "conduct research on issues" (Standard 7), and they "use written language...to accomplish their own purposes" (Standard 12). However, beyond

Figure 18. Matrix of Standards Addressed by Readers Theatre

Standard	IRA/NCTE Standards for English Language Arts												California English-Language Arts Content Standards								NY State English Language Arts Core Curriculum															
													Reading			Writing		Written and Oral Language	Listening and Speaking		Reading				Writing				Listening				Speaking			
	1	2	3	4	5	6	7	8	9	10	11	12	1.0	2.0	3.0	1.0	2.0	1.0	1.0	2.0	1	2	3	4	1	2	3	4	1	2	3	4	1	2	3	4
Reading																																				
Read wide range of print and nonprint	✓													✓	✓						✓															
Read wide range of literature from many periods in many genres		✓												✓	✓						✓															
Apply a wide range of strategies			✓										✓								✓	✓	✓													
Conduct research							✓							✓							✓	✓														
Use variety of technological and information resources								✓													✓		✓													
Participate as members of literary communities											✓													✓												
Writing																																				
Adjust use of written language to communicate effectively				✓												✓		✓							✓	✓	✓	✓								
Employ wide range of strategies					✓											✓		✓							✓	✓	✓									
Apply knowledge of language structures and conventions						✓										✓	✓	✓							✓	✓	✓									
Conduct research							✓		✓								✓	✓							✓	✓	✓									
ELL: Use of first language to develop competency and comprehension of English										✓																✓	✓	✓								
Participate as member of literary communities																											✓									
Use written language to accomplish purposes												✓													✓	✓	✓									

Figure 18. Matrix of Standards Addressed by Readers Theatre (continued)

Standard	IRA/NCTE Standards for English Language Arts												California English-Language Arts Content Standards								NY State English Language Arts Core Curriculum																
													Reading			Writing		Written and Oral Language	Listening and Speaking		Reading				Writing				Listening				Speaking			
	1	2	3	4	5	6	7	8	9	10	11	12	1.0	2.0	3.0	1.0	2.0	1.0	1.0	2.0	1	2	3	4	1	2	3	4	1	2	3	4	1	2	3	4
Listening and Speaking																																				
Adjust use of spoken language to communicate effectively				✓														✓	✓	✓													✓	✓	✓	✓
ELL: Use of first language to develop competency and comprehension of English										✓								✓	✓														✓	✓	✓	✓
Participate as member of literary community											✓								✓										✓	✓	✓	✓	✓	✓	✓	✓
Use spoken language to accomplish purposes												✓							✓										✓	✓	✓	✓	✓	✓	✓	✓
Other																																				
Develop understanding and respect for diversity in language									✓															✓				✓				✓				✓

the creation of introductions, transitions, and conclusions, writing opportunities in Readers Theatre are usually limited because of time constraints within the classroom.

The shorter the time frame for Readers Theatre, the more teacher-directed it is, with the teacher responsible for creating and assigning scripts, groups, and individual roles, and leading the discussion with students about their reading, staging, and performance. Conversely, if the script is longer or if students have experience with Readers Theatre (thus making the process more student-directed), a longer time frame is necessary or possible (see Figure 19). An extended activity may focus on students' reflective writing (Standard 11) or their response to the process or performance of Readers Theatre.

Finally, the performance aspect of Readers Theatre, with students preparing for a public presentation and speaking to an audience, allows them to "adjust their use of spoken…language to communicate effectively" (Standard 4) and to "use spoken language…to accomplish their own purposes" (Standard 12). Students become a part of a literacy community through their performance, and as they perform to a variety of audiences (peers, students in other grades, parents), they become active "members of a variety of literacy communities" (Standard 11). This performance aspect also addresses the viewing inherent in communication today as noted in Standard 4 (visual language), Standard 7 (nonprint text, artifacts, people), Standard 8 (video), and Standard 12 (visual language).

California English-Language Arts Content Standards for Grade 6

The content standards for California (California Department of Education, 1998) focus on reading, writing, written and oral English language conventions, and listening and speaking. Most of these general standards have specific subtopics which clarify that standards use and provide a focus for instruction. For example, in Reading 2.0: Reading Comprehension (see below), the subtopic "Structural features of informational materials" refers to the organization of nonfiction or informational text or other print materials. This organization alludes to specific text structure, such as description, sequence, or compare and contrast, and may also include the use of an index or glossary, text features unique to nonfiction. For more details on each subtopic, see the full text for the standards online at www.cde.ca.gov/be/st/ss/engmain.asp.

Reading

1.0 Word Analysis, Fluency, and Systematic Vocabulary Development

Students use their knowledge of word origins and word relationships, as well as historical and literary context clues, to determine the meaning of specialized

Figure 19. Matrix of Standards Addressed by Readers Theatre, Organized by Two-Day, Five-Day, and Ten-Day Schedules

	IRA/NCTE Standards For English Language Arts												California English-Language Arts Content Standards								NY State English Language Arts Core Curriculum															
													Reading			Writing		Written and Oral Language	Listening and Speaking		Reading				Writing				Listening				Speaking			
Standard	1	2	3	4	5	6	7	8	9	10	11	12	1.0	2.0	3.0	1.0	2.0	1.0	1.0	2.0	1	2	3	4	1	2	3	4	1	2	3	4	1	2	3	4
Two-Day Schedule																																				
Day 1	✓		✓									✓	✓	✓	✓			✓	✓	✓	✓	✓								✓			✓	✓		
Day 2		✓	✓	✓							✓	✓	✓	✓	✓			✓	✓	✓	✓	✓		✓					✓						✓	✓
Five-Day Schedule																																				
Day 1	✓	✓	✓	✓							✓	✓	✓	✓				✓	✓	✓	✓	✓							✓	✓	✓	✓	✓	✓	✓	✓
Day 2		✓	✓	✓		✓			✓	✓	✓	✓	✓	✓	✓			✓	✓	✓	✓	✓	✓	✓					✓	✓	✓	✓	✓	✓	✓	✓
Day 3		✓	✓	✓		✓			✓	✓	✓	✓	✓	✓	✓			✓	✓	✓	✓	✓	✓	✓					✓	✓	✓	✓	✓	✓	✓	✓
Day 4		✓	✓	✓							✓	✓	✓	✓	✓			✓	✓	✓	✓								✓	✓	✓	✓	✓	✓	✓	✓
Day 5		✓	✓	✓							✓	✓	✓	✓	✓			✓	✓	✓									✓	✓	✓	✓	✓	✓	✓	✓
Ten-Day Schedule																																				
Day 1	✓	✓	✓	✓					✓	✓	✓	✓	✓	✓	✓			✓	✓	✓	✓	✓	✓	✓					✓	✓	✓	✓	✓	✓	✓	✓
Day 2		✓	✓	✓					✓	✓	✓	✓	✓	✓	✓			✓	✓	✓	✓	✓	✓	✓					✓	✓	✓	✓	✓	✓	✓	✓
Day 3		✓	✓	✓		✓					✓	✓	✓	✓	✓			✓	✓	✓	✓	✓	✓	✓					✓	✓	✓	✓	✓	✓	✓	✓
Day 4		✓	✓	✓		✓	✓				✓	✓	✓	✓	✓			✓	✓	✓	✓	✓	✓	✓					✓	✓	✓	✓	✓	✓	✓	✓
Day 5		✓	✓	✓		✓	✓	✓			✓	✓	✓	✓	✓			✓	✓	✓	✓	✓	✓	✓					✓	✓	✓	✓	✓	✓	✓	✓
Day 6		✓	✓	✓		✓	✓	✓			✓	✓	✓	✓	✓			✓	✓	✓	✓	✓	✓	✓					✓	✓	✓	✓	✓	✓	✓	✓
Day 7		✓	✓	✓		✓	✓	✓			✓	✓	✓	✓	✓			✓	✓	✓	✓	✓	✓	✓					✓	✓	✓	✓	✓	✓	✓	✓
Day 8		✓	✓	✓		✓	✓	✓			✓	✓	✓	✓	✓			✓	✓	✓	✓	✓	✓	✓					✓	✓	✓	✓	✓	✓	✓	✓
Day 9		✓	✓	✓							✓	✓	✓	✓	✓			✓	✓	✓	✓	✓	✓	✓					✓	✓	✓	✓	✓	✓	✓	✓
Day 10		✓	✓	✓							✓	✓	✓	✓	✓			✓	✓	✓	✓	✓	✓	✓					✓	✓	✓	✓	✓	✓	✓	✓

vocabulary and to understand the precise meaning of grade-level–appropriate words.

- *Word Recognition*
- *Vocabulary and Concept Development*

2.0 Reading Comprehension (Focus on Informational Materials)

Students read and understand grade-level–appropriate material. They describe and connect the essential ideas, arguments, and perspectives of the text by using their knowledge of text structure, organization, and purpose.

- *Structural Features of Informational Materials*
- *Comprehension and Analysis of Grade-Level–Appropriate Text*
- *Expository Critique*

3.0 Literary Response and Analysis

Students read and respond to historically or culturally significant works of literature that reflect and enhance their studies of history and social science. They clarify the ideas and connect them to other literary works.

- *Structural Features of Literature*
- *Narrative Analysis of Grade-Level–Appropriate Text*
- *Literary Criticism*

Reprinted, by permission, California Department of Education. This grant of permission does not constitute endorsement.

There are three main components under reading, and each one is easily met through Readers Theatre. The first component focuses on the reading process, "Word Analysis, Fluency, and Systematic Vocabulary Development" (Reading, 1.0) and is addressed easily by Readers Theatre because its focus is reading fluency and word recognition. The second component, "Reading Comprehension (Focus on Informational Materials)" (Reading, 2.0), may be met through the use of nonfiction materials as shown in chapter 5 and Appendix B. Then, the third component, "Literary Response and Analysis" (Reading, 3.0), is an integral part of Readers Theatre because students must analyze the literature they are reading with performance as one form of their response.

Writing

1.0 Writing Strategies

Students write clear, coherent, and focused essays. The writing exhibits students' awareness of the audience and purpose. Essays contain formal introductions, supporting evidence, and conclusions. Students progress through the stages of the writing process as needed.

- *Organization and Focus*
- *Research and Technology*
- *Revising and Evaluating Writing*

2.0 Writing Applications (Genres and Their Characteristics)

Students write narrative, expository, persuasive, and descriptive texts of at least 500 to 700 words in each genre. Student writing demonstrates a command of standard American English and the research, organizational, and drafting strategies outlined in Writing Standard 1.0.

Reprinted, by permission, California Department of Education. This grant of permission does not constitute endorsement.

As noted previously, Readers Theatre offers limited opportunities for writing. However, the standard for writing may be met through the use of Readers Theatre if time permits and if students adapt the text to script format themselves by developing introductions, transitions, and conclusions. The two main components under writing include "Writing Strategies" (Writing, 1.0) and "Writing Applications (Genres and Their Characteristics)" (Writing, 2.0).

"Writing Strategies" refer to the clarity, focus, and organization of students' writing, their use of the writing process, and their awareness of audience and purpose. It also relates to the research and use of technology inherent in much of students' writing. Each of these comes into play when adapting a text to script format for a performance (editing or creating meaningful and logical speaker roles and deleting extraneous material). Writing may also include summarizing sections of text and substituting or paraphrasing words more familiar to an audience. In addition, students may write an introduction, many transitions, and a conclusion to the script. Although writing is not the focus of Readers Theatre, students certainly benefit from these writing exercises. However, because of limited class time, the teacher is usually responsible for the adapting of a text to script format or the selection of an existing script.

A Readers Theatre script must be clearly written if it is to be understood by the audience. Students work through the writing process as a group with the teacher's feedback and a focus on revising and evaluating to ensure that their written script facilitates a successful performance. Finally, because performance serves as a strong motivator for students, they are very aware of audience in their writing.

The second component, "Writing Applications" (Writing, 2.0), refers to students' writing of "narrative, expository, persuasive, and descriptive text" and to their command of standard English. The adaptability of Readers Theatre allows for each of these genres to be used in the performance text. Narrative (fiction) and expository or informational text (nonfiction) are noted in chapters 5 and 6, respectively. A narrative text, with the adapted script for performance, tells a story using narrative devices. This includes dialogue and persuasive evidence to validate the story's conclusion. Narrative devices also support the main idea with description as spoken by the narrator or one of the characters.

Written introductions, transitions, and conclusions in the script, whether fiction or nonfiction, often provide descriptions.

Written and Oral English Language Conventions

1.0 Written and Oral English Language Conventions

Students write and speak with a command of standard English conventions appropriate to this grade level.

- *Sentence Structure*

- *Grammar*

- *Punctuation*

- *Capitalization*

- *Spelling*

Reprinted, by permission, California Department of Education. This grant of permission does not constitute endorsement.

The California English-Language Arts Content Standards are unique in that they address a component called "Written and Oral English Language Conventions" which focuses on students' ability to write and speak standard English. This standard addresses mechanics such as sentence structure, grammar, punctuation, capitalization, and spelling. One of the benefits of Readers Theatre is students' exposure to quality literature that models these mechanics. Again, if time permits and students are able to adapt a text to script format themselves, they will address the mechanics of standard English in their writing and in their oral performance.

Listening and Speaking

1.0 Listening and Speaking Strategies

Students deliver focused, coherent presentations that convey ideas clearly and relate to the background and interests of the audience. They evaluate the content of oral communication.

- *Comprehension*

- *Organization and Delivery of Oral Communication*

- *Analysis and Evaluation of Oral and Media Communications*

2.0 Speaking Applications (Genres and Their Characteristics)

Students deliver well-organized formal presentations employing traditional rhetorical strategies (e.g., narration, exposition, persuasion, description). Student speaking demonstrates a command of standard American English and the organizational and delivery strategies outlined in Listening and Speaking Standard 1.0.

Reprinted, by permission, California Department of Education. This grant of permission does not constitute endorsement.

The standards of listening and speaking are combined and have two main components. The first is "Listening and Speaking Strategies" where students deliver "focused, coherent presentations" and evaluate oral communication (Listening and Speaking, 1.0). The strength of Readers Theatre as an instructional strategy lies in its attention to the language arts skills of speaking and listening. Students need to understand what they are reading aloud and to be aware that their listeners (the audience) also understand. The scripting of text in Readers Theatre allows for specific "organization and delivery of oral communication" (California Department of Education, 1998). Rehearsals, an inherent part of Readers Theatre, offer a forum for the analysis and evaluation of this communication by providing the teacher and audience with many opportunities to give feedback, and the presenters a chance for reflection and self-assessment.

The second main component is "Speaking Applications (Genres and Their Characteristics)" where students deliver a variety of genre presentations, demonstrating a command of standard English (Listening and Speaking, 2.0). As previously noted in the writing standard 2.0, Reader Theatre supplies text of "narration, exposition, persuasion, and description" that is read aloud to an audience (California Department of Education, 1998).

Many of the supplementary activities in chapter 7 address these listening and speaking standards, and the matrix in Figure 20 illustrates this. Because Readers Theatre focuses on the oral reading of a script, it has the capacity to address these components as it did in the writing standard. In addition, Readers Theatre is a performance which indicates not only the need for a "focused, coherent presentation" but also the existence of an audience—listeners who hear, evaluate, and attempt to understand the oral performance of a written text.

New York State English Language Arts Core Curriculum

There are four standards for the English language arts core curriculum of New York State (New York State Education Department, 1996). Each addresses reading, writing, listening, and speaking.

New York State English Language Arts Core Curriculum

Reading, Writing, Listening, and Speaking

1. Students will read, write, listen, and speak for information and understanding.

2. Students will read, write, listen, and speak for literary response and expression.

3. Students will read, write, listen, and speak for critical analysis and evaluation.

Figure 20. Matrix of Standards Addressed by Readers Theatre Supplementary Activities

Standard	IRA/NCTE Standards for English Language Arts												California English-Language Arts Content Standards								NY State English Language Arts Core Curriculum															
													Reading			Writing		Written and Oral Language	Listening and Speaking		Reading				Writing				Listening				Speaking			
	1	2	3	4	5	6	7	8	9	10	11	12	1.0	2.0	3.0	1.0	2.0	1.0	1.0	2.0	1	2	3	4	1	2	3	4	1	2	3	4	1	2	3	4
Character Profile			✓	✓	✓		✓					✓		✓	✓	✓	✓	✓			✓	✓	✓	✓	✓	✓	✓									
Letter to the Character			✓	✓	✓		✓		✓			✓		✓		✓	✓	✓			✓	✓	✓	✓	✓	✓	✓									
New Endings			✓	✓	✓	✓	✓		✓			✓	✓	✓		✓		✓	✓	✓	✓	✓	✓	✓		✓	✓	✓		✓	✓	✓	✓	✓	✓	✓
Research Project			✓	✓	✓	✓	✓	✓				✓	✓	✓	✓	✓		✓			✓	✓	✓	✓	✓	✓	✓	✓								
Inside the Character			✓	✓	✓	✓	✓	✓	✓			✓		✓		✓		✓			✓	✓	✓	✓	✓	✓	✓									
Mural	✓		✓	✓		✓						✓		✓	✓			✓			✓	✓	✓	✓												
Poster			✓	✓	✓	✓						✓		✓	✓	✓		✓			✓	✓	✓	✓												
Puppetry			✓	✓	✓				✓	✓	✓	✓	✓	✓				✓		✓	✓	✓	✓	✓					✓	✓	✓	✓	✓	✓	✓	✓
Setting the Scene			✓	✓	✓							✓		✓		✓	✓	✓			✓	✓	✓			✓	✓									
Story Sequence Strip			✓	✓								✓	✓	✓	✓	✓		✓			✓	✓	✓	✓		✓	✓									
Video Production			✓	✓		✓		✓		✓		✓	✓	✓				✓		✓	✓	✓	✓	✓	✓				✓	✓	✓	✓	✓	✓	✓	✓
Audiotape Recording			✓	✓		✓						✓	✓	✓				✓		✓	✓	✓	✓	✓	✓				✓	✓	✓	✓	✓	✓	✓	✓
Choral Reading			✓	✓					✓	✓		✓	✓	✓				✓		✓	✓	✓	✓	✓	✓				✓	✓	✓	✓	✓	✓	✓	✓
Dialogue Practice			✓	✓					✓	✓		✓	✓	✓				✓		✓	✓	✓	✓	✓					✓	✓	✓	✓	✓	✓	✓	✓
The Family Connection			✓	✓		✓						✓	✓	✓	✓			✓		✓	✓	✓	✓	✓	✓				✓	✓	✓	✓	✓	✓	✓	✓
Partnered Oral Reading			✓	✓								✓	✓	✓				✓		✓	✓	✓	✓	✓	✓				✓	✓	✓	✓	✓	✓	✓	✓
Radio Drama			✓	✓		✓			✓			✓	✓	✓				✓		✓	✓	✓	✓	✓					✓	✓	✓	✓	✓	✓	✓	✓
Real People, Real Stories	✓	✓	✓	✓								✓	✓	✓				✓			✓	✓							✓	✓	✓	✓	✓	✓	✓	✓
Reading Buddy			✓	✓			✓		✓	✓		✓	✓	✓		✓		✓		✓	✓								✓	✓	✓	✓	✓	✓	✓	✓
Role Playing			✓	✓		✓	✓					✓						✓		✓			✓	✓									✓	✓	✓	✓
Vocabulary Race			✓	✓	✓	✓	✓					✓	✓	✓		✓		✓		✓	✓		✓	✓					✓	✓	✓	✓	✓	✓	✓	✓
Who Am I?			✓	✓			✓					✓	✓	✓	✓			✓		✓	✓		✓						✓	✓	✓	✓	✓	✓	✓	✓

4. Students will read, write, listen, and speak for social interaction.

Reprinted with the permission of the New York State Education Department.

Readers Theatre has the potential to address each of these four standards. For example, the language arts involved in gaining information and understanding that information (Standard 1) are enacted through an adaptation of material to a written script, repeated readings and rehearsal of that script, the oral reading or speaking of that script in performance, and the listening of the audience.

Literary response and expression (Standard 2) is evident in Readers Theatre because of the nature of its process; that is, Readers Theatre encourages students to respond to literature in a variety of ways, specifically to the content, emotions, and production elements such as visuals, sound, and staging. Individual students may respond through a journal or other reflective writing activities regarding their understanding and feelings of the process or the performance of Readers Theatre. Group members respond verbally, visually, and actively to the text selected to perform. This response may be the way in which the text is adapted to a script as well as students' oral expressive reading of that script. Performers respond to the audience, and the audience responds to the performance.

Just as the process of Readers Theatre facilitates literary response and expression, it also engages students in a critical analysis and evaluation (Standard 3) of what they are reading, writing, listening, and speaking. The oral performance, preceded by necessary analytical readings and editing of the script, gives both the performers and the audience an opportunity to evaluate what is heard. Finally, social interaction (Standard 4) is inherent in the group membership, roles, and interaction required in Readers Theatre. Because the final performance provides a meaningful context for students' work and presents that work in a public forum, they are more motivated to work together for the common goal of a successful performance. The rehearsals provide a structured forum where constructive criticism within each group is sought, confidence is gained, and a higher comfort level for all group members is often achieved.

Literacy standards, as guideposts for teachers to ensure that all their students have the opportunities and resources needed in reading, writing, listening, and speaking, are addressed through the use of Readers Theatre in the classroom. Listening and speaking skills, often neglected or at least deemed difficult to assess, are the skills upon which Readers Theatre heavily relies. In using quality literature, in promoting group collaboration, and in focusing on fluent reading with the end result of performance, teachers may create through Readers Theatre a place where all readers are successful, students are motivated, and standards are met.

REFERENCES

California Department of Education. (1998). Grade Six. In *English-Language Arts Content Standards for California Public Schools, Kindergarten Through Grade Twelve*. Sacramento, CA: Author. Retrieved December 6, 2006, from http://www.cde.ca.gov/be/st/ss/enggrade6.asp

International Reading Association & National Council of Teachers of English. (1996). *Standards for the English language arts*. Newark, DE; Urbana, IL: Authors. Retrieved December 6, 2006, from http://www.reading.org/resources/issues/reports/learning_standards.html

New York State Education Department. (1996). *Learning Standards for English Language Arts*. Albany, NY: Author. Retrieved December 6, 2006, from http://www.emsc.nysed.gov/ciai/ela.html

CHAPTER 10

Assessing Readers Theatre

As with any viable activity in the classroom, assessment depends upon the specific objectives of that activity. Readers Theatre leaves a rich trail of students' reading, writing, listening, speaking, and viewing skills, and its assessment is directly related to the objectives focused on these skills. Both formative assessment (ensuring that students learn better and teachers teach more effectively) and summative assessment (translating student growth to a grade) can be used to assess each of these skills.

This chapter provides assessments for the core components of the Readers Theatre process. First, assessment instruments and methods for the process of Readers Theatre as a whole are discussed. This is followed by an identification and discussion of the assessment forms and methods for more specific components of Readers Theatre. Reproducible assessment forms are provided in Appendix C.

For students to be successful, they must know what they have to do to be successful, particularly if they are engaged in a new venture. Therefore, it is recommended that the assessment (rubric, checklist, etc.) be given to students before they begin the process of Readers Theatre.

General Readers Theatre Assessments

The final Readers Theatre performance has been successfully performed. Students have worked hard individually and as a group. Each student has fulfilled specific roles and participated in the final performance. The next challenge is to determine how all the work students have done translates into a grade.

Because Readers Theatre is a complex activity promoting a variety of skills and because students have worked individually and as a group, it is essential that a grade reflects this variety. Assessment for the overall process of Readers Theatre may focus on the group process, the individual role, the group performance, and the individual performance. The following breakdown of points is one way to highlight the process of Readers Theatre and various components of the process as well as honoring both the individual and the group.

Group Process 20%

Individual Role 30%

Group Performance 20%

Individual Performance......30%

This breakdown allows for more points to be given to the individual grade than the group grade; however, the percentages can easily be changed by the teacher.

The group process component would include group dynamics as well as work that may be done within the group, such as script development and staging. The individual role focuses on each student's specific role within the group. It may be formalized with specific expectations for each role noted in a handout or it may be a general overview of the student's participation and responsibility taken within the group.

Group performance refers to the group's rehearsals and final performance. The individual performance, including rehearsals and final performance, is probably the area that can be most comprehensively assessed. It looks at the individual student's speaking and listening skills, reading fluency and comprehension, performance, attitude toward reading, and reflection or self-assessment.

Assessment Instruments

The "Readers Theatre Preparation Chart" in Figure 21 focuses on the individual student and his or her role and participation during the process of Readers

Figure 21. Readers Theatre Preparation Chart

	Student Name	Attendance: Student is prompt and regularly attends classes during preparation days.	Preparation: Student is prepared for class with required class materials.	Listening Skills: Student listens when others talk, both in group and in class.	Engagement: Student proactively participates by asking questions and offering ideas.	Anecdotal Record: Any observations made during class or group work.
Date						

Theatre. Including attendance, preparation, listening skills, and engagement, it does not look at the student's performance. This chart allows the teacher to observe and easily assess all students working independently or within their groups with a check in the appropriate box. It also provides space for brief comments the teacher may wish to make. The daily use of such a chart will provide adequate information if the teacher wishes to give an individual grade. This chart format is easily adaptable by changing the headings and their specific information to address what the teacher would like to observe and assess.

The "Rubric for Readers Theatre" in Figure 22 looks at both the individual and group performance. This rubric may be used to give feedback to each group

Figure 22. Rubric for Readers Theatre

While observing students during rehearsals and performances, the following are focus areas for assessing individual students.

Name _____ Date _____

4	3
Individual	**Individual**
• Student always speaks clearly.	• Student often speaks clearly.
• Student always speaks at an appropriate pace.	• Student often speaks at an appropriate pace.
• Student always speaks fluently, using appropriate intonation, expression, and emphasis.	• Student often speaks fluently, using appropriate intonation, expression and emphasis.
• Student contributed appropriately to this production.	• Student usually contributed appropriately to this production.
Group	**Group**
• Students' script accurately retells the text the group chose.	• Students' script retells the text the group chose with only a few inaccuracies.
• Students prepared and used appropriate props.	• Students prepared and used appropriate props.
• Students encouraged participation from the audience.	• Students participated actively in participation and rehearsals.
• Students participated actively in preparation and rehearsals.	

2	1
Individual	**Individual**
• Student rarely speaks clearly.	• Student is unable to be heard or is difficult to understand.
• Student rarely speaks at an appropriate pace.	• Student uses no intonation, expression, or emphasis in reading.
• Student rarely speaks fluently, using appropriate intonation, expression, and emphasis.	• Student rarely contributed appropriately to this production.
• Student contributed appropriately to this production on occasion.	
Group	**Group**
• Students' script that retells the **text the group** chose has several inaccuracies and/or is difficult to understand.	• Students' script that retells the text the group chose is completely inaccurate.
• Students struggle to participate actively in preparation and rehearsals.	• Students rarely participated actively in preparation and rehearsals.

as they rehearse or may be an assessment tool for their final performance. The rubric looks at the individual's speaking skills and overall participation and also at the group's scripting, staging, and performance. Any of these descriptions may be changed and adapted to individual classroom needs. For example, a teacher interested in students' attitudes, group dynamics, or critical thinking skills may adapt language to reflect these criteria.

The "Grading Checklist for Presentations" in Figure 23 focuses on poetry presentations of the group but is easily adapted to fiction or nonfiction presentations. It would be used by the teacher as students work together to prepare for their performance ("participation"). It would also evaluate the

Figure 23. Grading Checklist for Presentations

Name _____ Class Period _____

Group # _____ Theme _____

Group Members _____

Poem #1 _____

Poem #2 _____

1. **Performance Script (15 points)** _____
   Turn in one copy for teacher and use copies to read from for your presentations.
   Script should include: group number; group members' names; theme; poem titles and authors; who says what in what order; description of background, props, music selection.

2. **Participation (15 points)** _____
   All group members participate in the planning, organizing, rehearsal, and performance.
   Participation is equally distributed (one member is not clearly doing all the work while the others do less).

3. **Visual Aid (15 points)** _____
   Backdrop related to theme
   Costumes/clothing
   Other items, including props that add to presentation

4. **Music Selection (15 points)** _____
   Appropriate for poems and/or theme
   Adds to but does not distract from performance

5. **Performance (40 points)** _____
   States theme, titles, and authors of poems
   Tone/atmosphere is appropriate for poems
   Appears to understand the poems' meanings
   Short interpretation of poems and their relationship to the theme

Comments:

script, staging ("visual aid" and "music selection"), and the "performance" according to the criteria noted. The points given may be changed as well to reflect what the teacher wishes to assess.

Other Readers Theatre Assessment Methods

Other methods to generally assess Readers Theatre are conferences, student self-assessment, and portfolios. Each allows the teacher and student to consider what is happening or what has happened during the group work, scripting, staging, rehearsal, and performance of Readers Theatre.

Conferences. Conferences allow the teacher to meet one-on-one with individual students or to meet with the group to discuss, clarify, direct, and provide feedback. Conferences provide for focused interaction between teachers and their students and also allow the teacher to address issues of concern. Initially, a whole-class discussion about Readers Theatre to establish the ground rules, text selection, roles, and so forth is necessary. However, after students begin to work in groups, it will also be necessary to conduct periodic conferences with each group. During these group conferences, the teacher should monitor the group's dynamics, observe if students are effectively fulfilling their roles, and determine if students understand the text in terms of both surface-level understanding and deep understanding. The teacher also has an opportunity at this time to help students problem solve, to model specific components of the Readers Theatre process, and to facilitate students' communication of the text through their written script and expressive reading. If individual students need more help, more focus, or more support, a short one-on-one conference is beneficial as long as it is not used as a disciplinary measure.

Student Self-Assessments. Student self-assessment requires students to reflect and think critically about their own actions and talk. Allowing students to assess themselves helps to create ownership in what they have accomplished. It also provides the teacher with valuable feedback. Student self-assessment could be in the form of a checklist or rating scale that each student fills out (see Figures 21, 22, and 23 for criteria regarding process and performance that may be used for student self-assessment). It may also be a one-page handout that students respond to with or without identifying themselves. Some possible prompts for this handout include the following:

Prompts for Student Self-Assessment

1. What was the best part about Readers Theatre? Why?

2. What was the most difficult part of Readers Theatre? Why?

3. I like Readers Theatre because _____.

4. Readers Theatre is hard for me because _____.

5. This was my role: _____. I could have done better _____.

   I was really good _____.

6. As a group member, I was successful at _____.

7. As a group member, I could have been better at _____.

8. My group worked together successfully to _____.

9. My group was not very good at _____.

10. My performance in Readers Theatre _____.

11. One thing I understand about _____ is _____.

12. One thing I do not understand about _____ is _____.

If students are asked to assess their group, the teacher should provide general prompts such as the following:

1. My group worked together successfully to _____ because _____.

2. My group was not very good at _____ because _____.

Such prompts may induce students to think more critically and help reduce personal criticism (see Appendix C for reproducible versions of these prompts).

Portfolios. The portfolio provides documentation of what the student has done and what the student thinks; its strength lies in highlighting students' accomplishments and growth over the school year. Each student should have a performance folder that includes a script marked with his or her roles and actions, a final performance script, and a list of individual accomplishments in the group role. If portfolios are in use in the classroom, a teacher may require students to keep a Readers Theatre log to document their thoughts, their understanding of the process, or to answer teacher-selected prompts ("What is your role and how is it difficult?"). A videotape of each group's final performance serves as an excellent artifact for the students' portfolios and could be used for other classes as a model of the Readers Theatre process, as a vehicle to showcase students' accomplishments, or simply for enjoyment and sharing. Videos may also serve as a significant contribution to an open house or a parent–teacher conference.

Teachers should select the assessment tools that best suit their teaching and their students' learning. It is recommended, however, that a variety of tools be used during the Readers Theatre process because each tool will highlight students' different strengths. The assessment tools discussed here are meant to serve as templates, with teachers plugging in the content or specific components they wish to assess.

Assessing Specific Components of Readers Theatre

Readers Theatre is a process composed of the following elements:

1. group dynamics
2. reading fluency
3. reading comprehension
4. script development
5. staging (which includes creating the whole picture; postures, gestures, and actions; and the design and execution of production elements such as sound, props, costumes, and backdrops)
6. rehearsal and the final performance
7. speaking and listening skills
8. students' attitudes toward reading
9. critical thinking

Each of these components can be effectively evaluated by using the appropriate assessment instruments.

Group Dynamics

Group dynamics focus on how a group functions throughout the process of Readers Theatre (see chapter 2, page 19). An excellent way to assess group dynamics is through observation and anecdotal records of those observations.

Observation is a form of constant informal assessment. As the teacher moves about the room, he or she may have a clipboard and paper to jot down notes throughout the class period. These anecdotal records are an open-ended documentation of what is seen and heard and may be global (whole classroom or group) and specific (individual students). A focus is helpful, however, so a teacher may choose to observe specific groups as they discuss their scripts or may observe several individuals each day and note important comments made as well as each student's actions and attitudes.

The teacher may also want to document his or her own interactions with groups and individuals, especially as the Readers Theatre process moves into rehearsal and performance, with such comments as "I can't hear you" and "If you are so sad, what would your voice sound like? How would your body move?" Done over a period of time to allow for patterns to emerge, anecdotal records are a valuable assessment tool that often best supplement other forms of assessment. Figure 24 provides sample anecdotal records of individual students.

Figure 24. Anecdotal Records of Individual Students

Focus: *Group dynamics*   Date: 3/21/05

Group A: *All members on task and very excited. ER taking lead. LS: "I can't wait for the class to hear this."*

Group B: *MT not participating. Others urging her to practice. JN: "Come on, we all have to do this. It's important."*

Focus: *Student BD*   Date: 3/22/05

BD prepared and motivated but seems distracted by costumes. Has brought in extra material and is trying to convince group that all should wear hats. When asked about her practice of reading role, she said, "It's OK. Maybe I should read it over again." Did so, and wearing hat, was very expressive. Maybe this costume does help with reading!

Reading Fluency

Reading fluency means that students are decoding accurately, phrasing correctly, and using the proper intonation. Their reading is smooth and expressive. Anecdotal records (see Figure 24) help to document if an individual student's reading is fluent, and reading fluency can also be assessed through the use of running records, a notation system developed by Clay (1985) with which most reading specialists and primary-grade teachers are familiar. The use of running records to assess students' reading fluency in Readers Theatre is recommended for those who are knowledgeable in its use and find it productive. In addition to providing data on a student's fluency, this one-on-one holistic recording of a student's ability to read text helps to evaluate text difficulty and monitor the student's progress. If students are reading fluently, they are reading with a high level of accuracy, comprehension, and confidence. Therefore, comparing students' reading rates with the following table (Table 2) is another way to assess fluency.

The table notes each grade level with its corresponding rate of words per minute read with comprehension. A teacher times the student reading a specific text with a predetermined number of words and decides if he or she is reading on grade level. For examples, if an eighth grader reads 410 words in two minutes and, after brief questioning, shows an understanding of what was read, the teacher can determine that he or she was reading on grade level.

Another appropriate assessment is the "Reading Fluency Checklist" in Figure 25. This checklist, of use with any text genre, may be used before the initial rehearsal and after the dress rehearsal to document an individual student's fluency.

Table 2. Average Reading Rates

	Grade Level											
	1	2	3	4	5	6	7	8	9	10	11	12
Rate of Words per Minute (WPM) with comprehension	80	115	140	160	175	185	195	205	215	225	235	250

Adapted from Kibby & Dechert, 2003.

Figure 25. Reading Fluency Checklist

Student Name _____ Date _____

The student:	Yes	Sometimes	No
1. Reads word by word.			
2. Reads with long pauses between words.			
3. Misses many words.			
4. Reads with little expression.			
5. Reads with little evidence of the use of punctuation.			
6. Has a reading rate that is slow and laborious.			

Reading Comprehension

A variety of instruments are discussed in the following section for assessing students' reading comprehension: a retelling form, comprehension checklists, and graphic organizers.

Retelling Form. If a teacher wishes to assess students' reading comprehension, the retelling strategy embodied in Figure 26 is simple and effective. Retelling, whether oral, written, or drawn, allows students to organize their thoughts and tell what they have read in their own words. For a fiction text, as shown, students demonstrate their understanding of story structure and sequence, moving from the beginning of the story to the end.

For nonfiction, students note the key concepts and ideas in the text. The retelling of poetry depends on the type of poem read. A narrative poem could follow the retelling format for fiction with its specific story structure. Other types of poetry may be retold with a restating of their theme and key concepts.

In Figure 26, the "Part" refers to the place in the story. Blank space is left for "Student's Independent Retelling" because the teacher will make brief notes

Figure 26. Readers Theatre Retelling Form for Fiction

Name _____

Date _____

Story _____

Part	Student's Independent Retelling	Prompts	Student's Aided Retelling
Beginning		What happened in the beginning? Where and when did this story take place? Who are the main characters? What is the problem in the story?	
Middle		What happened next? What did _____ do?	
End		What happened to _____? What happened in the end? How was the problem solved? What is the author trying to say?	

Adapted from Tompkins, 1998.

there of what the student is saying. The questions under "Prompts" offer guidance to teachers in what questions to ask if the student is unable to retell. Space is left under "Student's Aided Retelling" for the teacher to record what the student has said in response to the specific prompts noted.

This assessment strategy may be adapted to a rewriting or a visualization of fiction and narrative poetry such as that in the activity "Inside the Character" (see Chapter 7, page 132) where key ideas are translated into a visual representation. To use this retelling form with nonfiction text, the teacher can replace the key headings with "Main Ideas" and "Key Vocabulary." As the student identifies some of each, the teacher fills in the blank spaces under the headings with the student responses.

Comprehension Checklists. Another form of assessment for comprehension is the comprehension checklists (see Figures 27 and 28). These checklists may be used one-on-one with a specific student or given to all students for self-assessment.

Graphic Organizers. Another viable assessment for the comprehension of any genre is the use of graphic organizers. These visual representations of text information enable readers to see relationships between concepts, events, or characters in fiction or nonfiction texts. Webbing, or mapping, one of the most familiar graphic organizers, helps students to categorize and structure information. Vocabulary development may also be enhanced through webbing or mapping with the key phrase in the middle circle and associated words identified and placed in surrounding connecting circles (see Figure 29).

Figure 27. Comprehension Checklist for Fiction or Narrative Poetry

Student correctly identifies	Yes	No
1. Setting (time and place)	⎯⎯	⎯⎯
2. Main characters	⎯⎯	⎯⎯
3. Theme	⎯⎯	⎯⎯
4. Key plot events	⎯⎯	⎯⎯
5. Resolution	⎯⎯	⎯⎯
Comments:		

Figure 28. Comprehension Checklist for Nonfiction Text

Student correctly identifies	Yes	No
1. Main ideas	⎯⎯	⎯⎯
2. Important themes	⎯⎯	⎯⎯
3. Key descriptors	⎯⎯	⎯⎯
4. Content vocabulary	⎯⎯	⎯⎯
Comments:		

Figure 29. Webbing Graphic Organizer

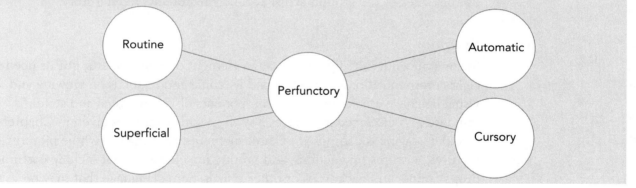

Script Development

As discussed in chapter 2, script development may focus on writing introductions, transitions, and conclusions. Further, depending on the time and focus devoted to Readers Theatre in the classroom, the students may adapt the text to scripts themselves or even create or retell a script (see Figure 26 for an assessment of retelling). During this time, the teacher may need to conference with students to help them revise and edit their work. If students are creating the introduction, transitions, and conclusion to a script, a teacher conference with the group is very helpful. A checklist is another effective way of evaluating script development. Figure 30 provides a checklist for assessing a student-adapted script.

Figure 30. Checklist for Assessing Script Adaptation

Focus _____ Date _____

Yes No

___ ___ 1. Does the material meet the criteria on the handout for a good Readers Theatre script?

___ ___ 2. Are the transitions prepared so the performance flows?

___ ___ 3. Are the narrator roles effective?

___ ___ 4. Are the lines divided up meaningfully?

___ ___ 5. Is there an understanding of who is saying what and why?

___ ___ 6. Are clear directions for performance noted in the script?

Comments:

Because script development includes both a process and a final product and focuses on writing, there are many effective ways to assess it. The process may be documented both for individuals and groups through anecdotal records (see Figure 24).

A ratings scale is also a good way to assess script development, and it is easily adaptable for individual students. A rubric could focus specifically on the script and its development, or it could include components as noted in Figure 22 that assesses the group's script accuracy if students retell a story.

Staging

Staging may not initially be seen as an element of language arts, but its need for clear communication in speaking and listening and its focus on viewing and visual language are all important components of U.S. national and state standards. As discussed in chapter 3 with specific examples given in Chapters 4, 5, and 6, staging is composed of three elements: creating the whole picture; gestures, postures, and actions; and production elements that include costumes, props, sound, and backdrops or other visuals. Some language that may be helpful in focusing on assessment for the viewing and visual language inherent in staging would be as follows:

- effective whole picture presented
- effective posture and actions used
- effective use of props and costumes
- sound supports the reading
- backdrop helps to create a setting

The assessment of staging may also be addressed through anecdotal records, checklists (see Figure 31) and rating scales. The rubric in Figure 22 also has a component with specific references to staging elements.

Figure 31. Checklist for Assessing Staging

Focus _____ Date _____

Yes No

___ ___ 1. Are the readers arranged to create an interesting stage picture?

___ ___ 2. Do students know how to enter and exit?

___ ___ 3. Are these entrances and exits clear to the audience?

___ ___ 4. If stools, chairs, or other props are used, are they used effectively?

___ ___ 5. Do performers focus so that the audience understands where the described action or focus is?

___ ___ 6. Are movements clear?

___ ___ 7. Do actions illuminate the text?

___ ___ 8. If sound effects are used, do they serve the purpose intended?

___ ___ 9. Can sound effects be performed easily and heard clearly?

___ ___ 10. If props and costumes are used, are they used easily and effectively?

___ ___ 11. Are scripts in good shape: pages securely fastened, nondistracting?

Comments:

Rehearsal and Performance

It is not necessary to assess rehearsal, but if assessed, the focus should be on students' participation and attitude. These may be assessed through anecdotal records (see Figure 24). Any assessment of the final performance could also be used after the students' dress rehearsal and serve as a forum for feedback.

Assessment of the final performance encompasses a number of skills such as staging, speaking, and listening. It may also address students' attitudes or behaviors. While the checklist in Figure 31 focuses on staging, Figure 32 looks at the overall performance.

Teachers may also want to assess students' behavior during the planning, process, rehearsal, and final performance. Figure 33 presents a ratings scale for teachers to use to evaluate behavior throughout the Readers Theatre process. Students may also use this scale for self-assessments addressing specific prompts.

Speaking and Listening

Speaking and listening are a vital part of language arts skills, and Readers Theatre is a forum that promotes these skills. Speaking is embodied in students' oral reading of the script before an audience, with reading fluency as a key component. Using standards (as outlined in chapter 9) as a guide may help the teacher to create appropriate statements regarding speaking and listening for use in checklists, rating scales, and rubrics. These skills may be assessed throughout the Readers Theatre process with anecdotal records. Specific focus points for speaking could be fluency, expressive reading, appropriate volume, and confidence.

Another excellent source for assessment is the website of the Canadian province of Saskatchewan regarding English language arts. Its focus on speaking

Figure 32. Checklist for Assessing Performance

Focus _____ Date _____

Yes No

___ ___ 1. Is the script smoothly performed without breakdowns and interruptions?

___ ___ 2. Is speech clear and consistent?

___ ___ 3. Do performers show an understanding of what they are reading?

___ ___ 4. Do performers avoid word-by-word delivery?

___ ___ 5. Is expressive reading successfully employed?

___ ___ 6. Do readers create believable characters and good mental images?

___ ___ 7. Do readers listen to each other and react meaningfully?

___ ___ 8. Do readers handle scripts unobtrusively and efficiently?

___ ___ 9. Does the performance come to a definite ending?

Comments:

skills may be of value when creating assessment tools for Readers Theatre (Saskatchewan Education, 1998). Discussing oral language development, it highlights a variety of types of speaking activities and provides specific assessments (peer, self, and teacher) for each type of activity.

The scale in Figure 33 has several statements related to speaking and listening. The chart in Figure 21 mentions listening skills, and the rubric in Figure 22 includes some components of speaking for the individual.

Students' Attitudes Toward Reading

Assessing an affective quality such as attitude is difficult. However, by looking at specific student behavior before and after the use of Readers Theatre and supporting this data with other assessments, it is possible to gain a sense of students' attitude toward reading. Some key language that may be used in checklist or rating scales includes the following:

- enjoys reading
- is proud of his or her reading
- shares books, recommends books
- has developed a preference for reading
- reads beyond classroom
- learns from reading
- talks about books read
- buys or borrows books

The rating scale (see Figure 33) assesses student behavior within the context of Readers Theatre. Attitude or behavior may also be assessed through anecdotal records (see examples in Figure 24) and through students' responses to prompts in their self-assessment.

Critical Thinking

Critical thinking skills look at an individual's ability to comprehend, interpret, analyze, and synthesize information. Reading comprehension, noted earlier, is an aspect of critical thinking. In addition, the use of anecdotal records may provide information that helps a teacher understand if a student "gets the big picture." Questions such as "Are the lines divided up meaningfully?" and "Is there an understanding of who is saying what?" (Figure 30), "Do actions illuminate the text?" (Figure 31), and "Do performers show an understanding of what they are reading?" (Figure 32) are helpful in determining students' critical thinking skills.

Figure 33. Scale for Assessing Student Behavior and Engagement With Readers Theatre

Name _____

Date _____

Directions:
Rate each item on the basis of four points: 4=excellent, 3=very good, 2=average, 1=fair, 0=poor or lacking.

0 1 2 3 4   1. Enthusiasm for overall Readers Theatre project
0 1 2 3 4   2. Eagerness to seek out materials for possible use in the project
0 1 2 3 4   3. Eagerness to read and reread a part in the group script
0 1 2 3 4   4. Contributions of ideas for the creation and staging of the script
0 1 2 3 4   5. Receptiveness to ideas generated by classmates
0 1 2 3 4   6. Listens respectfully to reading by classmates
0 1 2 3 4   7. Comprehension of the literature used
0 1 2 3 4   8. Appreciation of literature used
0 1 2 3 4   9. Fulfillment of role in group
0 1 2 3 4   10. Improvement in oral reading skills
0 1 2 3 4   11. Overall response to Readers Theatre
0 1 2 3 4   12. Overall participation in Readers Theatre process
0 1 2 3 4   13. Overall performance of specific group job (i.e., director, recorder, etc.)

Comments:

Journal prompts such as "One thing I understand about _____ is..." and "One thing I do not understand about _____ is..." allow students to verbalize their own sense of comprehension, analysis, and possibly synthesis.

These suggestions are very fluid, and many of the assessment tools may be adapted to focus on the group, the individual, or both. For example, checklists could be used to document the dynamics of the group and, with specific students' names noted, they could also monitor individual students.

REFERENCES

Clay, M. (1985). *The early detection of reading difficulties: A diagnostic survey with recovery procedures*. Portsmouth, NH: Heinemann.

Kibby, M.W., & Dechert, D. (2003). *Teacher modeling-guided repeated readings (TMgRR)*. Buffalo, NY: Center for Literacy and Reading Instruction. Retrieved December 6, 2006, from http://www.readingcenter.buffalo.edu/center/resear4ch/tmgrr.html

Tompkins, G.E. (1998). *50 literacy strategies: Step by step*. Englewood Cliffs, NJ: Merrill.

Saskatchewan Education. (1998). English language arts, 2.0: A curriculum guide for the secondary level. Regina, SK: Saskatchewan Education. Retrieved December 6, 2006, from http://www.sasked.gov.sk.ca/docs/ela20/teach2.html

Sources and Resources for Scripts

RECOMMENDED BOOKS FOR READERS THEATRE SCRIPTS

Barchers, S.I. (2004). *Judge for yourself: Famous American trials for Readers Theatre*. Englewood, CO: Teacher Ideas Press.

Barchers, S.I. (2006). *More Readers Theatre for beginning readers*. Englewood, CO: Teacher Ideas Press.

Barnes, J.W. (2004). *Sea songs: Readers Theatre from the South Pacific*. Englewood, CO: Teacher Ideas Press.

Bauer, C.F. (1987). *Presenting Reader's Theatre: Plays and poems to read aloud*. New York: H.W. Wilson.

Cobb, L.K. (2004). *Literary ideas and scripts for young playwrights*. Englewood, CO: Teacher Ideas Press.

Fredericks, A.D. (1993). *Frantic frogs and other frankly fractured folktales for Readers Theatre*. Englewood, CO: Teacher Ideas Press.

Fredericks, A.D. (2000). *Silly salamanders and other slightly stupid stuff for Readers Theatre*. Englewood, CO: Teacher Ideas Press.

Glasscock, S. (Ed.). (1999). *Ten American history plays for the classroom*. New York: Scholastic.

Haven, K. (1996). *Great moments in science experiments and Readers Theatre*. Englewood, CO: Teacher Ideas Press.

Jenkins. D.R. (2004). *Just deal with it! Funny Readers Theatre for life's not-so-funny moments*. Englewood, CO: Teacher Ideas Press.

Kroll, J.L. (Ed.). (2003). *Simply Shakespeare: Readers Theatre for young adults*. Englewood, CO: Teacher Ideas Press.

Sloyer, S. (2003). *From the page to the stage: The educators complete guide to Readers Theatre*. Englewood, CO: Teacher Ideas Press.

Smith, C.R. (2004). *Extraordinary women from U.S. history: Readers Theatre for grades 4–8*. Englewood, CO: Teacher Ideas Press.

RECOMMENDED WEBSITES FOR READERS THEATRE SCRIPTS

Aaron Shepard's Readers Theatre page: www.aaronshep.com
This excellent website has information about everything from scripting to performance. The homepage allows you to access a Readers Theatre page, and from there you can easily get to "Scripts and Tips for Readers Theatre." Included are many stories—some are adaptations of popular children's literature and many are folk tales. The scripts range from 3 to 20 minutes and may be downloaded at no charge from this site. Highly recommended.

Lisa Blau's Readers Theatre site: www.lisablau.com/plays.html
Seven reasonably priced books of scripts are noted here. Each features a brief annotation and a table of contents.

Literacy Connections—Readers' Theater: www.literacyconnections.com/ReadersTheater.html
This extensive site includes links to guides for implementing Readers Theatre (many of which have samples scripts), links to books about Readers Theatre and books filled with scripts, and links to Readers Theatre scripts online. Activities described supplement the teacher's use of Readers Theatre scripts.

Lois Walker's Readers Theatre site: http://scriptsforschool.com
This website features a number of Readers Theatre scripts ranging from kindergarten to adult use, many of which are folktales and nonfiction. These scripts are available for purchase and are a good investment if Readers Theatre is a schoolwide activity. The scripts are accessed by grade level, curriculum level, or special theme. If you go to a section on her site (www.loiswalker.com), you can get some free scripts and a teacher's guide.

Playbooks: www.playbooks.com
This commercial site sells the "playbook" stories that offer leveled Readers Theatre scripts. Each story is complete with basic directions, suggestions for use in the classroom, reader assignment with the percentage of reading done, labels from easy reader to advanced, character summaries, and color-coded script parts. This site is useful and presents many possibilities, with most materials available for purchase.

Reader's Theatre Basics: http://bms.westport.k12.ct.us/mccormick/rt/RTHOME.htm
On this site, Readers Theatre is defined, suggestions for adapting scripts are made, and actor goals are identified. There are all-fiction scripts included for grade 3 to grade 9.

Readers Theatre Digest: www.readerstheatredigest.com
This site connects you to an online quarterly magazine where experts and fans of Readers Theatre share their experiences and ideas. The subscription to the online magazine includes a free monthly newsletter.

Readers Theatre Script Service: www.readerstheatreinstitute.com
Script packets available for purchase range from elementary level to adult. The scripts are varied with some content. In addition, the site provides information about workshops offered throughout the country.

Readers Theatre Workshop: www.readers.org
This site provides an exciting look at Readers Theatre as a performance medium. Comparable to the programs about artists in the schools, Readers Theatre Workshop is a New York City–based organization that offers workshops and performances in schools but that does not appear to be directed toward student performance.

Storycart Press: www.storycart.com
Storycart's website provides five free sample scripts as well as a variety of individual scripts and books for sale.

Cross-Curricular Connections

Readers Theatre can easily extend beyond the use of narrative fiction and poetry into expository text or nonfiction. When using such informational text with Readers Theatre, there may be a stronger focus on students' grasp of specific content and concepts as well as students' reading fluency and comprehension. In addition, the use of nonfiction serves as a natural forum for student research, summarization, and even scripting if the teacher has time to assist in moving expository text to script format.

The use of Readers Theatre should not be relegated solely to language arts. All the content areas have stories to tell, concepts to explore, and individuals to discover. Stories are essential to learning and to understanding. For educators, stories told through the venue of Readers Theatre may be one way to attract students' attention and to also help them understand and remember key concepts.

> We live by narrative,...narrative is the human way of working through a chaotic and unforgiving world.... Facts presented in stories, as opposed to lists, are much easier to remember. Likewise, facts that stir up intense emotions are quickly and easily stored in our brains...and well-told stories are a great way to tie emotions to facts. (Wilson, 2002, p. 10)

This power of story to communicate content is supported by a number of researchers. Their studies have found that students exposed to historical material or stories were better able to grasp related content concepts (Egan, 1987; Irwin, 2000; Kauffman, 1989; Klopfer & Cooley, 1961; Lonsbury & Ellis, 2002; Martin & Brouwer, 1991; Roach & Wandersee, 1993; Seker & Welsh, 2006; Solomon, Duveen, & Scot, 1992; Yager & Wick, 1966). Another benefit in using nonfiction with Readers Theatre is its appeal to boys, making them more motivated to read, research, write, and perform.

Egan (1987), an educational psychologist, states that elements of story (such as events or plot and people or characters) that engage the reader may be used to teach any subject at any level. By using the literary device of dialogue in telling stories, readers in Readers Theatre enhance the emotional content of the stories.

The following is a summary of reasons why story, often interpreted as history, should be incorporated into content instruction:

1. Stories promote better comprehension of content concepts.
2. Stories support the development of individual thinking with the development of specific content concepts.
3. The story of specific content areas is intrinsically worthwhile. Important episodes in the story of any content—the Civil War, Darwinism, the discovery of penicillin, the development of zero and the decimal system, and so on—should be familiar to all students.
4. Stories are necessary to understand the nature of any discipline.
5. Elements of story counteract the dogmatism commonly found in content texts and classes.
6. Stories, by examining the life and times of individuals, humanize the subject matter, making it less abstract and more engaging.
7. Stories allow connections to be made within topics and disciplines; they display the integrated and interdependent nature of human achievements.

(Adapted from Matthews, 1994, p. 50.)

Although Matthews (1994) focused on science instruction, the reasons listed above have been adapted and found to be applicable for all content areas.

Using nonfiction sources in Readers Theatre requires a strict attention to detail and accuracy, with such a focus providing an alternative to the traditional research paper. Nonfiction themes may be narrow and specific, such as the Underground Railroad or Isaac Newton. They may also be more general, such as immigration or outer space.

The development of a script, whether by the teacher, students, or both, may be based upon a single work, and yet some of the most interesting scripts for specific content areas are the results of a compilation of various sources and types of literature. For example, in creating a script for Readers Theatre supporting a unit on the South Pole, information about the weather, the people, the animals, and the topography could be pulled from many sources. In addition, the incredible story of Sir Ernest Shackleton's expedition, which would place the weather, people, animals, and topography in context, could be included.

Creating a story-form organization with content material means envisioning content within a human context, therefore making the context familiar through story and meaningful and engaging (Egan, 1986). It must be noted that, although content areas such as social studies may be very applicable to Readers Theatre because of its dependence upon story, the forum for its presentation (in this case, Readers Theatre) can present only concepts which students are ready to grasp due to their developmental level and prior knowledge. Therefore, Readers Theatre should not be seen as a panacea for students' lack of content comprehension but as one way in which content may be introduced, taught, and reinforced. The key to successful teaching of any content area through Readers

Theatre is to focus on main concepts as well as related human emotions and actions and then, through the script, illustrate and elaborate upon these.

Social Studies

The content of social studies is composed of the basic components of story: events (plot), intentions and values (theme), specific times and places (setting), individual people and groups (characters), and conflict. Therefore, the content of social studies lends itself easily to Readers Theatre. Consider a unit on World War II with novels such as *Number the Stars* (Lowry, 1989) and true stories like *The Upstairs Room* (Reiss, 1972) and *The Diary of a Young Girl by Anne Frank* (Frank, 1947). Each book tells of young people forced into hiding and, coupled with brief yet grim statistics from the death tolls in concentration camps, would provide a personalized and riveting glimpse of a time and events far removed from students' lives today.

Biographies or their excerpts paired with relevant poetry or even primary documents (e.g., *Lincoln: A Photobiography* [Freeman, 1987] paired with "O Captain, My Captain!" by Walt Whitman [1992], and "The Gettysburg Address" by Lincoln himself, as cited in Commager [1963]) can give life to specific individuals and specific documents as well as the times in which those individuals lived. In addition to trade books available through the school library or book clubs, there are many social studies materials that lend themselves to Readers Theatre. For example, Harmon, Riney-Kehrberg, and Westbury (1999) looked at Readers Theatre as a teaching tool and created a script of the first women's rights convention held in New York in 1848. They pulled information from newspaper and periodical articles of that time as well as an attendee's own journal accounts, declaring that the presentation was best served by Readers Theatre because "such productions are engaging and relatively easy to stage" (p. 525). Another source, Muir (2000), put together a collection of biographical sketches of both military and civilians during World War II. These stories are short, fact filled, and easy to read, making them very accessible to middle school and high school students and prime material for Readers Theatre.

Finally, in looking at how Readers Theatre may support U.S. standards in social studies, an article in *The History Teacher* ("Exploring the national," 1995) discusses Readers Theatre as one way to enact dramatic readings of famous speeches. In exploring the national history Standard 4: Struggle for racial and gender equity and extension of civil liberties, Readers Theatre is offered as a way to explain the issues in the U.S. Supreme Court case Brown vs. Board of Education (1954).

Science

Science has long been considered a content area far removed from fiction, drama, and poetry. Increasingly, however, scientists and writers have begun to blur the boundaries and have found that "the common thread that holds imaginative works and scientific works together is a celebration of the sense of wonder and awe that comes with addressing big questions—even ultimate questions—about the nature of humankind and the universe our species inhabits" (Westcott & Spell, 1999, p. 70). The teaching of science concerns not only scientific information but also scientific methods and thinking. To get at these bodies of knowledge, students must go beyond memorizing dry facts and doing experiments. Through narrative, that which is central to Readers Theatre, the human stories of science and its scientists become comprehensible and interesting to students. Placing a scientific concept within a specific context allows for its history, its discovery, its events, and its characters to be explored.

Working with middle school students, Solomon, Duveen, and Scot (1992), referring to the teaching of science history, concluded "studying the history of a change in theory may make the process of conceptual change a little easier" (p. 419). Using short stories grounded in science history, Roach and Wandersee (1993) helped high school students understand that science is a dynamic process of continuous searching. Other proponents for the use of story within science education are Martin and Brouwer (1991) who argue that, through stories, students may begin to better understand science and its place in their lives and the world.

Seker and Welsh (2006) found that stories from scientists' personal lives created student interest in science. Such stories parallel real life and invite students into a specific time and place. Thus, the forum of Readers Theatre is one way to share these stories and to motivate students through a personal connection, to read and think about specific scientists and their work. Sagan's book *Cosmos* (2002) is an excellent example of a writer using "literary techniques to break the wall down between the artistic and scientific" (Westcott & Spell, 1999, p. 71).

Science abounds with dramatic stories and discoveries. Wilson (2002) advocates teaching science through the power of story. Aside from the motivational factor, he notes that our brains function best by creating narratives or stories to communicate, to explain, and to understand:

> Science consists of millions of stories.... These accounts become science when they can be tested and woven into cause-and-effect explanations to become part of humanity's material worldview. But they also constitute a fascinating narrative, which can be the key to helping the non-scientist understand the great ideas of science. (p. 10)

The annual volumes of *The Best American Science and Nature Writing* contain stories with scientists as the main characters and provide fertile ground for Readers Theatre ideas. Hakim (2002) uses "The Story of the Atom" to tell middle school students about the scientific detective work that convinced the world that the atom actually exists. She discusses the development of the atomic theory, which began as early as 400 BC when the Greek philosopher Democritus theorized that if matter were divided into finer and finer parts, it would eventually reach a point where it could no longer be divided. Hence, the atom, from the Greek word meaning "not cuttable." Although her narrative is filled with difficult concepts, its story and cast of fascinating characters (i.e., real scientists) carry the reader away. Science is filled with stories to tell—consider the story of Copernicus, the founder of astronomy, who developed the theory that Earth is a moving planet. In addition to nonfiction such as Joanna Cole's Magic School Bus series, biographies are an excellent resource for Readers Theatre ideas, offering scientific information in an appealing and uncomplicated manner.

Mathematics

By integrating story with mathematics, the content becomes less an abstract, distinct, and unconnected realm. Mathematics is usually seen as a set of computational skills to be mastered. Through stories, math's major concepts become more meaningful and interesting. Because mathematics was created to be used for human purposes—to enable humans to do difficult things easily and to solve problems—it is possible to humanize it, allowing students to recognize not a computation, but a solution.

The use of story in mathematics helps to create within students a sense of wonder regarding numbers and their uses. From this follows the motivation to use numbers. Again, stories about key mathematicians throughout history give insights on the connection, the context, and the humanity integral to these stories. Consider the story of Pythagoras, who believed that numbers were magic. Think about the fact that the Latin word for a *cut* is *talea*, leading to *tally* or the making of cuts on a stick to indicate the numbers and that the Latin word for *pebble* is *calculus*!

Other Content Areas: Physical Education, Health, and the Arts

The power of story discussed previously does indeed apply to these content areas. Physical education can be enhanced through Readers Theatre with narratives of great sports figures as well as dramatic stories of the Olympics. Such stories not only remind us of human drama but also provide a moral stance and a sense of time and place.

Health, akin to science with its focus on the human body and disease, is made more comprehensible if given a human face. This can be done through Readers Theatre with stories about doctors and disease throughout history, ranging from the discover that germs that spread disease, to the current concerns of E. coli and bird flu.

Finally, the arts (including writing, painting, sculpture, music, and theater) are a testament to human creativity, and each artistic endeavor has a variety of human stories to help us grasp its development, reasons, connections, and characters. Art is an undertaking that creates joy and beauty, that challenges and pleases, and that often uses concepts of social studies, science, and mathematics in its final product.

Because narrative or story helps students to construct meaning, provides a human context for key concepts, and creates motivation for students to pursue the content, Readers Theatre is an effective method to introduce, teach, and reinforce the teaching of all content areas. Assessment of Readers Theatre in a specific content area may be done through the use of a rubric or checklist, documenting key criteria that should be covered. Figure 34, the Rubric, Native American Unit Model, shows how assessment may occur across several content areas. There are

Figure 34. Rubric, Native American Unit Model

Rubric: Native American Unit

Names _____

Native American Nation _____

Social Studies Section
20 Points
- Accuracy of facts
- The scene shows the culture in action
- Human features are evident
- It is easy to see the connection between the people and their environment

0   2   4   6   8   10   12   14   16   18   20

English Section
20 Points
- Labels and posters are easy to read
- The model's actions help tell a story about the Native American Nation
- The poster includes a graphic organizer to display information
- The poster contains information on the biome and culture of the Native American Nation

0   2   4   6   8   10   12   14   16   18   20

Science Section
20 Points
- The biome elements are correctly depicted and labeled (specific type)
- Includes water resources (lakes, streams, oceans), at least three animals, and at least three plants
- You can see the use of resources

0   2   4   6   8   10   12   14   16   18   20

Math Section
20 Points
- Measurements are accurate
- The scale is included and is easy to understand
- The correct units are used for real-life measurements

0   2   4   6   8   10   12   14   16   18   20

Technology/Artistic Presentation
20 Points
- Different materials are used (an effort to create an authentic appearance)
- The quality of the construction and attention to detail is evident
- The written work enhances the visual appearance
- Products of technology are accurate to the era
- Illustrates how problems were solved with technology

0   2   4   6   8   10   12   14   16   18   20

Overall Score _____

myriad ways to tell an interesting story. Students' play with language, their search for facts, and their use of texts to bring meaning and coherence to a concept, an individual, a time, or an area of study create both a meaningful process as well as an interactive product through the use of Readers Theatre.

REFERENCES

Egan, K. (1986). *Teaching as story telling: An alternative approach to teaching and curriculum in the elementary school.* Chicago: University of Chicago Press.

Egan, K. (1987). The underused power of the story form in teaching. *Westminster Studies in Education, 10,* 77–82.

Exploring the national standards for U.S. history and world history. (1995). *The History Teacher, 28,* 335–357.

Hakim, J. (2002). The story of the atom. *American Educator, 26,* 12–25.

Harmon, S.D., Riney-Kehrberg, P., & Westbury, S. (1999). Readers Theatre as a history teaching tool. *The History Teacher, 32,* 525–545.

Irwin, A.R. (2000). Historical case studies: Teaching the nature of science in context. *Science Education, 84,* 5–26.

Kauffman, G.B. (1989). History in the chemistry curriculum. *Interchange, 20*(2), 81–94.

Klopfer, L.E., & Cooley, W.W. (1961). *Use of case histories in the development of student understanding of science and scientists.* Cambridge, MA: Harvard University Press.

Lonsbury, J.G., & Ellis, J.D. (2002). Science history as a means to teach nature of science concepts: Using the development of understanding related to mechanisms of inheritance. *Electronic Journal of Science Education, 7*(2). Retrieved from http://unr.edu/homepage/crowther/ejse/lonsbury.pdf

Martin, B.E., & Brouwer, W. (1991). The sharing of personal science and the narrative element in science education. *Science Education, 75*(6), 707–722.

Matthews, M.R. (1994). *Science teaching: The role of history and philosophy of science.* New York: Routledge.

Roach, L.E., & Wandersee, J.H. (1993). Short story science: Using historical vignettes as a teaching tool. *Science Teacher, 60*(6), 18–21.

Seker, H., & Welsh, L. (2006). The use of history of mechanics in teaching motion and force units. *Science & Education, 15*(1), 55–89.

Solomon, J., Duveen, J., & Scot, L. (1992). Teaching about the nature of science through history. *Journal of Research in Science Teaching, 29,* 409–421.

Westcott, W.B., & Spell, J.E. (1999). Tearing down the wall: Literature and science. *English Journal, 89*(2), 70–76.

Wilson, E.O. (2002). The power of story. *American Educator, 26,* 8–11.

Yager, R.E., & Wick, T.W. (1966). Three emphases in teaching biology—A statistical comparison of results. *Journal of Research in Science Teaching, 4,* 16–20.

LITERATURE CITED

Brown v. Board of Educ., 347 U.S. 483 (1954).

Commager, H.S. (Ed.). (1963). *Documents of American history* (7th ed.). New York: Apple-Century-Crofts.

Frank, O.H. (Ed.). (1947). *The diary of a young girl by Anne Frank.* New York: Doubleday.

Freeman, R. (1987). *Lincoln: A photobiography.* New York: Clarion.

Lowry, L. (1989). *Number the stars.* New York: Houghton Mifflin.

Muir, M., Jr. (Ed.). (2000). *The human tradition in the World War II era.* Wilmington, DE: SR Books.

Reiss, J. (1972). *The upstairs room.* New York: HarperCollins.

Sagan, C. (2002). *Cosmos.* New York: Random House.

Whitman, W. (1992). *Leaves of grass: The deathbed edition.* New York: Simon & Schuster.

Reproducible Forms

Student Preparation Checklist

Reminders

- Readers Theatre scripts don't need to be memorized. They are a dramatic reading of a piece of writing. This does not mean, though, that you can read your scripts word for word. You need to practice them enough to make the reading interesting for your audience.

- Use your voice and movements to make your scripts more entertaining.

- Remember the audience. The audience needs to understand the story you are trying to tell.

- When performing, don't stand with your back to the audience. It makes it difficult to hear you—not to mention difficult to see your face.

To-Do List

☐ As a group, decide which text will be the best choice for Readers Theatre.

☐ Read through the text once again. This time, make a note of the number of characters you will need to tell the story. Remember to include the narrator(s).

☐ Help each other to read and adapt the script. You may want a narrator to describe the setting and establish characters in your script. Your script should take between 5 and 10 minutes to read. Anything longer may be difficult for your audience to follow. Focus on important events.

☐ While you read your script, make sure you also discuss different voices and movements that will improve the quality of your performance.

☐ Feel free to add a part for your audience—the audience members will love it! You can create a cue card for them to read from.

☐ Be sure to plan how you will introduce your text to the audience. You should share your names, the name of the story, and the characters that you will play. If you choose to include your audience in the act, you may want to explain what you want to them to do or say during this time.

☐ Once the script is complete, discuss any small costume pieces or props that could be used to help your audience follow your story. Really consider this if you are reading more than one part.

☐ When you are finished, you should decide as a group how you want to share the script with each other. Is the written copy neat enough for everyone to read? Could each of you type a section of it at home and bring it in Friday? Is someone willing to type it for the group while others create costume pieces or props? Once your decisions are made, please know that you need enough copies of the script for everyone in your group to have one. (If you give a copy to [teacher's name] she can make copies for everyone.) [Teacher's name] needs a copy as well. You will hand it in with a copy of the original myth by [due date].

Readers Theatre Poetry Project Checklist

☐ With your group, choose the poem you would like to work with.

☐ Let [teacher's name] know which poem you have chosen so that [teacher's name] can make copies for you.

☐ As a group, break your poem into parts. Don't forget to decide who will
    ☐ Introduce the poem and poet.
    ☐ Introduce the people in your group.
    ☐ Share information about your poet.
    ☐ Give an explanation of the poem that you will perform.

☐ Practice, practice, practice!

☐ Write a summary of your section of the poem to share with your group.

☐ Practice, practice, practice again!

☐ Share your summaries and combine them to create one complete interpretation of your poem to share during your presentation.

☐ Practice, practice, practice some more!

☐ Decide on any small props that you might make or bring in for the presentations to add to your performance. Remember—the most important tools your group has are your voices and gestures. Any additional props should be used to clarify parts of the poem for the audience, or possibly to invite the audience to participate.

Readers Theatre Poetry Project Guidelines

Readers Theatre Poetry Presentations
Presentation Date:
Dress Rehearsal Date:

Introduction
Include the following:
- Group members' names
- Name of poem
- Author
- Explanation of mural

Script
- Your script should be well rehearsed.
- Your script should be read with emotion.
- Appropriate use of expression is expected.

Music
- Background music only
- Appropriate for the poem
- Instrumental only, if possible

Murals
- Two team members responsible: _____
  _____

- Should illustrate your interpretation of the poem
- Should show images from the poem

Costumes
- Should represent interpretation of the poem
- Groups may choose to have "uniform" costumes (for example, all dressed in a particular color)

Poster To-Do List

☐ Research information about your poster topic and record that information on your graphic organizer. Complete a works cited page for the sources you use in your research.

☐ As a group, use your graphic organizer to create a rough draft of the poster. Review your graphic organizer as a group to make sure that your rough draft is complete. Remember, your final copy will be seen by lots of people! ☺

☐ Using poster paper, begin creating the final draft. Use pictures, markers, colored paper, and any other materials that you can think of to make your poster a clear and creative representation of all the work you have done. This is your opportunity to show us what you've learned!

☐ You may want to assign each other some homework here. You may want to type some of the information. Someone in your group may have a color printer at home that will make great pictures or decorations for your poster. Talk about it and plan what to do. Write down any tasks that you are supposed to complete on your own so that you don't forget.

☐ Check your works cited page. Make sure all of your resources have been listed. If any are missing, **neatly** write the resources on the page. Here is another guide for the citation of a book:
> Author's last name, First initial. <u>Title of book</u>. Date. Publishing Company: City/State/Country where published.

☐ Tape or glue the works cited page to the back of the poster.

☐ Make sure all of your names are on the back of the poster.

☐ Find a safe place for your poster so that it will be ready to hang up on [<u>due date</u>].

☐ Congratulate each other on a job well done!

Readers Theatre Preparation Chart

Student Name	Attendance: Student is prompt and regularly attends classes during preparation days.	Preparation: Student is prepared for class with required class materials.	Listening Skills: Student listens when others talk, both in group and in class.	Engagement: Student proactively participates by asking questions and offering ideas.	Anecdotal Record: Any observations made during class or group work.
Date					

Rubric for Readers Theatre

While observing students during rehearsals and performances, the following are focus areas for assessing individual students.

Name _____ Date _____

4	3
Individual	**Individual**
• Student always speaks clearly.	• Student often speaks clearly.
• Student always speaks at an appropriate pace.	• Student often speaks at an appropriate pace.
• Student always speaks fluently, using appropriate intonation, expression, and emphasis.	• Student often speaks fluently, using appropriate intonation, expression and emphasis.
• Student contributed appropriately to this production.	• Student usually contributed appropriately to this production.
Group	**Group**
• Students' script accurately retells the text the group chose.	• Students' script retells the text the group chose with only a few inaccuracies.
• Students prepared and used appropriate props.	• Students prepared and used appropriate props.
• Students encouraged participation from the audience.	• Students participated actively in participation and rehearsals.
• Students participated actively in preparation and rehearsals.	

2	1
Individual	**Individual**
• Student rarely speaks clearly.	• Student is unable to be heard or is difficult to understand.
• Student rarely speaks at an appropriate pace.	• Student uses no intonation, expression, or emphasis in reading.
• Student rarely speaks fluently, using appropriate intonation, expression, and emphasis.	• Student rarely contributed appropriately to this production.
• Student contributed appropriately to this production on occasion.	
Group	**Group**
• Students' script that retells the text the group chose has several inaccuracies and/or is difficult to understand.	• Students' script that retells the text the group chose is completely inaccurate.
• Students struggle to participate actively in preparation and rehearsals.	• Students rarely participated actively in preparation and rehearsals.

Grading Checklist for Presentations

Name _____ Class Period _____

Group # _____   Theme_____

Group Members _____

Poem #1 _____

Poem #2 _____

1. **Performance Script (15 points)** _____
   Turn in one copy for teacher and use copies to read from for your presentations.
   Script should include: group number; group members' names; theme; poem titles and authors; who says what in what order; description of background; props, music selection.

2. **Participation (15 points)** _____
   All group members participate in the planning, organizing, rehearsal, and performance.
   Participation is equally distributed (one member is not clearly doing all the work while the others do less).

3. **Visual Aid (15 points)** _____
   Backdrop related to theme
   Costumes/clothing
   Other items, including props that add to presentation

4. **Music Selection (15 points)** _____
   Appropriate for poems and/or theme
   Adds to but does not distract from performance

5. **Performance (40 points)** _____
   States theme, titles, and authors of poems
   Tone/atmosphere is appropriate for poems
   Appears to understand the poems' meanings
   Short interpretation of poems and their relationship to the theme

Comments:

Prompts for Student Self-Assessment

1. What was the best part about Readers Theatre? Why? _____
_____

2. What was the most difficult part of Readers Theatre? Why? _____
_____

3. I like Readers Theatre because _____
_____.

4. Readers Theatre is hard for me because _____
_____.

5. This was my role: _____. I could have done better _____
_____.

    I was really good _____
_____.

6. As a group member, I was successful at _____.

7. As a group member, I could have been better at _____.

8. My group worked together successfully to _____
_____.

9. My group was not very good at _____.

10. My performance in Readers Theatre _____
_____.

11. One thing I understand about_____ is _____
_____.

12. One thing I do not understand about _____ is _____
_____.

Anecdotal Records of Individual Students

Focus Group: Date:

Focus Group: Date:

Focus Group: Date:

Reading Fluency Checklist

Student Name _____ Date _____

The student:	Yes	Sometimes	No
1. Reads word by word.			
2. Reads with long pauses between words.			
3. Misses many words.			
4. Reads with little expression.			
5. Reads with little evidence of the use of punctuation.			
6. Has a reading rate that is slow and laborious.			

Readers Theatre Retelling Form for Fiction

Name _____

Date _____

Story _____

Part	Student's Independent Retelling	Prompts	Student's Aided Retelling
Beginning		What happened in the beginning? Where and when did this story take place? Who are the main characters? What is the problem in the story?	
Middle		What happened next? What did _____ do?	
End		What happened to _____? What happened in the end? How was the problem solved? What is the author trying to say?	

Adapted from Tompkins, G.E. (1998). *50 literacy strategies: Step by step.* Englewood Cliffs, NJ: Merrill

Comprehension Checklist for Fiction or Narrative Poetry

Student correctly identifies	Yes	No
1. Setting (time and place)	_____	_____
2. Main characters	_____	_____
3. Theme	_____	_____
4. Key plot events	_____	_____
5. Resolution	_____	_____

Comments:

Comprehension Checklist for Nonfiction Text

Student correctly identifies	Yes	No
1. Main ideas	_____	_____
2. Important themes	_____	_____
3. Key descriptors	_____	_____
4. Content vocabulary	_____	_____

Comments:

Webbing Graphic Organizer

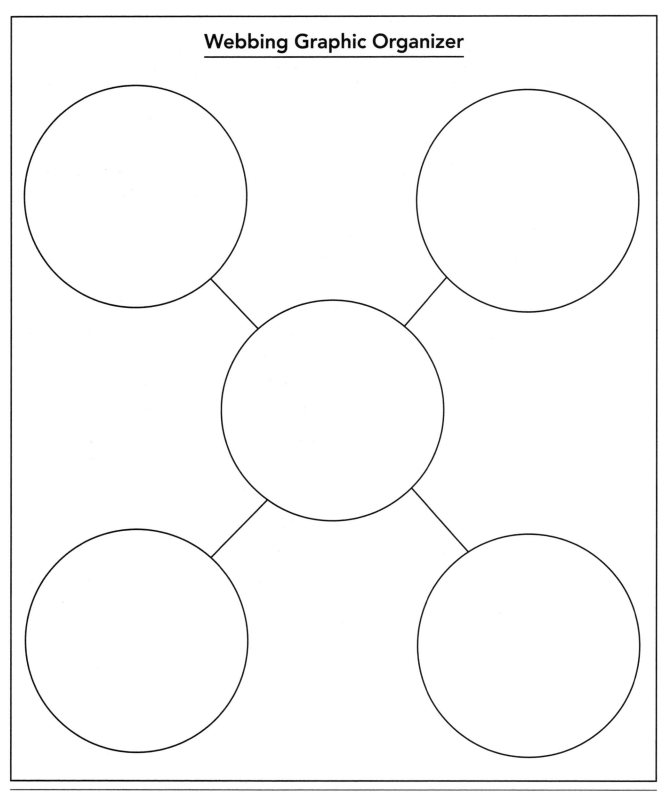

Checklist for Assessing Script Adaptation

Focus _____   Date _____

Yes   No

___   ___   1. Does the material meet the criteria on the handout for a good
                   Readers Theatre script?

___   ___   2. Are the transitions prepared so the performance flows?

___   ___   3. Are the narrator roles effective?

___   ___   4. Are the lines divided up meaningfully?

___   ___   5. Is there an understanding of who is saying what and why?

___   ___   6. Are clear directions for performance noted in the script?

Comments:

Checklist for Assessing Staging

Focus _____   Date _____

Yes   No

___   ___   1. Are the readers arranged to create an interesting stage picture?

___   ___   2. Do students know how to enter and exit?

___   ___   3. Are these entrances and exits clear to the audience?

___   ___   4. If stools, chairs, or other props are used, are they used effectively?

___   ___   5. Do performers focus so that the audience understands where the described action or focus is?

___   ___   6. Are movements clear?

___   ___   7. Do actions illuminate the text?

___   ___   8. If sound effects are used, do they serve the purpose intended?

___   ___   9. Can sound effects be performed easily and heard clearly?

___   ___   10. If props and costumes are used, are they used easily and effectively?

___   ___   11. Are scripts in good shape: pages securely fastened, nondistracting?

Comments:

Checklist for Assessing Performance

Focus _____   Date _____

Yes   No

___   ___   1. Is the script smoothly performed without breakdowns and
                   interruptions?

___   ___   2. Is speech clear and consistent?

___   ___   3. Do performers show an understanding of what they are reading?

___   ___   4. Do performers avoid word-by-word delivery?

___   ___   5. Is expressive reading successfully employed?

___   ___   6. Do readers create believable characters and good mental
                   images?

___   ___   7. Do readers listen to each other and react meaningfully?

___   ___   8. Do readers handle scripts unobtrusively and efficiently?

___   ___   9. Does the performance come to a definite ending?

Comments:

Scale for Assessing Student Behavior and Engagement With Readers Theatre

Name _____

Date _____

Directions: Rate each item on the basis of four points: 4=excellent, 3=very good, 2=average, 1=fair, 0=poor or lacking.

0 1 2 3 4   1. Enthusiasm for overall Readers Theatre project

0 1 2 3 4   2. Eagerness to seek out materials for possible use in the project

0 1 2 3 4   3. Eagerness to read and reread a part in the group script

0 1 2 3 4   4. Contributions of ideas for the creation and staging of the script

0 1 2 3 4   5. Receptiveness to ideas generated by classmates

0 1 2 3 4   6. Interest in listening to reading by classmates

0 1 2 3 4   7. Comprehension of the literature used

0 1 2 3 4   8. Appreciation of literature used

0 1 2 3 4   9. Fulfillment of role in group

0 1 2 3 4   10. Improvement in oral reading skills

0 1 2 3 4   11. Overall response to Readers Theatre

0 1 2 3 4   12. Overall participation in Readers Theatre process

0 1 2 3 4   13. Overall performance of specific group job (i.e., director, recorder, etc.)

Comments:

Standards

IRA/NCTE Standards for the English Language Arts

1. Students read a wide range of print and nonprint texts to build an understanding of texts, of themselves, and of the cultures of the United States and the world; to acquire new information; to respond to the needs and demands of society and the workplace; and for personal fulfillment. Among these texts are fiction and nonfiction, classic and contemporary works.

2. Students read a wide range of literature from many periods in many genres to build an understanding of the many dimensions (e.g., philosophical, ethical, aesthetic) of human experience.

3. Students apply a wide range of strategies to comprehend, interpret, evaluate, and appreciate texts. They draw on their prior experience, their interactions with other readers and writers, their knowledge of word meaning and of other texts, their word identification strategies, and their understanding of textual features (e.g., sound–letter correspondence, sentence structure, context, graphics).

4. Students adjust their use of spoken, written, and visual language (e.g., conventions, style, vocabulary) to communicate effectively with a variety of audiences and for different purposes.

5. Students employ a wide range of strategies as they write and use different writing process elements appropriately to communicate with different audiences for a variety of purposes.

6. Students apply knowledge of language structure, language conventions (e.g., spelling and punctuation), media techniques, figurative language, and genre to create, critique, and discuss print and nonprint texts.

7. Students conduct research on issues and interests by generating ideas and questions, and by posing problems. They gather, evaluate, and synthesize data from a variety of sources (e.g., print and nonprint texts, artifacts, people) to communicate their discoveries in ways that suit their purpose and audience.

8. Students use a variety of technological and information resources (e.g., libraries, databases, computer networks, video) to gather and synthesize information and to create and communicate knowledge.

9. Students develop an understanding of and respect for diversity in language use, patterns, and dialects across cultures, ethnic groups, geographic regions, and social roles.

10. Students whose first language is not English make use of their first language to develop competency in the English language arts and to develop understanding of content across the curriculum.

11. Students participate as knowledgeable, reflective, creative, and critical members of a variety of literacy communities.

12. Students use spoken, written, and visual language to accomplish their own purposes (e.g., for learning, enjoyment, persuasion, and the exchange of information). (International Reading Association & National Council of Teachers of English, 1996)

California English-Language Arts Content Standards for Grade 6

Reading

1.0 Word Analysis, Fluency, and Systematic Vocabulary Development
Students use their knowledge of word origins and word relationships, as well as historical and literary context clues, to determine the meaning of specialized vocabulary and to understand the precise meaning of grade-level–appropriate words.

- *Word Recognition*
- *Vocabulary and Concept Development*

2.0 Reading Comprehension (Focus on Informational Materials)
Students read and understand grade-level–appropriate material. They describe and connect the essential ideas, arguments, and perspectives of the text by using their knowledge of text structure, organization, and purpose.

- *Structural Features of Informational Materials*
- *Comprehension and Analysis of Grade-Level–Appropriate Text*
- *Expository Critique*

3.0 Literary Response and Analysis
Students read and respond to historically or culturally significant works of literature that reflect and enhance their studies of history and social science. They clarify the ideas and connect them to other literary works.

- *Structural Features of Literature*
- *Narrative Analysis of Grade-Level–Appropriate Text*
- *Literary Criticism*

Writing

1.0 Writing Strategies
Students write clear, coherent, and focused essays. The writing exhibits students' awareness of the audience and purpose. Essays contain formal introductions, supporting evidence, and conclusions. Students progress through the stages of the writing process as needed.

- *Organization and Focus*
- *Research and Technology*
- *Revising and Evaluating Writing*

2.0 Writing Applications (Genres and Their Characteristics)
Students write narrative, expository, persuasive, and descriptive texts of at least 500 to 700 words in each genre. Student writing demonstrates a command of standard American English and the research, organizational, and drafting strategies outlined in Writing Standard 1.0.

Written and Oral English Language Conventions

1.0 Written and Oral English Language Conventions
Students write and speak with a command of standard English conventions appropriate to this grade level.

- *Sentence Structure*
- *Grammar*
- *Punctuation*
- *Capitalization*
- *Spelling*

Listening and Speaking

1.0 Listening and Speaking Strategies
Students deliver focused, coherent presentations that convey ideas clearly and relate to the background and interests of the audience. They evaluate the content of oral communication.

- *Comprehension*
- *Organization and Delivery of Oral Communication*
- *Analysis and Evaluation of Oral and Media Communications*

2.0 Speaking Applications (Genres and Their Characteristics)
Students deliver well-organized formal presentations employing traditional rhetorical strategies (e.g., narration, exposition, persuasion, description). Student

speaking demonstrates a command of standard American English and the organizational and delivery strategies outlined in Listening and Speaking Standard 1.0.

New York Statei English Language Arts Core Curriculum

Reading, Writing, Listening, and Speaking

1. Students will read, write, listen, and speak for information and understanding.

2. Students will read, write, listen, and speak for literary response and expression.

3. Students will read, write, listen, and speak for critical analysis and evaluation.

4. Students will read, write, listen, and speak for social interaction.

Page numbers followed by *f* or *t* indicate figures or tables, respectively.

and struggling readers, 151;
establishing, 19–25; in high school
classrooms, 148; performance groups,
23–24; selecting groups, 23–24;
teachers meeting with students in
groups, 20, 20f
GUIDED READING, 21–22; definition of, 8t;
punctuation to help, 22

H

HAKIM, J., 194–195, 197
HAMILTON, V., 75
HANSEL AND GRETEL (FOLKTALE), 8
HARMON, S.D., 193, 197
HARRIS, V.J., 3, 6, 15, 18
HARSTE, J.C., 8, 17
HAVEN, K., 189
HEALTH, 195
HERMAN, P.A., 11, 17
HERRELL, A., 4, 6, 16–17
HESSE, K., 75, 125
HIGH SCHOOL CLASSROOMS: adaptations
for, 147–150; group dynamics in, 148,
151; recommended extension activities
for, 150
HILL, S., 12–13, 17
HIRSCHFELDER, A.B., 104
HISTORICAL DOCUMENTS, 76, 98–103;
adapting to script, 98–99; dividing for
script adaptation, 98; necessary script
additions, 98–99; sample script,
100–103; staging the script reading,
99; *The Universal Declaration of
Human Rights*, 77, 98–103
THE HISTORY TEACHER, 193, 197
HOLOCAUST, 77
HOMAN, S.P., 10, 17
HOPKINS, L.B., 125
HOYT, L., 9, 15, 17
HUGHES, L., 125
HULBERT, STEPHANIE, xiii
HUNTER, L., 104
"HUSH'D BE THE CAMPS TO-DAY"
(WHITMAN), 106, 114–120

I

IMMIGRANT VOICES UNIT, 88–97; sample
script, 91–97
"IN BEAUTY MAY I WALK," 106, 121–124,
137; adapting to script, 121–122;
dividing for script adaptation, 121;
essential reader information, 121;
necessary script additions, 121–122;
sample introduction, 121–122; sample
script, 123–124; staging the script
reading, 122
INSIDE THE CHARACTER (ACTIVITY), 132
INTERNATIONAL READING ASSOCIATION
(IRA), 172; Commission on
Adolescent Literacy, 3; Standards for
the English Language Arts
(IRA/NCTE), 159–164, 162f–163f,
165f, 170f, 217–218
INTERNET: websites, 189–190
INTERTEXTUALITY, 8t
INTERVIEWS, 76; adapting to script, 88–89;
dividing for script adaptation, 89; Ellis
Island oral histories, 88–97; necessary
script additions, 89; sample script,
91–97; staging the script reading, 89–90
INTRODUCTION, 3–18
IRA. *See* International Reading
Association
IRWIN, A.R., 191, 197

J

JACKDAW PHOTO COLLECTION, 90
JACKSON, E., 104
JENKINS, D.R., 189
JORDAN, M., 4, 6, 16–17
JOURNAL PROMPTS, 188
JOURNALS, 76

K

KAUFFMAN, G.B., 191, 197
KIBBY, M.W., 181f, 188
KLOPFER, L.E., 191, 197
KROLL, J.L., 189
KUKLIN, S., 104
KUMAR, S., 104